IMAGES
of America

FORKS

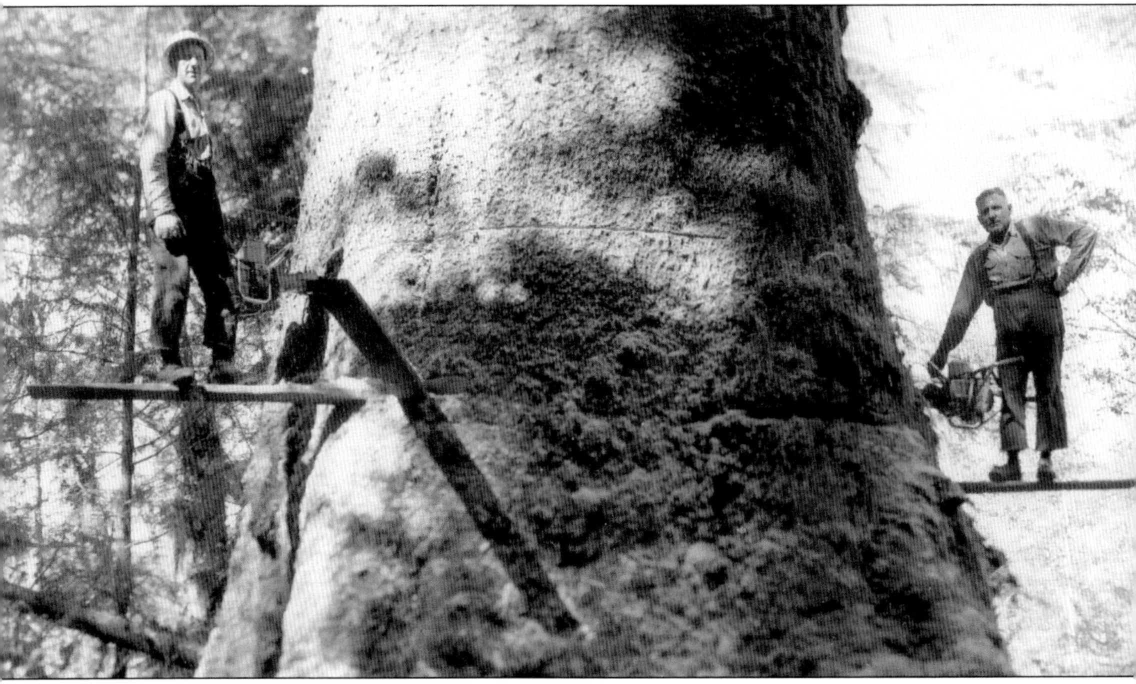

Duke Streeter (left) is seen felling a first-growth spruce on the Anderson place in 1952. Using chain saws while standing on springboards, he and another tree feller work in tandem. The loggers placed the springboards above the base of the huge trees to get a clean cut into solid wood and avoid what is known in logging jargon as swelled budding, or a swollen root structure, and tree rot. (Courtesy Forks Timber Museum Collection.)

ON THE COVER: Forks folk—young, old, and in between—enjoy a late-summer, dry-weather picnic in the forest at the first annual picnic of the IOOF Lodge of Forks on September 2, 1917. The lodge was an offshoot of and enjoyed ties to the Port Angeles IOOF, which was instituted in 1889. The men and women of the IOOF aimed to comfort and help the distressed, bury the dead, educate orphans, and visit the ill—their mission and services were practiced community-wide throughout Forks's history. (Courtesy Forks Timber Museum Collection.)

IMAGES
of America

FORKS

Forks Timber Museum,
Larry Burtness, and Chris Cook

ARCADIA
PUBLISHING

Copyright © 2011 by Forks Timber Museum, Larry Burtness, and Chris Cook
ISBN 978-0-7385-7553-7

Published by Arcadia Publishing
Charleston, South Carolina

Printed in the United States of America

Library of Congress Control Number: 2011903709

For all general information, please contact Arcadia Publishing:
Telephone 843-853-2070
Fax 843-853-0044
E-mail sales@arcadiapublishing.com
For customer service and orders:
Toll-Free 1-888-313-2665

Visit us on the Internet at www.arcadiapublishing.com

To the people of Forks, past and present, especially those who contributed the images pictured

Contents

FOREWORD

The Forks Timber Museum is here to develop a greater understanding of the city of Forks, Washington; its rural areas; and the community's logging heritage in particular.

The museum's collection of artifacts, photographs, illustrations, manuscripts, and books has provided most of the material in this pictorial history. In the blink of a camera's eye, the images we've gathered have captured the story of Forks.

The lands of Forks and nearby regions of the West End of the Olympic Peninsula have undergone many changes and seen numerous inhabitants: ancient coastal Native American tribes dependent on the land and sea for subsistence; Western explorers and traders in the late 1700s; American homesteaders who cleared sections of forest and farmed the land in the late 1800s; a timber industry–based community once widely known as the "logging capital of the world"; and a modern town set in the beauty of the western Olympic Peninsula rain forest and linked to the globe through telecommunications and modern highways. Each time period of our rich history is connected in some way to one or several of the following: change of climate, tsunami, the industrial revolution, world wars, forest fires, floods, and, most recently, fame as the setting for author Stephenie Meyer's global best-selling *Twilight* series of books and the resulting movies.

Located south of downtown, the Forks Timber Museum is across the road from the Forks Municipal Airport and adjacent to the Forks Visitor Center on Highway 101. The museum portrays a people that have handled life with grit, ingenuity, and verve, working to live a good life.

The Forks Timber Museum's own heritage dates back to 1981, when members of the community formed the Quillayute Valley Historical Society. In 1984, the organization was renamed and incorporated. The Forks Timber Museum collection was first put on display in September 1982 in a rented building on the north end of town and operated there through 1988. In that year, the museum leased property, which was located near the city's south entrance, from the City of Forks. Beginning in 1989, a two-story museum building was constructed there by Forks High School's carpentry class, community volunteers, and work crews provided by the Olympic Correction Center located in Clearwater, south of Forks.

The new Forks Timber Museum held its grand opening during the Old Fashioned Forks Fourth of July Celebration in 1990.

Piece by piece, through donations and acquisitions, we've created a superb collection that we see as a small jewel amid our green wonderland of towering forests and prairies.

The Forks Timber Museum is open May through October, Tuesday through Saturday, from 10:00 a.m. to 4:00 p.m. Private tours can be arranged by appointment for other times by calling (360) 374-9663 or sending an e-mail to forkstimbermuseum@hotmail.com.

We are proud of our past, the hardworking present, and hopeful for the future.

ACKNOWLEDGMENTS

The Forks Timber Museum thanks its board of directors and those who have contributed time, funding, photographs, and artifacts to its collection. Their support is the foundation for this book.

We thank Forks Timber Museum director Sherrill Fouts for sharing her wealth of logging knowledge, for her time and input, and for friendly assistance in creating this book.

Thanks to the following individuals and organizations who contributed to this project: Forks Library director Theresa Tetreau and staff, Florence Miles, Duane Miles, Ron Shearer, Dave McIrvin, John and Michelle Simpson, Fred Shaw, Steve Shaw, John and Edna Leppell, Charlene Cross, Rod Fleck, and Janet Hughes. Thanks also go to Chon Clayton and Mike Harmon for their insight on the Quillayute Naval Air Station.

All images pictured are from the Forks Timber Museum Collection unless noted otherwise.

Introduction

The city of Forks, with a population of around 3,100, is located in the West End of Clallam County in Western Washington. Forks is renowned for its rainfall, proudly claiming the title of the rainiest incorporated city or town in the contiguous 48 states. The town stands within what local residents call their "walls of green," which are made up of hundreds of rain forest plants; an island of homes, businesses, stores, government offices, restaurants, and visitor accommodations amidst huge stands of Douglas fir, hemlock, western red cedar, and spruce trees. US Highway 101 runs through the center of town and connects Forks to Port Angeles some 50 miles to the west.

Located in the northwest corner of the Olympic Peninsula, Forks was settled late in comparison to most regions of the United States. Early homesteading Americans chose to build their homes and barns on prairies that had, in the past, regularly been "burned over," or purposely set afire, by the Quileute tribe to attract elk and deer for hunting and to grow food and medicinal plants. The Quileute people are a coastal Native American tribe whose homeland at LaPush is about 30 minutes west of Forks on the Pacific coast. These settlers, drawn to the prairies by the reputation of Forks as a farming area with rich soil, arrived in the late 1870s, in the era following the Civil War. They joined a handful of trappers and traders already living in the densely forested region.

By the late 1800s, logging and milling operations had begun to harvest the towering first-growth trees of the West End, launching an industry that continues to provide the economic foundation for Forks into the 21st century.

The epochs of the 20th-century history of the United States reached out and touched the town. World War I brought high demand for spruce logs to meet aviation needs, fueling the development of modern bridges, a paved highway, and an airport. The continued need for the abundant forest resources helped float the town through the Great Depression. As happened in many rural towns, World War II scattered the young men of Forks across the nation and globe, and they returned with a new vision for their future. The postwar era saw a boom in logging and milling, with the devastating Forks fire of 1951 providing a windfall treasure of valuable timber to salvage.

Today, Forks is still reeling from an economic downturn brought on in the 1980s and 1990s by land-use restrictions, mostly of federal forestlands, aimed at protecting the habitat of the northern spotted owl.

Hispanic workers began arriving in the late 1970s, gathering salal and other ground cover foliage from the forest for the wholesale floral industry. As of 2010, the Hispanic community makes up about 15 percent of the resident population.

The people of Forks continue to live out their logging and frontier-infused lifestyle. They withstand any gloom cast by the economy and the wet, rain forest climate while moving into the future with a growing tourism industry that received a momentous boost through Forks's being the main setting in author Stephenie Meyer's *Twilight* series.

One

The Pioneers

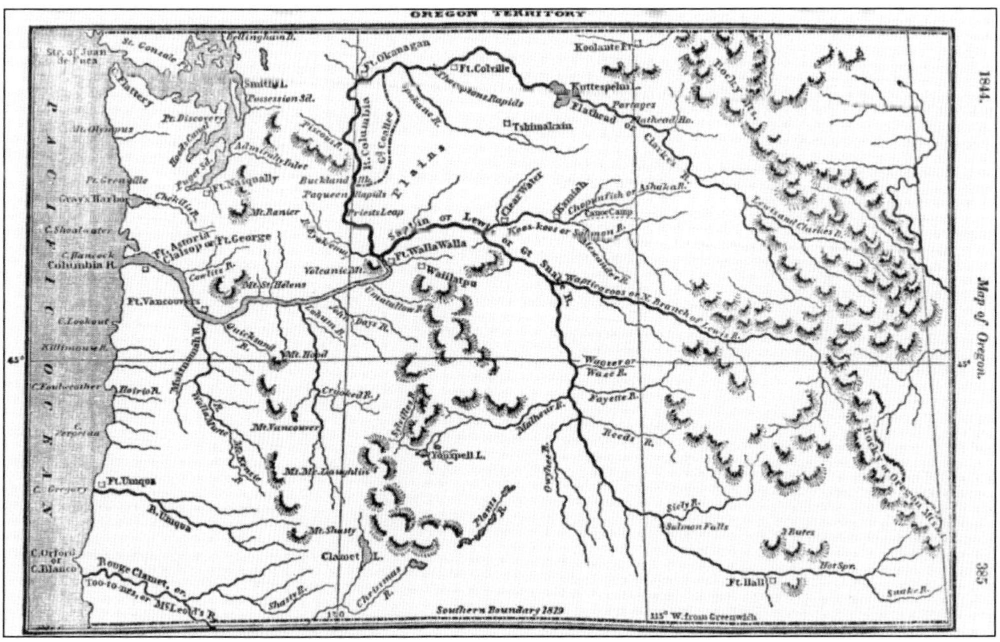

Except for Cape Flattery, named by Capt. James Cook in 1778, the place names of the North Olympic Peninsula are not marked on this 1844 Oregon Territory map published in Boston by *Missionary Herald* magazine. The Pacific Northwest was the last inhabitable section of the globe that Western explorers sailed to, resulting in development decades later than most sections of the United States. In 1808, Anna Petrovana Bulygin, the wife of Capt. Nikolai Bulygin of the Russian navy, came ashore at Rialto Beach, north of LaPush, making her the first Western woman to set foot in Washington State.

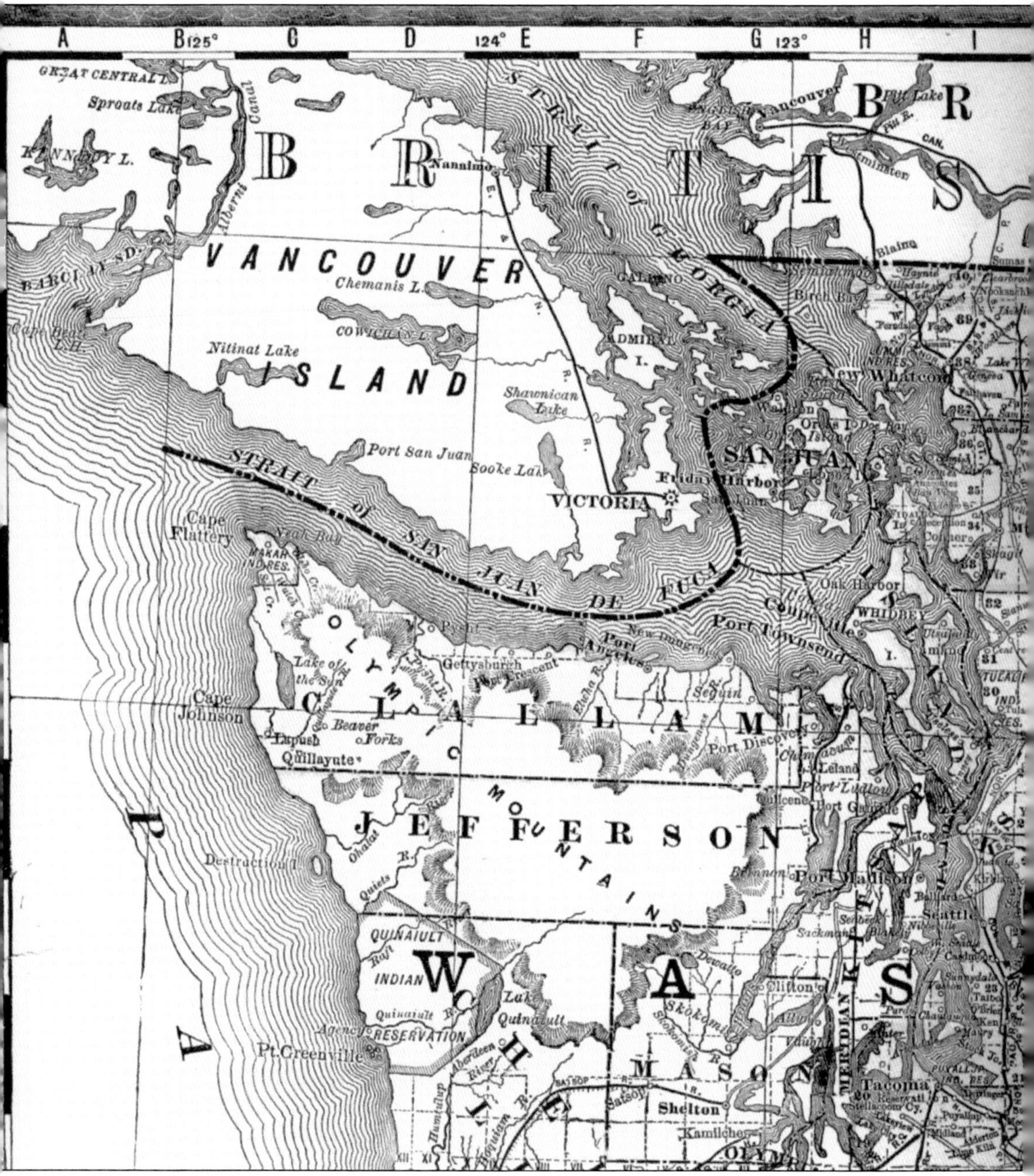

By 1895, Forks was on the Rand McNally map of the Pacific Northwest, Washington Territory had become a state, a reservation for the Quileute tribe had been created, and Clallam and Jefferson Counties had been surveyed and their boundaries mapped. The heavy rainfall of Forks would provide notoriety for the town when it was declared the wettest in the continental United States. The rainy climate was ideal for the growth of huge spruce, Douglas fir, hemlock, and cedar trees—an abundant resource that would support a timber industry in the "logging capital of the world."

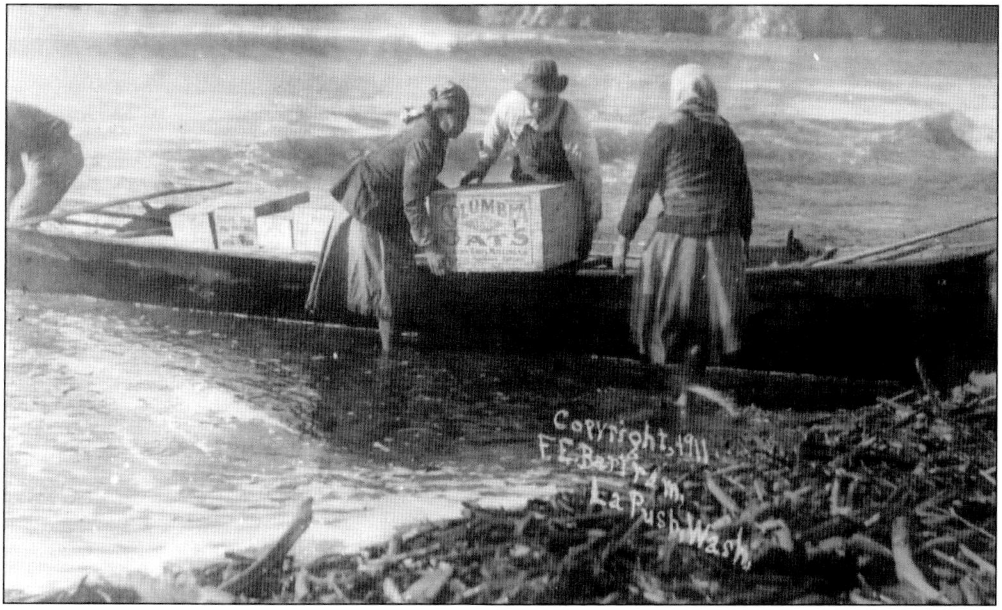

The family of Civil War veteran Luther Ford ventured out in 1878 to the West End of the Olympic Peninsula in search of fertile farmland on which to homestead. Ford left behind an offer of 80 acres of land in what would become downtown Seattle for the West End wilds. He and his family traveled from the Makah Reservation at Neah Bay aboard an oceangoing canoe, which was probably larger than the canoe pictured here. Later settlers would arrive in steamers, which anchored offshore, and then be transported to the beach in such canoes.

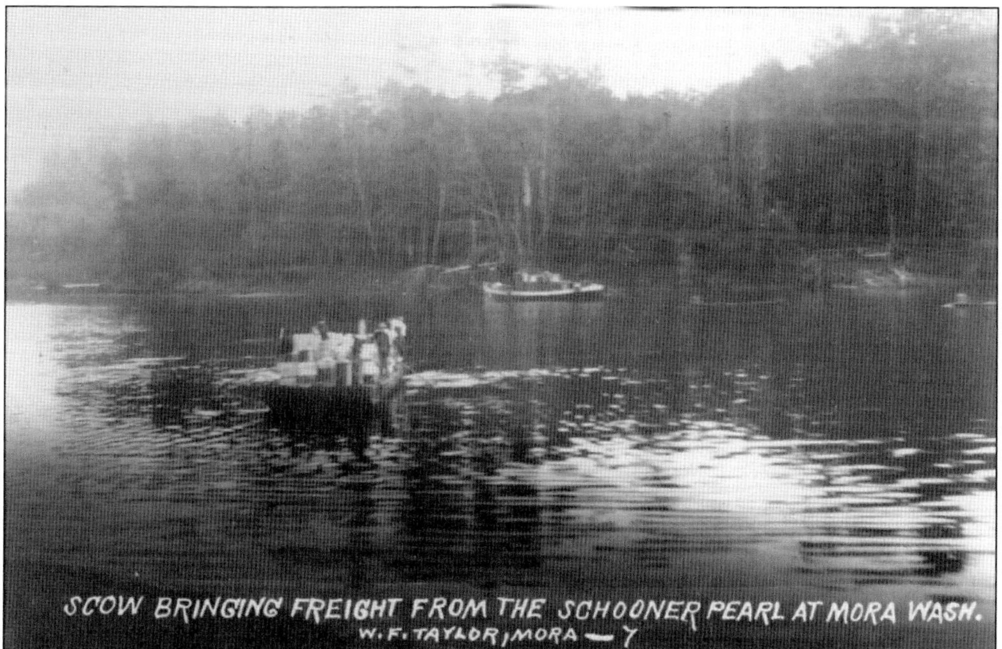

Supplies and settlers made the trek upriver from the Pacific coast to the Forks prairie by scow or canoe and by foot along traditional tribal trails and independently created paths. This scene at Mora shows a scow crossing the river with a load of supplies brought upriver aboard a schooner.

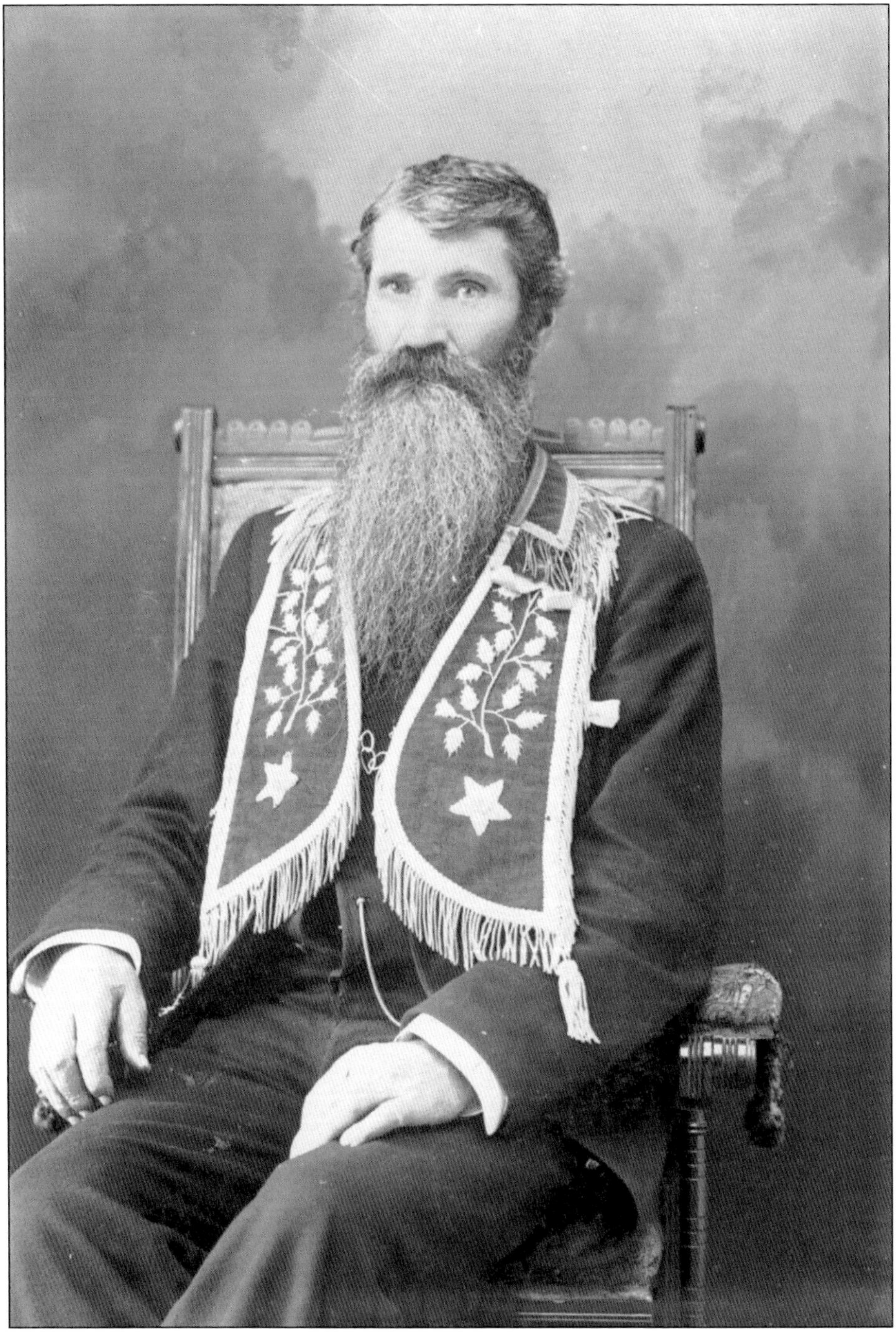

Luther Ford, garbed in International Order of Odd Fellows regalia, is shown in this photograph, which was, perhaps, taken when he was named the first Nobel Grand of the Forks chapter on May 6, 1893, the founding date of the Odd Fellows Lodge in Forks. The original town name, Ford's Prairie, was rejected by the post office because a town in central Washington already claimed the name. Instead, Forks was chosen due to the prairie, an area of flat land between the Calawah River immediately to the north and the Bogachiel River to the south of town.

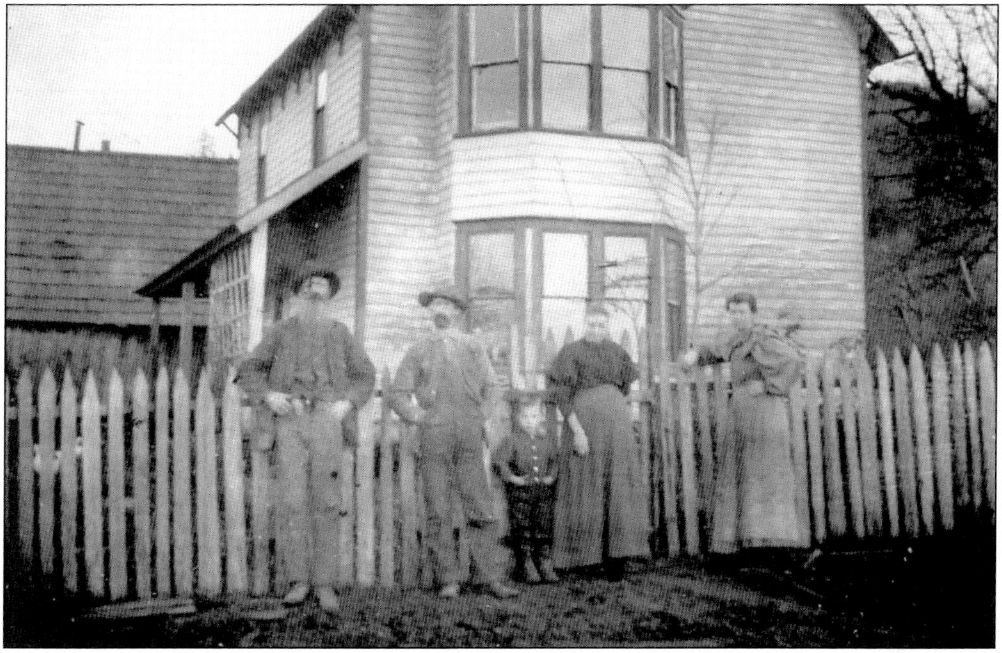

Luther (far left) and Esther Ford (second from right) and family stand in front of the bay windows of their farmhouse on the Forks prairie. The Ford's 160-acre homestead was the first on the Forks prairie. The family set up a ranch, which is still worked today, about a mile south of downtown. The town of Forks developed by 1890, becoming a center for the farming and logging community. Their children were Florence, Winifred (far right), Myrtle, and Oliver.

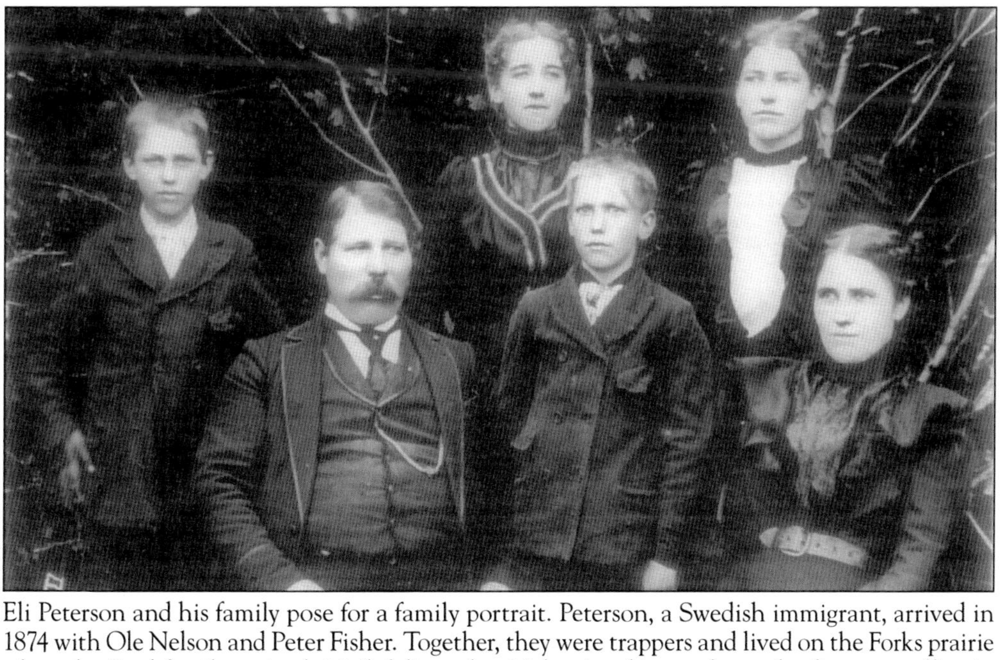

Eli Peterson and his family pose for a family portrait. Peterson, a Swedish immigrant, arrived in 1874 with Ole Nelson and Peter Fisher. Together, they were trappers and lived on the Forks prairie when the Ford family arrived. Mail delivered to Nelson's cabin made up the first post office in Forks. Pictured are, from left to right, (first row) Elias Levi (father), Morton, and Winifred "Mamie" (daughter of Luther Ford); (second row) Oscar Allen, Myrtle, and Elma.

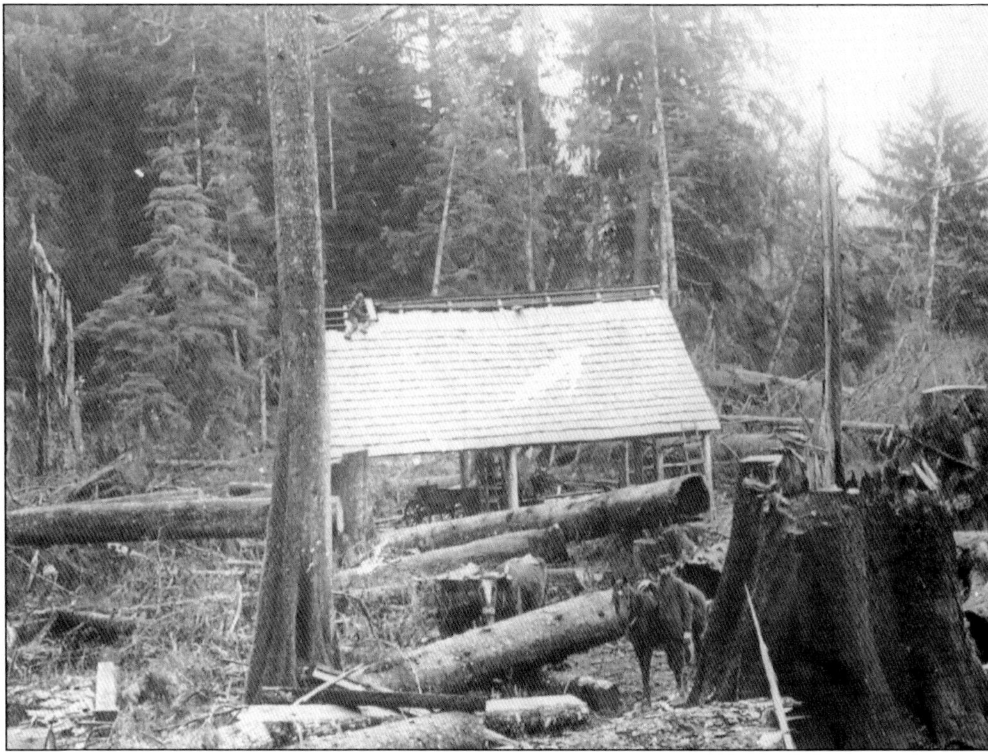

Homesteaders were lured to the Forks area with the promise of fertile farmland and having been told tree trunks could easily be burned out. They discovered that felling tall trees, rooting out huge stumps, and hauling timber were also part of the deal. Here, a cedar-shake roofed barn is under construction with a wagon beneath its cover.

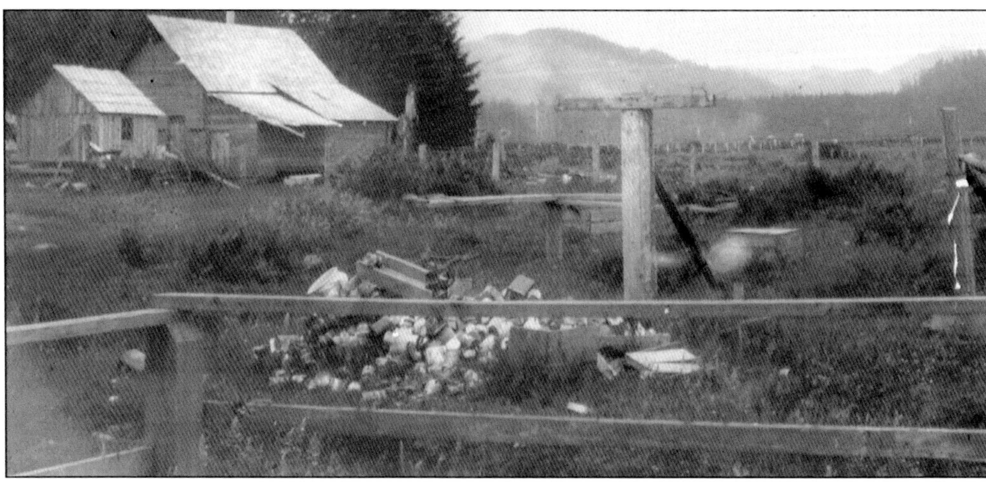

After the struggle of clearing trees and stumps, homesteaders found locally milled lumber and shakes—fine materials for building farmhouses and work sheds on their acreage in Forks. Vegetable and flower patches and brush took the place of a grassy lawn. The homesteaders traded produce for manufactured goods at two trading posts near the mouth of the Quileute River: the Washington Fur Company post operated by Seth Baxter at La Push and the trading post operated by Frank Balch at Boston, later called Mora.

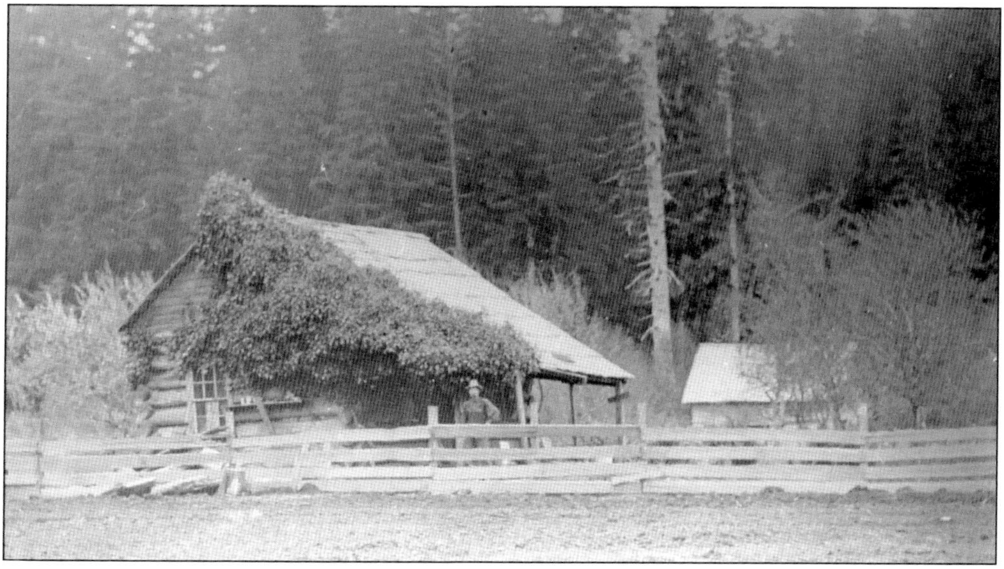

This is the original house on the Merchant family homestead built in 1882. Those known in the picture below are William (second from left) and Martha Maybury (third from left), Maude-Liz-Deede Merchant, and Callie McMillan (far right). The log cabin with wide shake roofing would have been heated with a fireplace or woodstove. From a bird's-eye view, patches of flowers provided a vast display of color when in bloom, and split cedar rails made sturdy fences. Dressing up for church on Sunday and social events helped to brighten the lives of those on the Forks and Quillayute prairies. Suspenders, sturdy boots (often homemade), and tough pants and shirts made up the men's wardrobe.

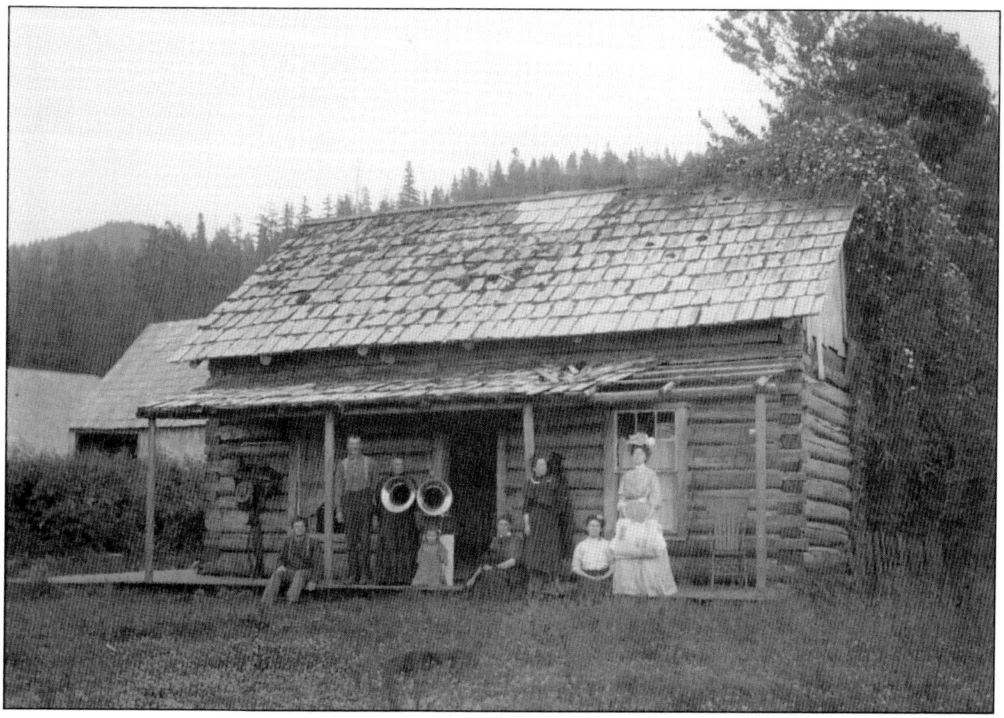

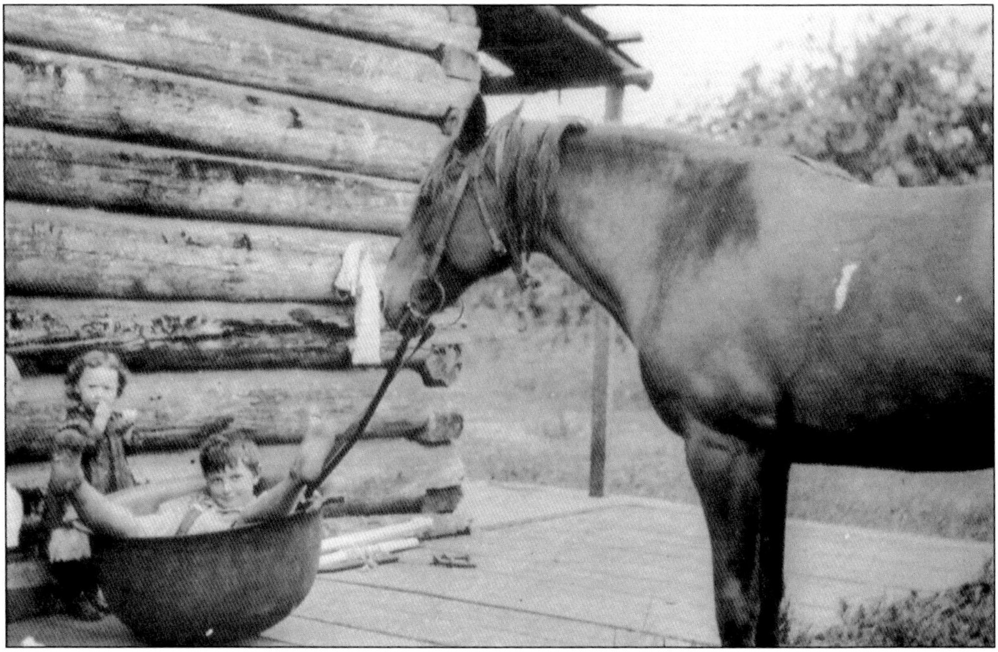

Plopped down inside the pot that was perhaps used for making lard, young Mickey Merchant plays around with his sister and the family horse. The Merchants were among the first pioneer families to homestead in Forks in the 1880s and 1890s and were faced with the same challenges of settlers heading west 50 years earlier.

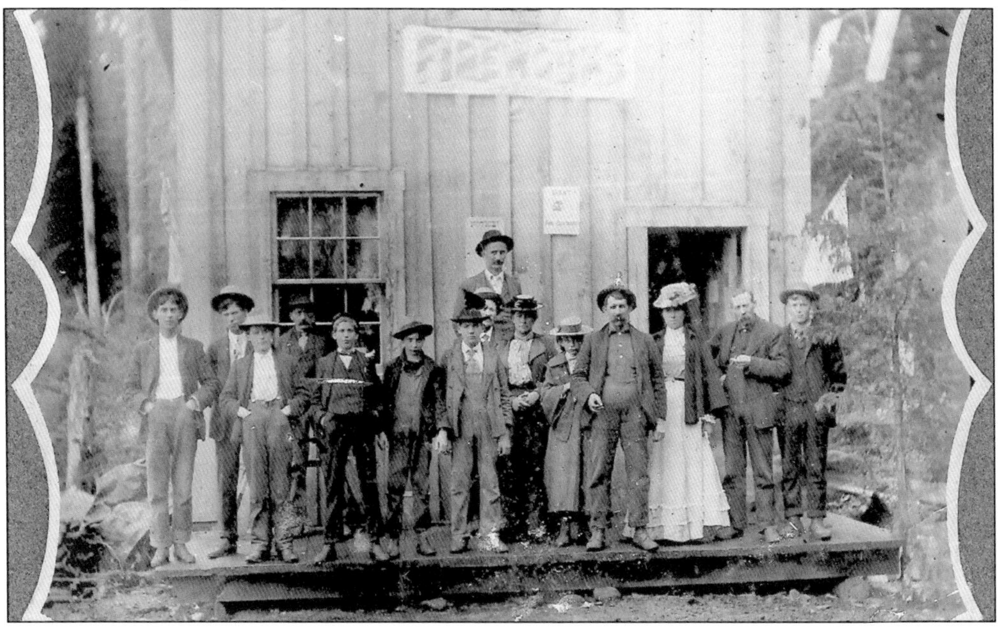

Fireworks are for sale at this general store in Forks. Dressed up for what is likely a Fourth of July celebration, this group of Forks area residents includes Earl Wilson, Jake Hahn, Martin Peterson, Ray Whittier, Mrs. Bowers, Jim Henry, Mrs. Densmore, and shop owner F.M. Ackerly. Note the wooden foundation that the board-and-batten–sided building rests on; it was designed to keep the wet soil away from the shop floor.

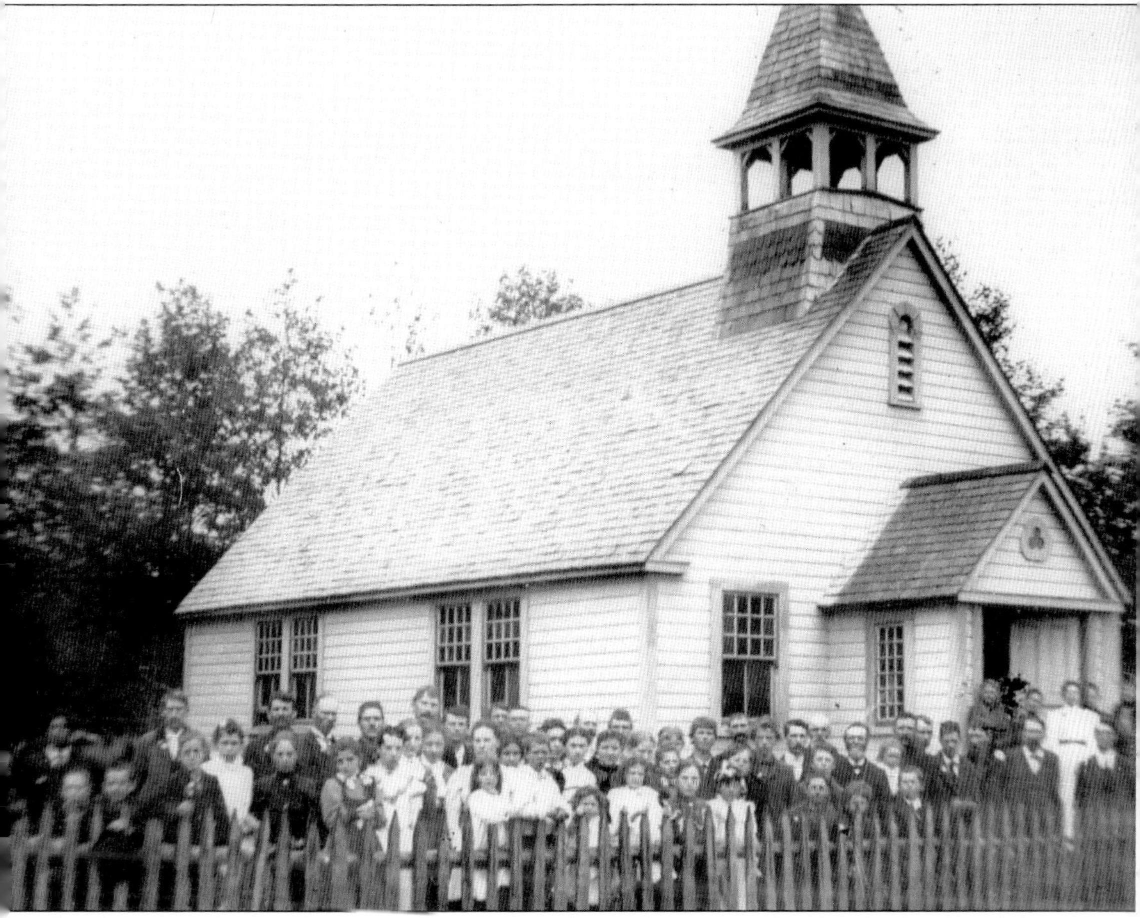

Churches were community centers. Congregational minister Reverend Rufus Fletcher founded the Quillayute Congregational Church. Fletcher served in the 1880s as a church planter, breaking the ice with the community through his medical abilities. He later departed but returned in 1902 to found the Forks Congregational Church in 1903.

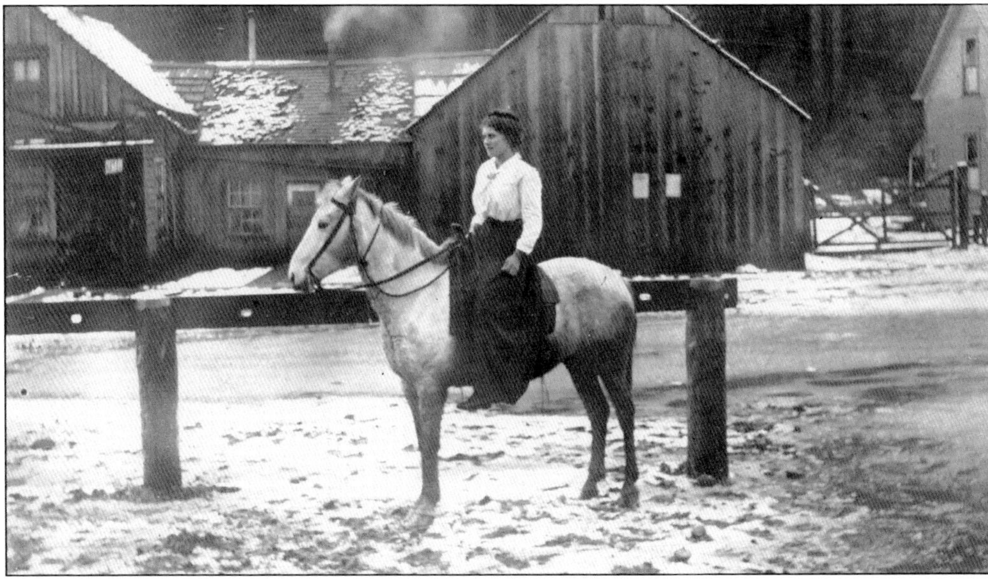

Horsewoman and rancher Mary (Schutz) Clark is shown in 1915 in front of the Cottage Hotel in Forks. Her family ranch was located east of Forks, past Sappho. Mary Clark Road at Sappho is named after her; the Schutz family homesteaded in the Sappho area. Born in LaGrande, Oregon, on October 31, 1883, Jim Clark, Mary's husband, was a Clallam County commissioner for many years, and his family came to the Forks area around 1890. The right-side portion of the building is still standing in Forks, behind the Native to Twilight store. It is acknowledged to be the oldest building in Forks, dating from around 1880.

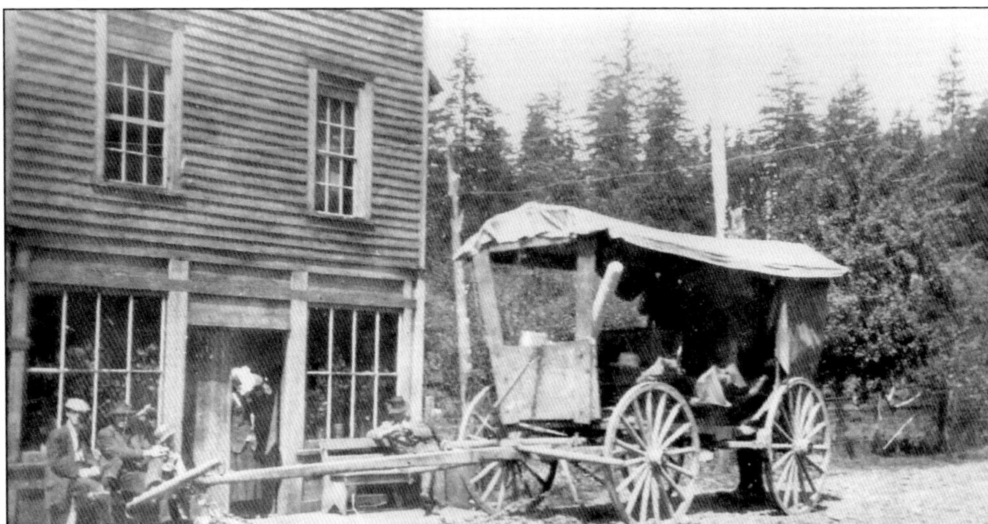

Fred Ackerly homesteaded in Sappho, east of Forks, in 1895. At this time, a grocery store and a small newspaper, the *Leader*, were established. Here, Clallam Bay stagecoach, with its canvas top, stands outside the Sappho Hotel waiting for a new team of horses to continue its journey. The hotel provided a place for locals to socialize, discuss community issues, and gossip. Rooms served as housing for newcomers and visitors.

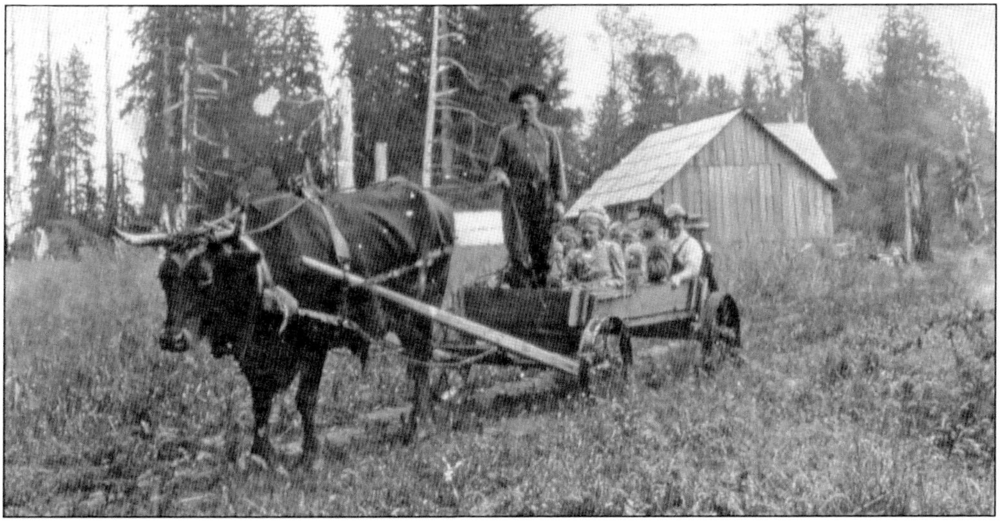

A pioneer farmer at the reins of his oxen cart employs a family work animal for transportation from their West End homestead. The cart followed well-worn paths that provided access to the homestead and later may have become city streets.

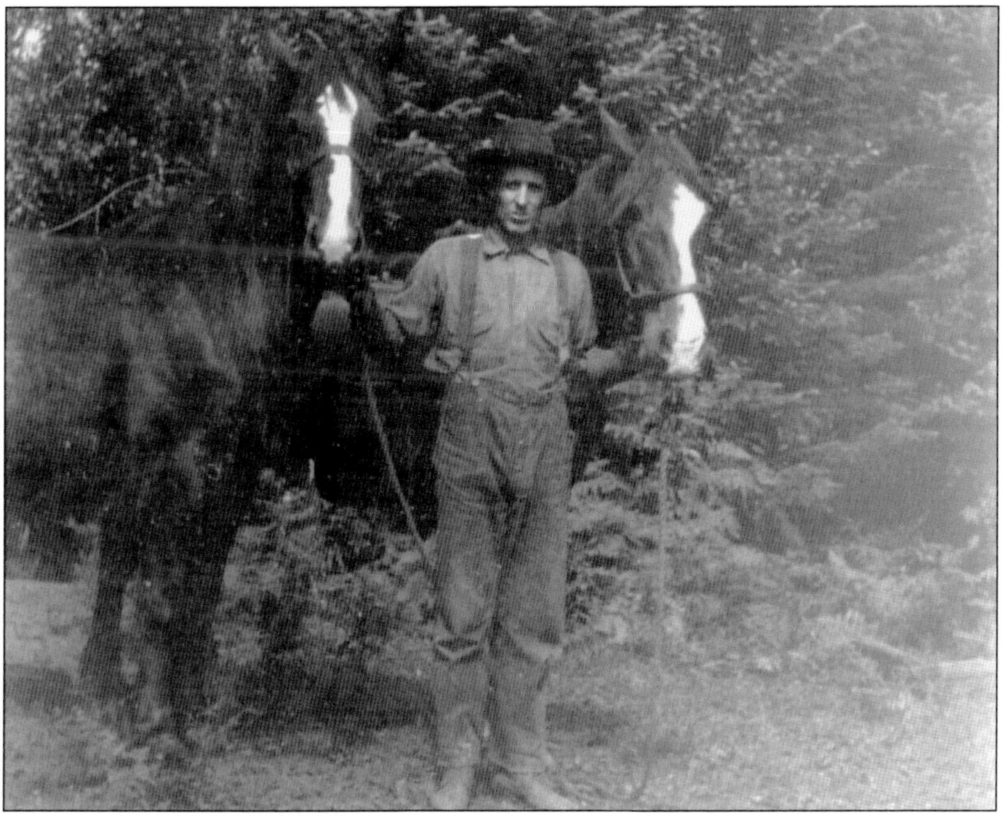

Horses were critical to the survival of pioneer families living on the Forks prairie, as well as being prized, well cared for possessions. Homesteaders rode horses and hitched them to wagons for transportation, used them to drag plows, and were dependent on their strength to haul logs in clearing land for farming and building lots.

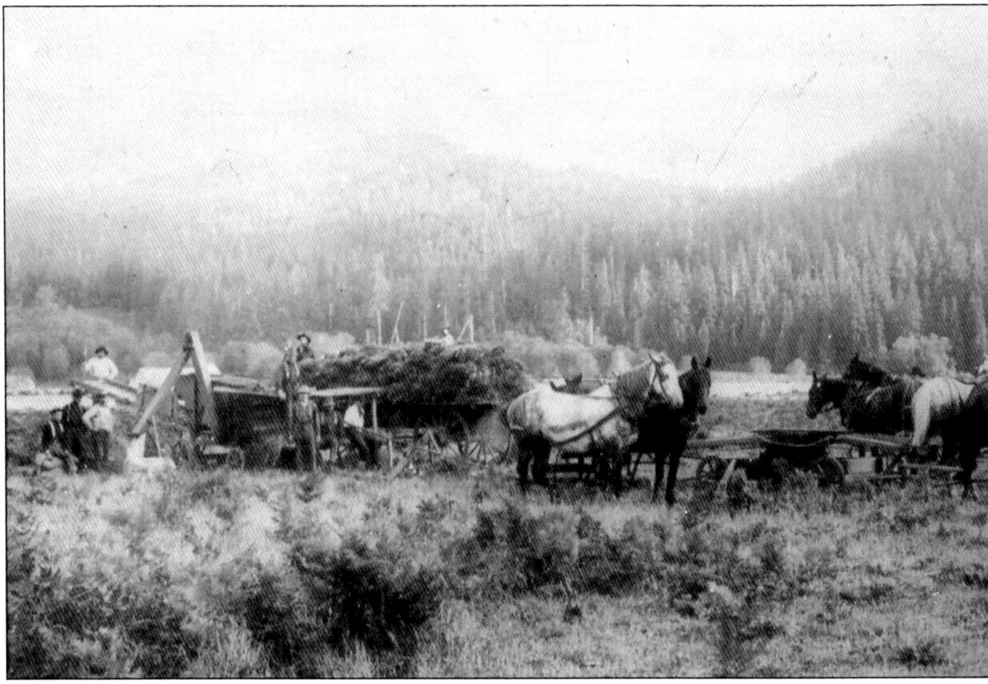

It took manpower and teamwork to thresh oats grown in a prairie clearing. Using nonmechanized tools speeded up the job. Harry Maxfield's thresher was used by a team of men who threshed fields belonging to the various different homesteads in the area.

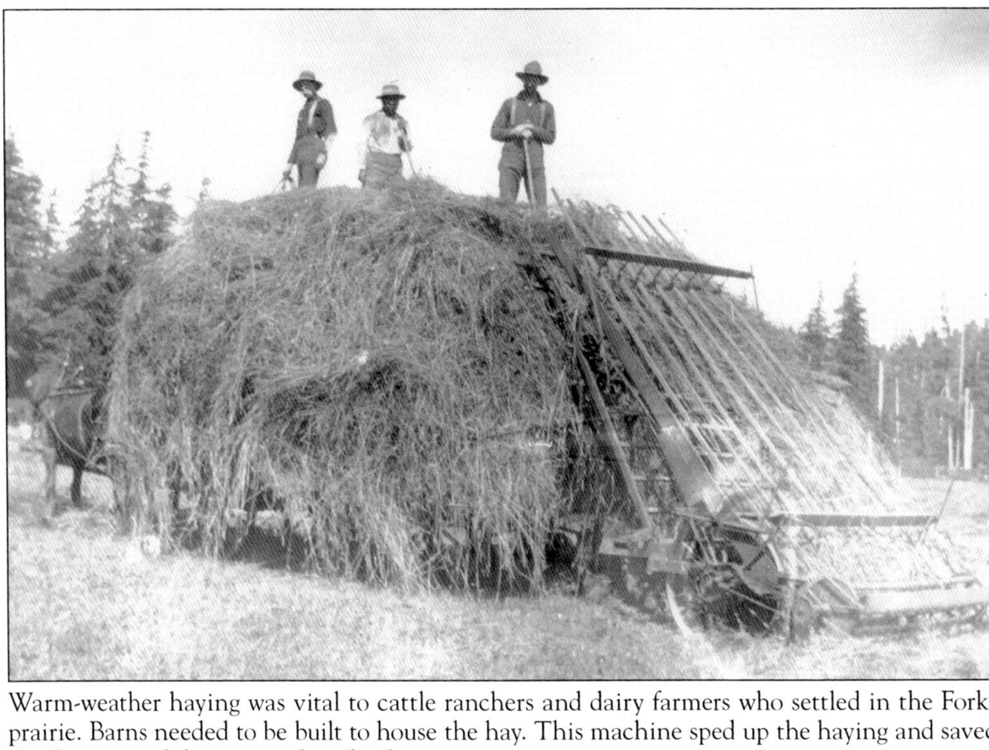

Warm-weather haying was vital to cattle ranchers and dairy farmers who settled in the Forks prairie. Barns needed to be built to house the hay. This machine sped up the haying and saved the farmers and dairymen a lot of toil.

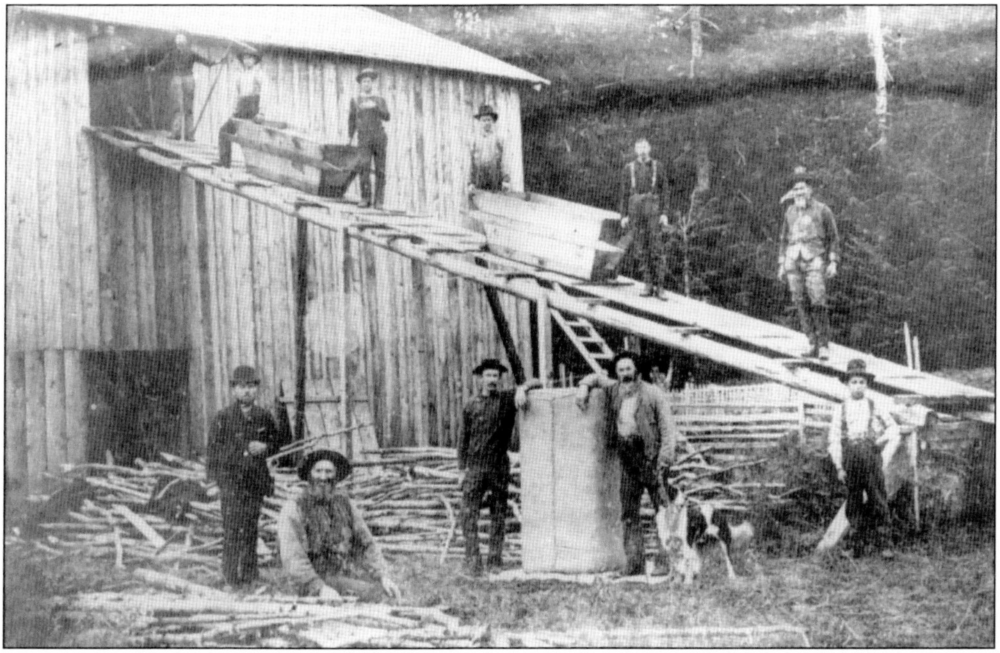

A hops house near Forks is shown in mid-production. Hops were hauled up the ramp in wooden bins and spread on the floor of the loft, which had small holes cut in it. A wood fire on the ground floor dried the hops. The cured hops were packaged in burlap sacks and sent to brewers in Seattle. The hops barn was used for dances on Saturday nights.

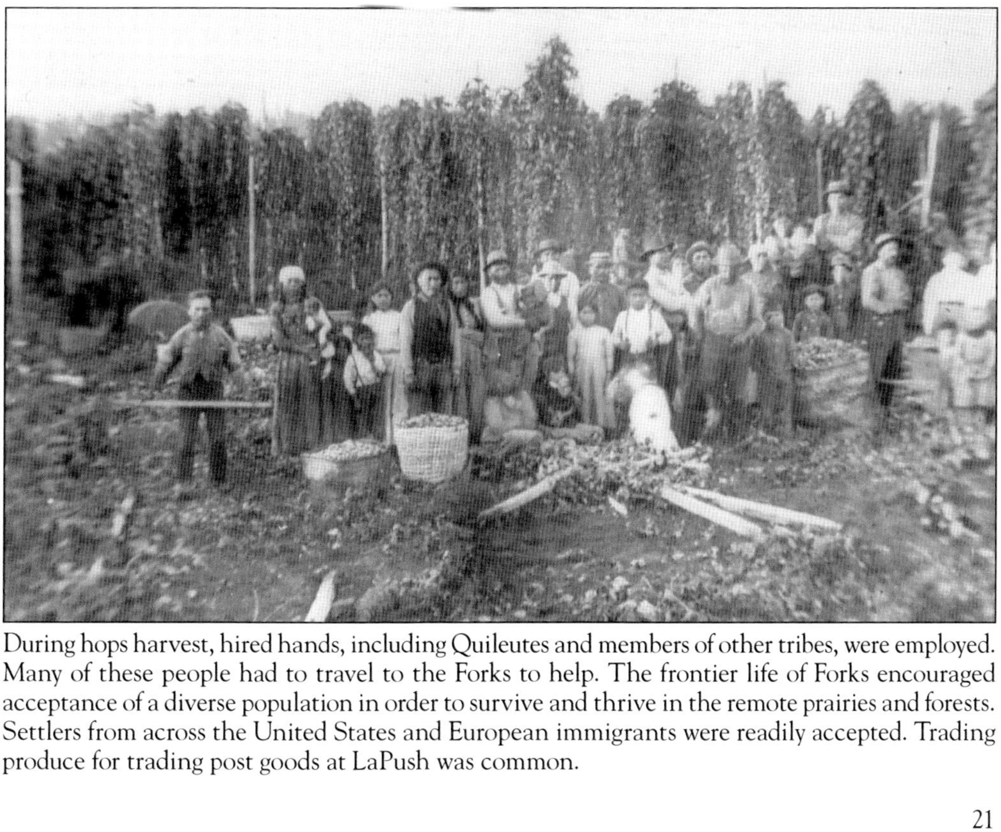

During hops harvest, hired hands, including Quileutes and members of other tribes, were employed. Many of these people had to travel to the Forks to help. The frontier life of Forks encouraged acceptance of a diverse population in order to survive and thrive in the remote prairies and forests. Settlers from across the United States and European immigrants were readily accepted. Trading produce for trading post goods at LaPush was common.

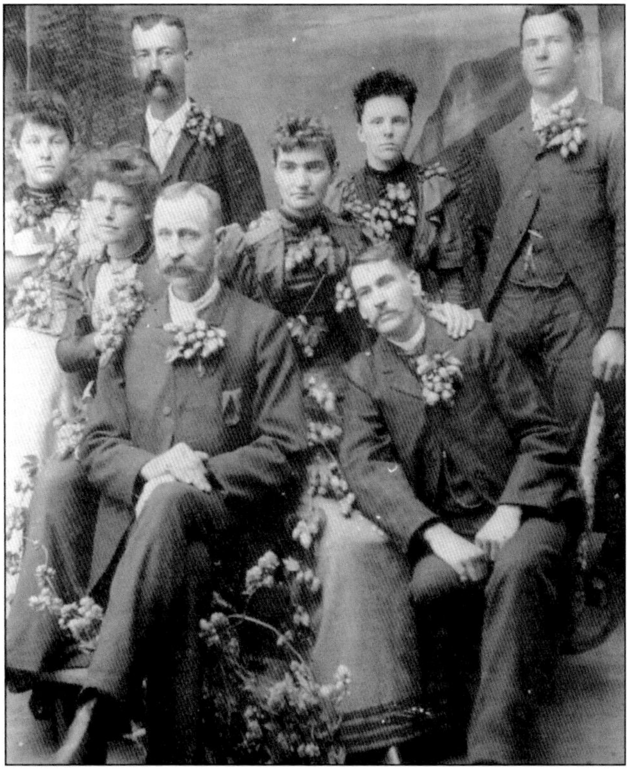

Hops grew extremely well on the prairie if the summer weather was long and hot. Big two-story buildings were used to dry hops. The hope that hops would provide a steady cash crop was celebrated with a hops festival, which featured sprigs of hops for decorations. Unfortunately, the crop became unprofitable when dampness ruined shipments waiting on the coast for transport to ships offshore.

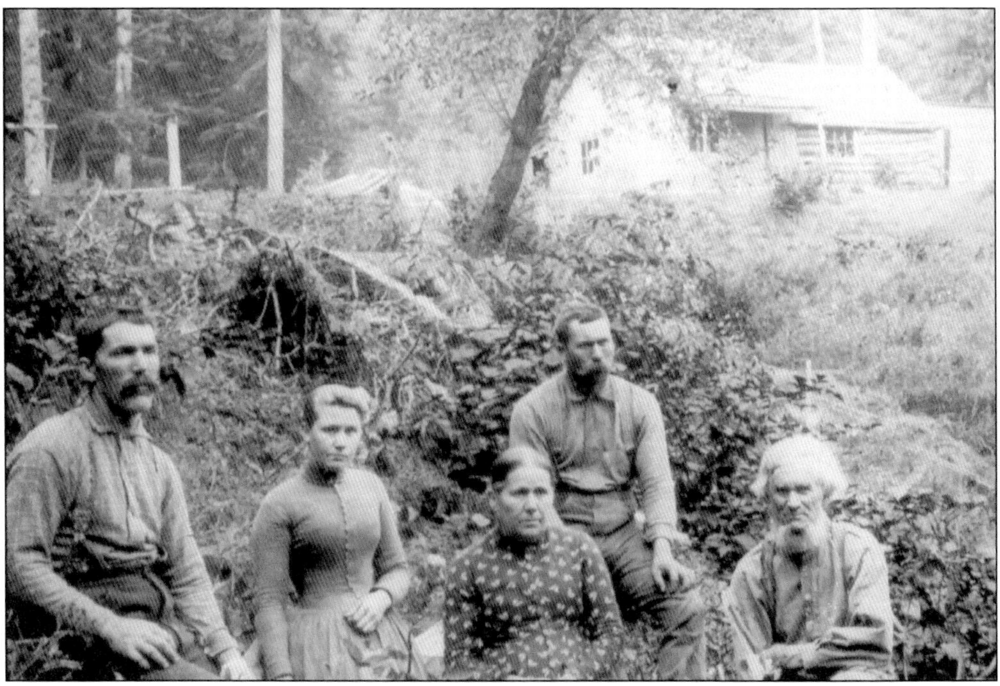

The Crawford family lived at the east end of Forks prairie and raised hops in 1889. Their cabin was on the bank of Elk Creek. Documentation of this family can be found in Forks's Pioneer Club's album.

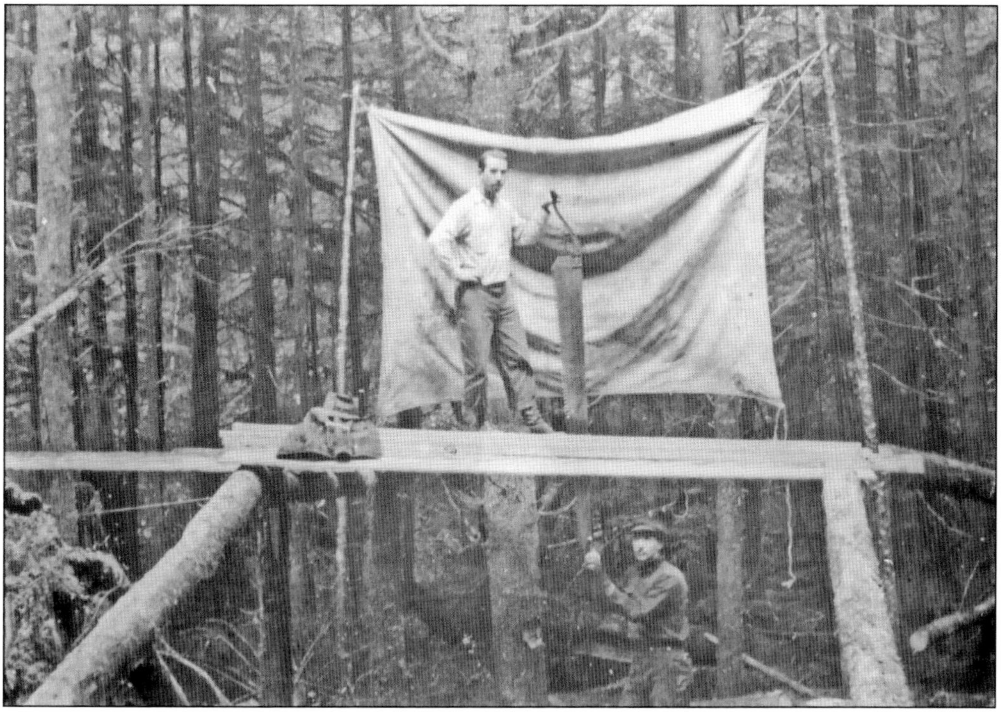

Perhaps the worst job was being the sawdust-covered man standing in the pit below a whipsawing platform when a beginner sawyer is learning how to cut timber by hand.

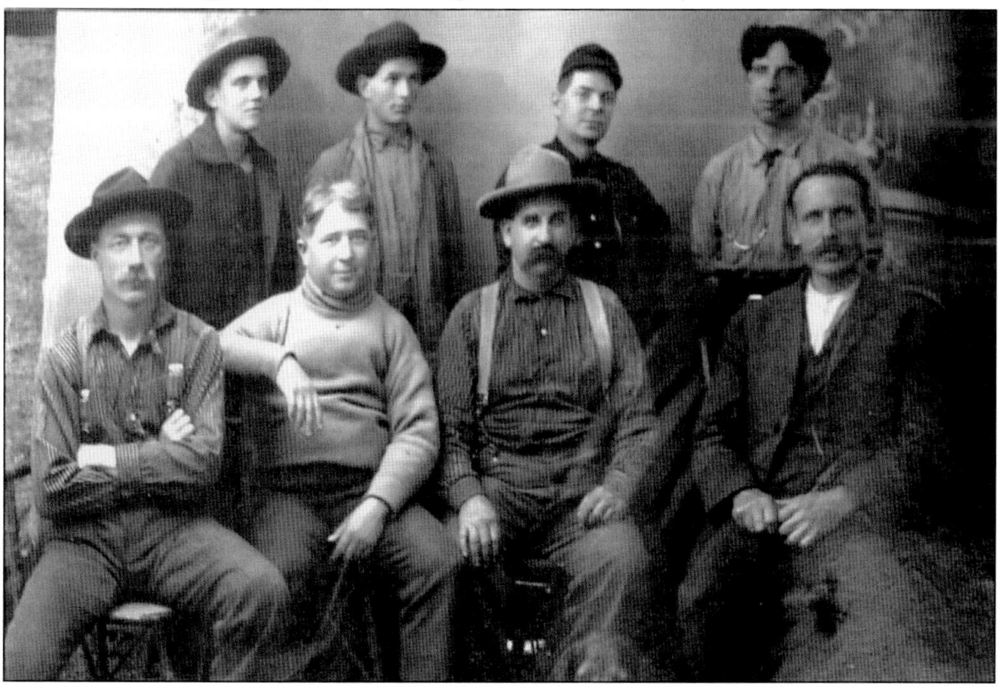

Forks pioneer men are seen posing for a studio photographer. Pictured are, from left to right, (first row) Jim Kay, Dr. Meade (dentist), Jim Henry, and Mr. Scott (teacher); (second row) Peter Schutz, Fred Fletcher, Charles Sult, and Jack Fraker.

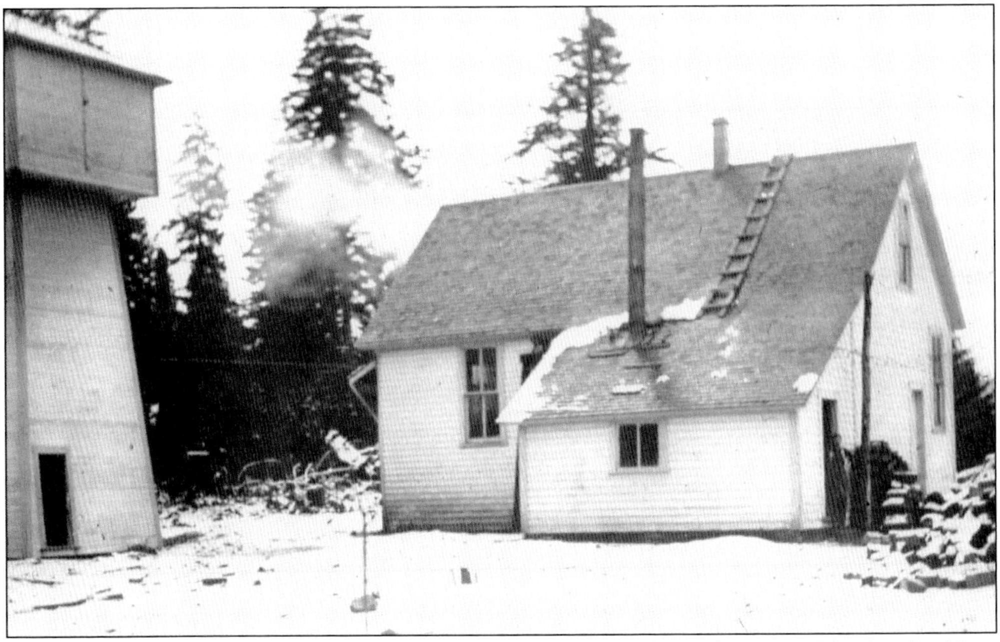

The Forks Cooperative Creamery (above) was established in the early 1990s. The first building burned down in 1922, and then the firm merged with Angeles Creamery in 1938. The structure on the left appears to be a hop-drying tower. The creamery business grew due to a need for milk for children. As dairy herds increased and outstripped the needs of homesteaders, the milk was put to commercial use. Dairyman Emil Bork drove his one-horse wagon to and from dairy farms and the creamery. Oversized metal milk cans slid into slots and hung suspended below his wagon seat.

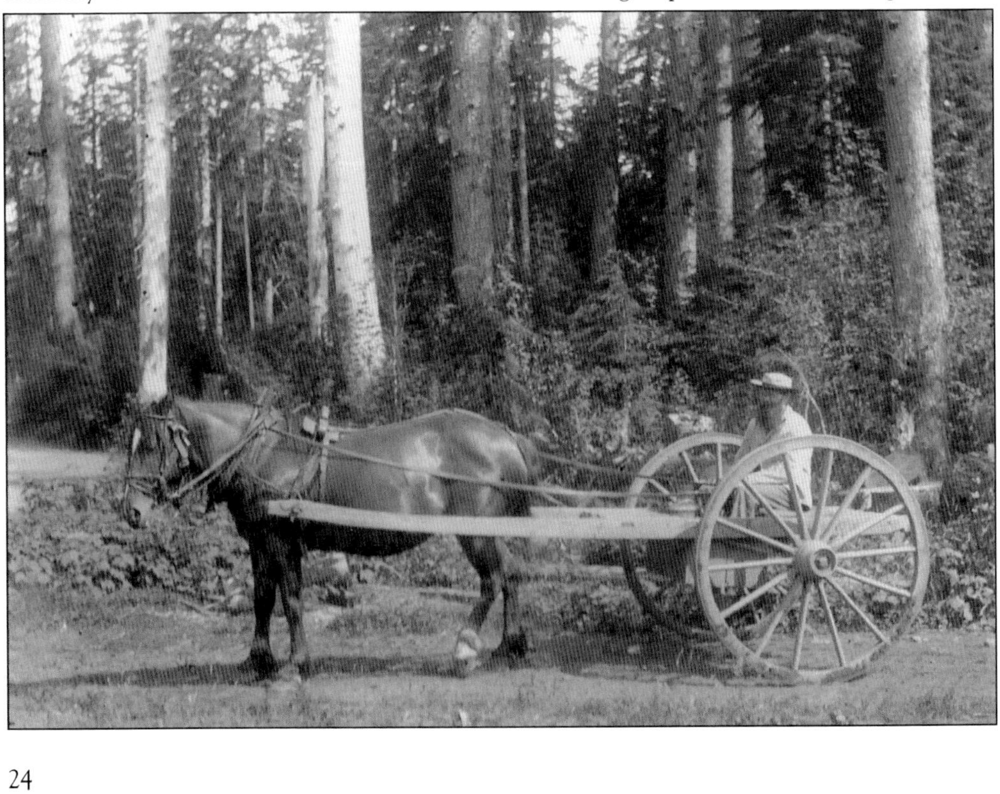

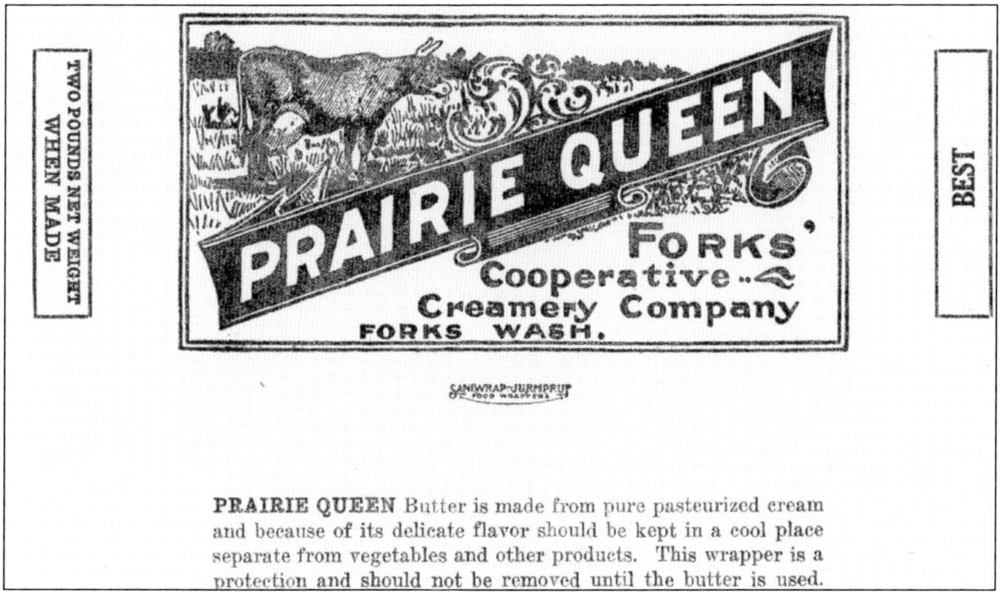

Here is a butter wrapper labeled with the Forks Cooperative Creamery's Prairie Queen brand.

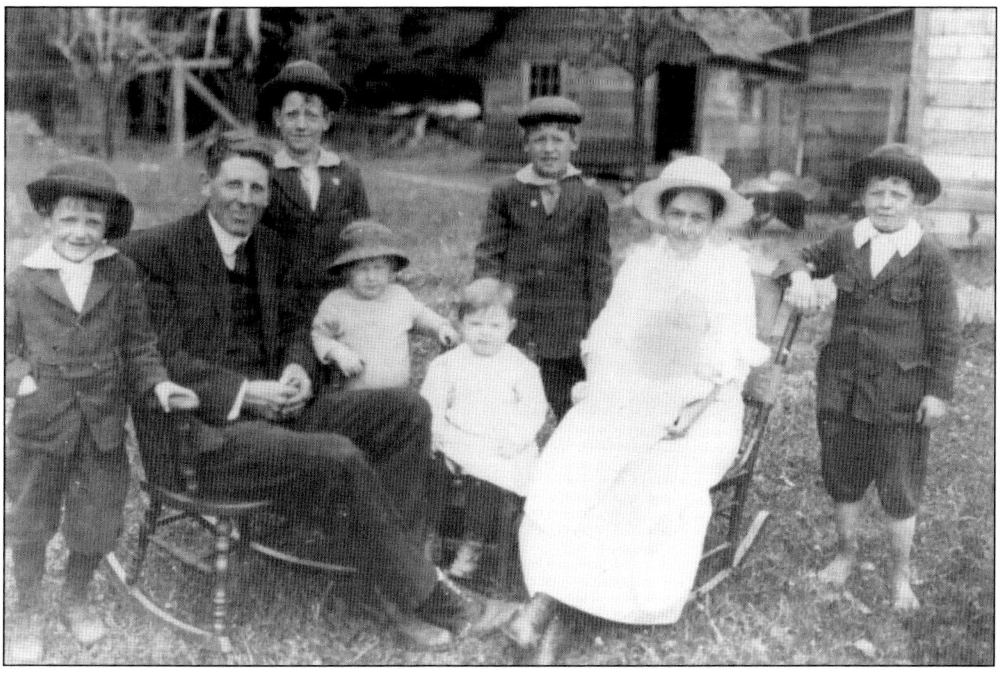

Casper Maxfield was born on May 30, 1879, on the Quillayute prairie and was the son of Jesse Maxfield, one of the first to settle on the prairie in 1872. Pictured from left to right around 1920 are Maxfield family members: Dudley, Casper, Arthur, Donald, Gloria, Jess, Daisy holding Darrell (born January 21, 1919), and Freemont. Eleanor Thornton, a daughter of Casper and Daisy, is not in this picture. Casper Maxfield died February 25, 1936, when the logging truck he was driving went into Lake Crescent.

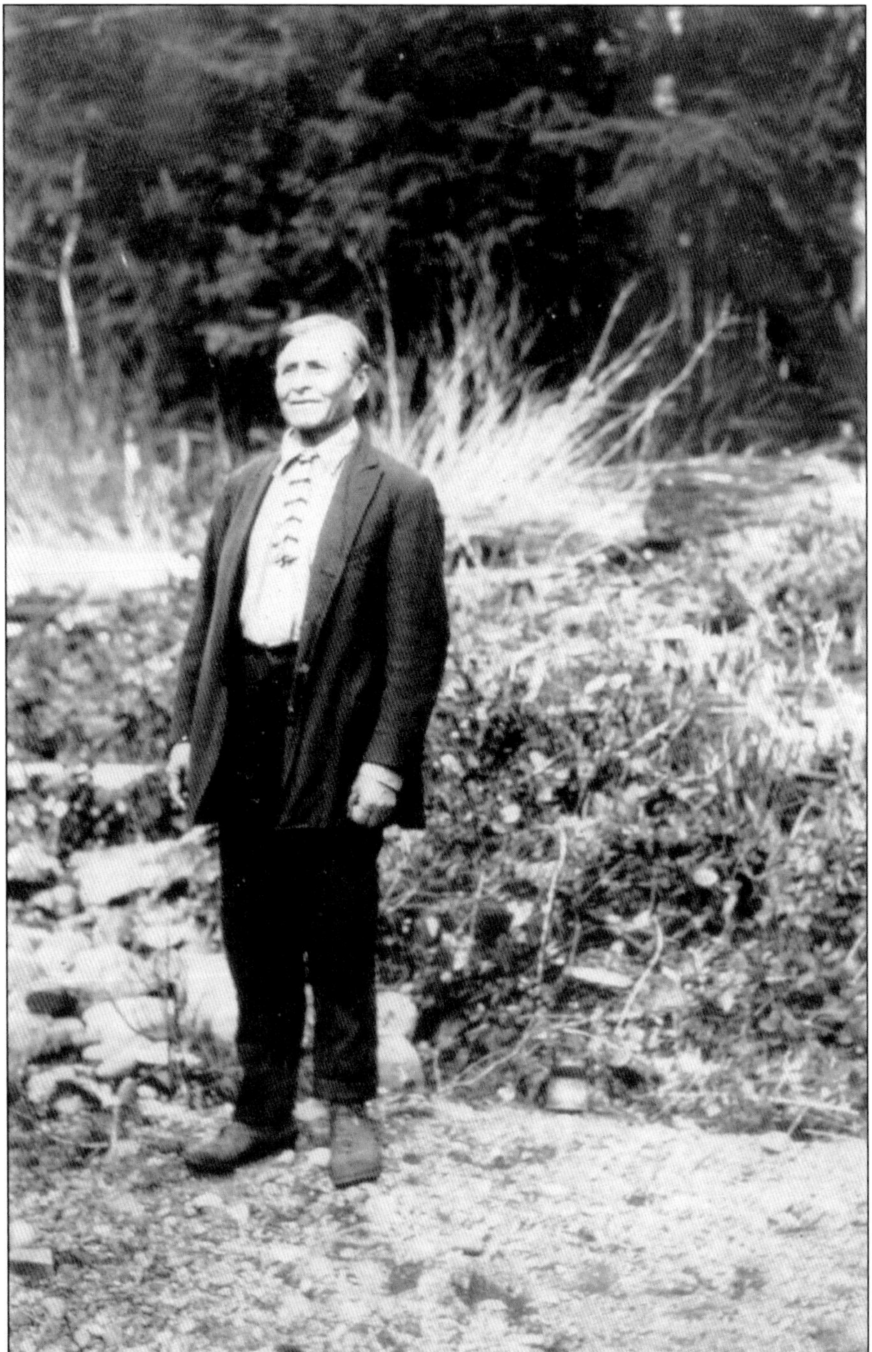

The Quileute have long-standing traditional hunting and fishing areas around Forks, and several Quileute tribal members established homesteads in the Quileute and Bogachiel river valleys. Quileute tribe member Tommy Payne settled along the Forks prairie. The need to cooperate to survive and thrive in the West End forest drew together pioneers from the United States and Europe. The tribes of the West End especially enjoyed joining Fourth of July activities, often winning the horse races.

Two

Early Logging Years

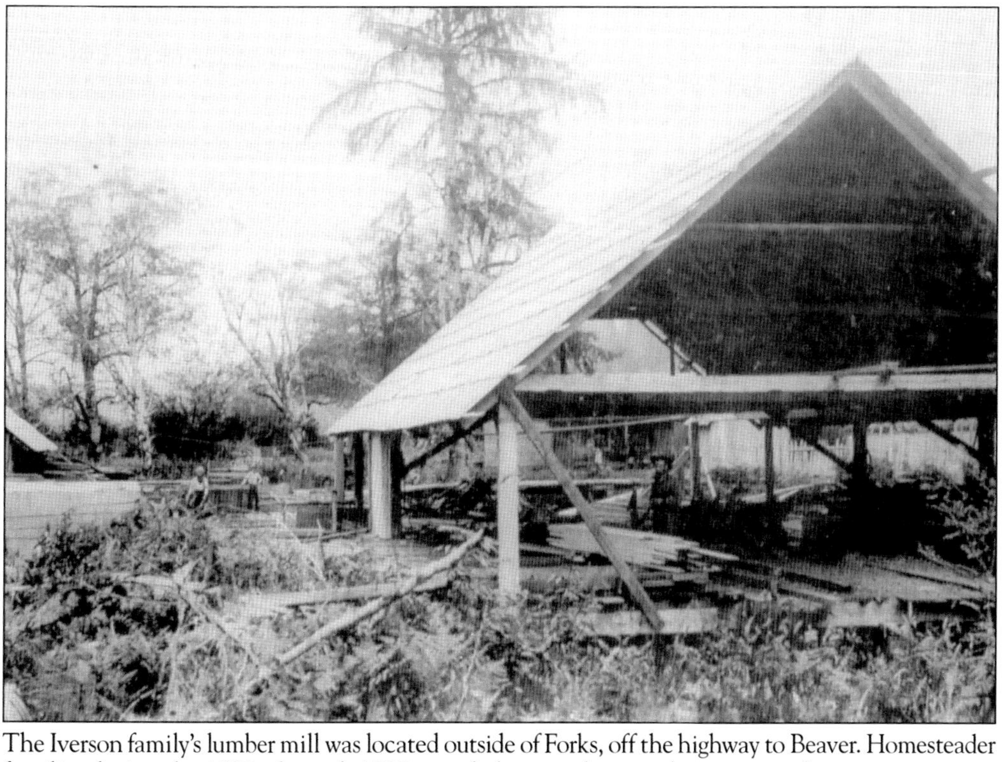

The Iverson family's lumber mill was located outside of Forks, off the highway to Beaver. Homesteader families during the 1880s through 1900s needed to supplement their income from growing crops and raising livestock, and some took to logging and milling, a first step in creating the timber industry in Forks.

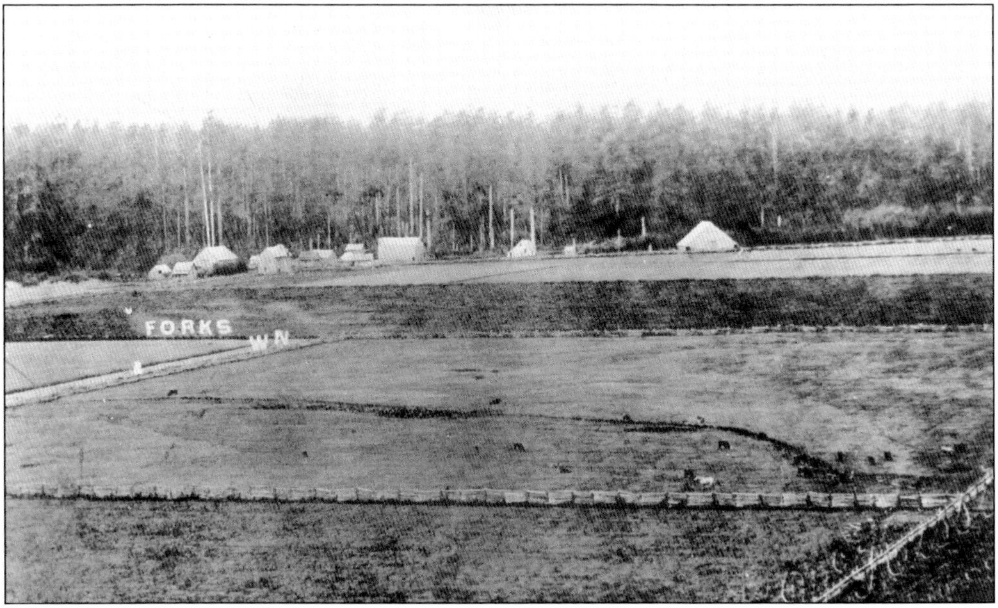

The Forks prairie was a frontier settlement lying between the Calawah and Bogachiel Rivers in the Olympic wilderness, with a few homes and commercial buildings in the late 1890s—the seeds for Forks's future.

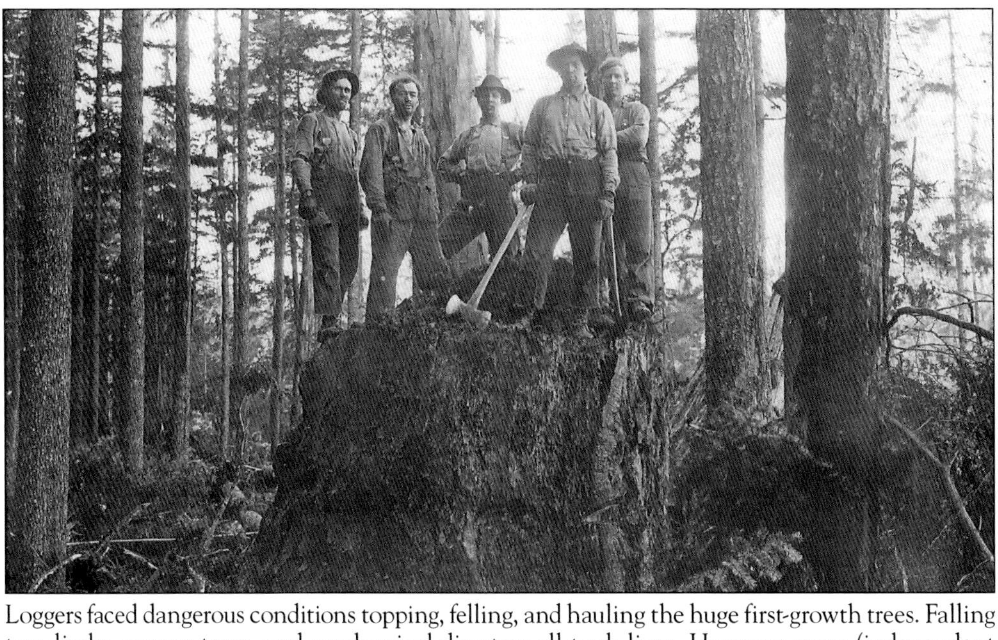

Loggers faced dangerous conditions topping, felling, and hauling the huge first-growth trees. Falling tree limbs, sprung trees, and mechanical disasters all took lives. However, gypo (independent lumbermen who worked under contract to logging companies) and company-hired loggers all shared a colorful heritage with their own jargon, dress, and pride in their hard work.

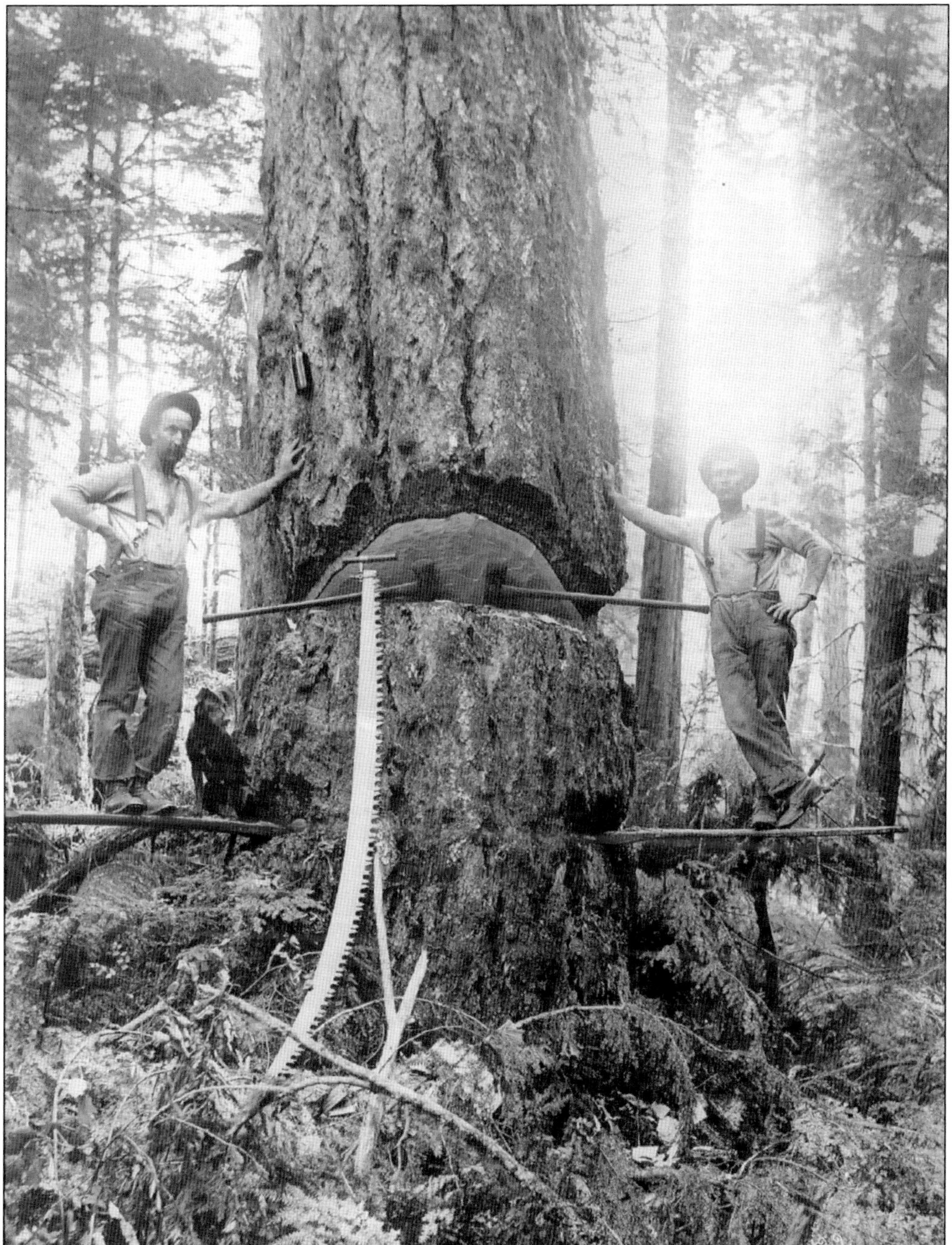

Tree fellers, finished with their first cut in a Douglas fir, pose on springboards in this staged photograph with their long-handled double-bit axes, crosscut saw, and faithful pet dog. Springboards allowed loggers to avoid cutting into hard-to-cut, tangled root sections of the tall trees. The bark of Douglas fir trees in the Olympic Peninsula's West End is noticeably thicker than that of the Douglas firs found in Oregon.

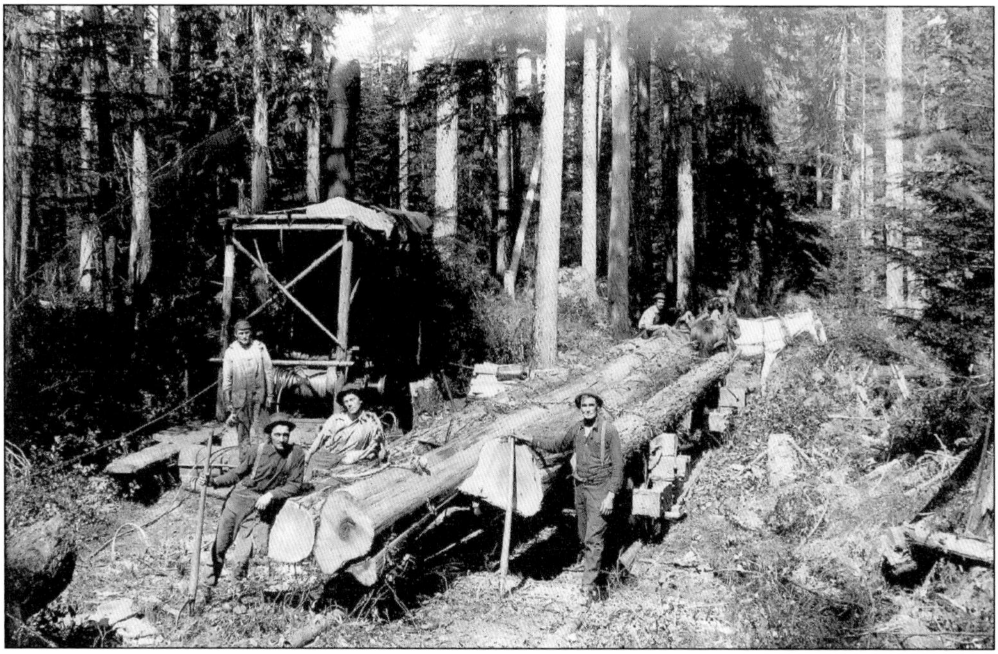

Using harnessed horses, a portable steam donkey, cables, metal chain chokers wrapped around logs, the peavey sticks held in their hands, and hours of hard work, this crew could move felled trees from the forest to mills. Every crew of timber felling had a unique personality. "It depends" was the stock answer when estimating work time, equipment, and manpower needed.

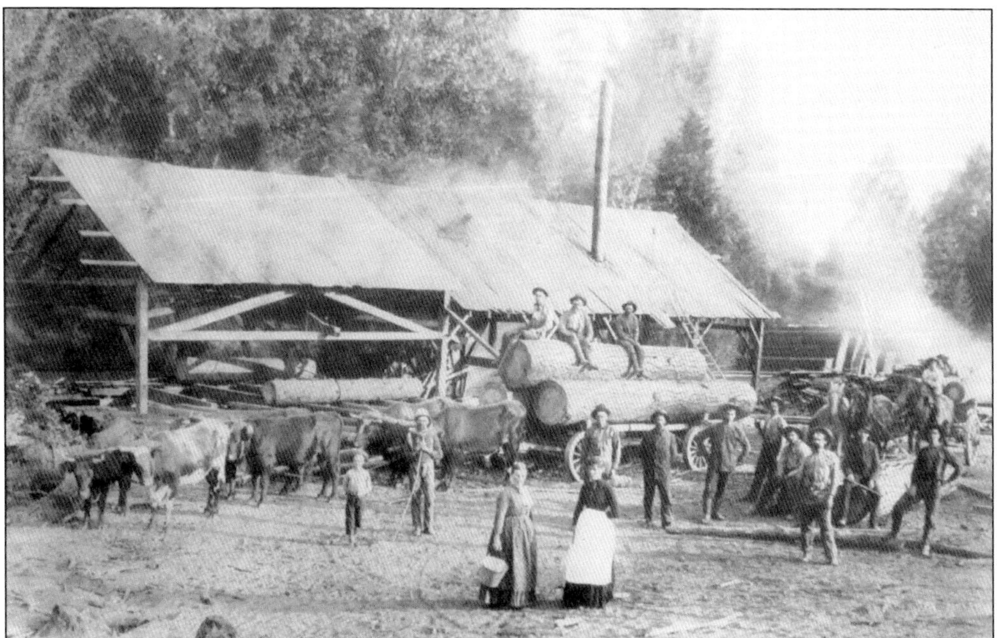

An early lumber mill scene provides a comprehensive look at life in the early days of Forks logging. An oxen team pulls a wagon loaded with first-growth logs. Two women, one with a wash pail and one wearing an apron, stand ready to attend to their hardworking men. The stack from a steam donkey pokes through a rough-hewn mill roof.

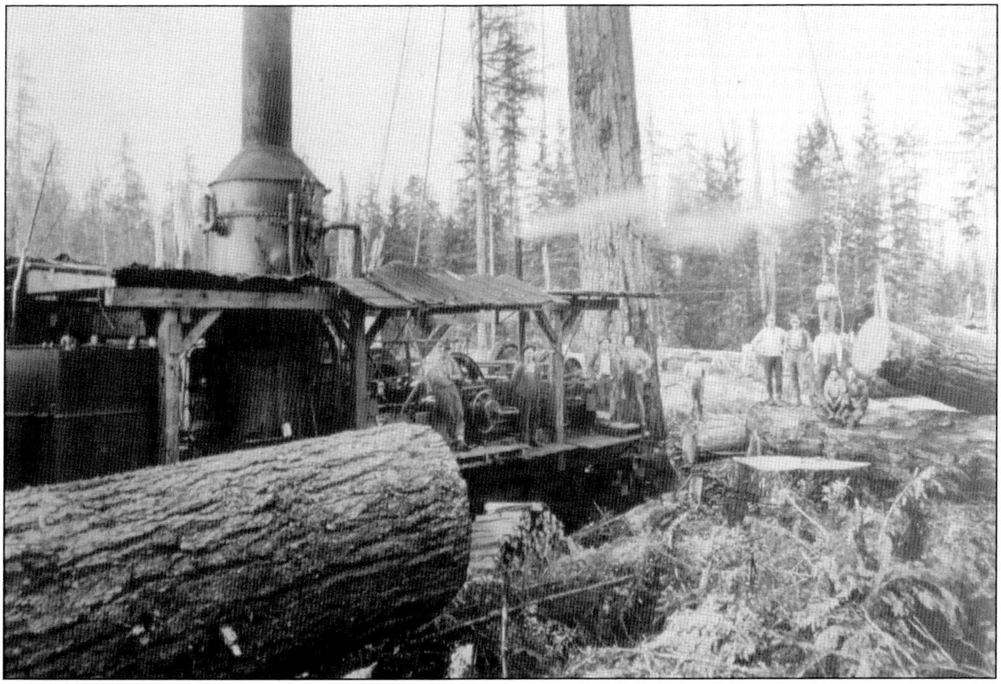

Workmen stand alongside a large stream donkey near a spar tree with high-lead cables draped down beside them from above. The spar tree provided leverage for moving the huge first-growth logs onto railroad cars and logging trucks.

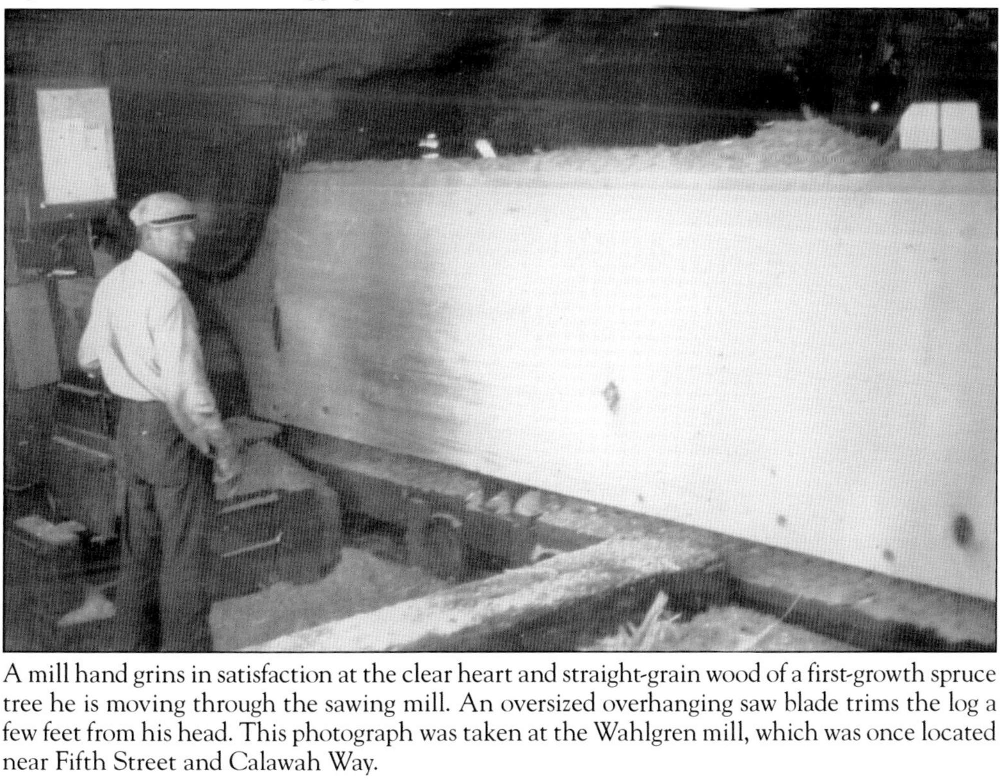

A mill hand grins in satisfaction at the clear heart and straight-grain wood of a first-growth spruce tree he is moving through the sawing mill. An oversized overhanging saw blade trims the log a few feet from his head. This photograph was taken at the Wahlgren mill, which was once located near Fifth Street and Calawah Way.

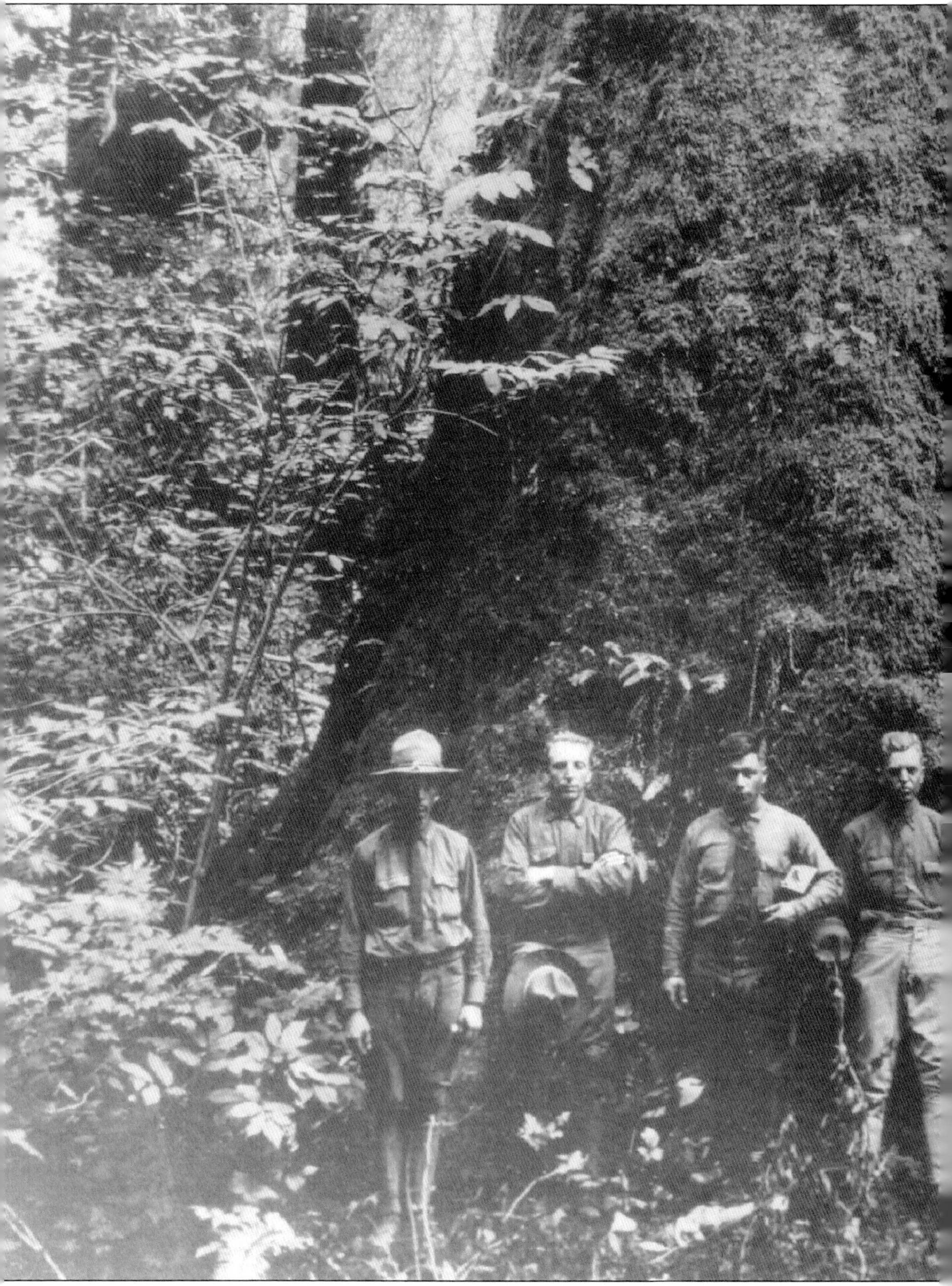

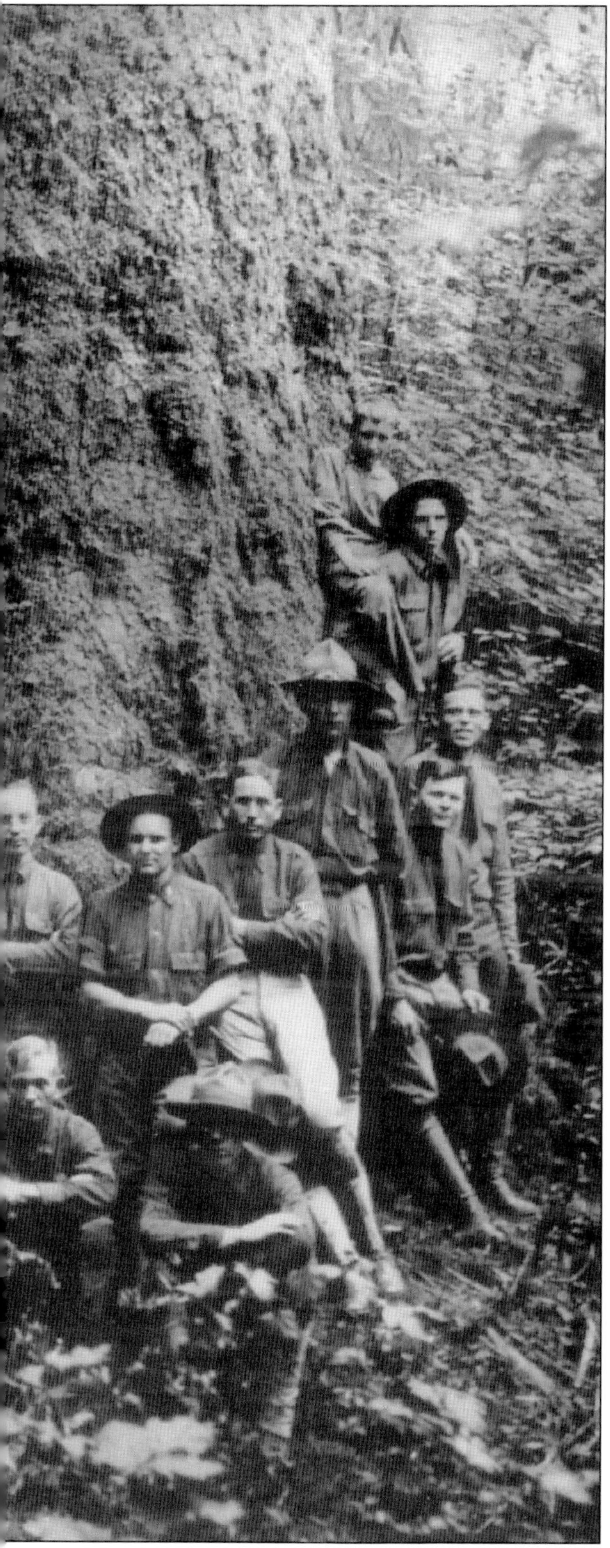

Men from the Spruce Division marvel at the size of the trees of the West Olympic Peninsula. Their job was to provide clear spruce wood for World War I combat airplanes and ships.

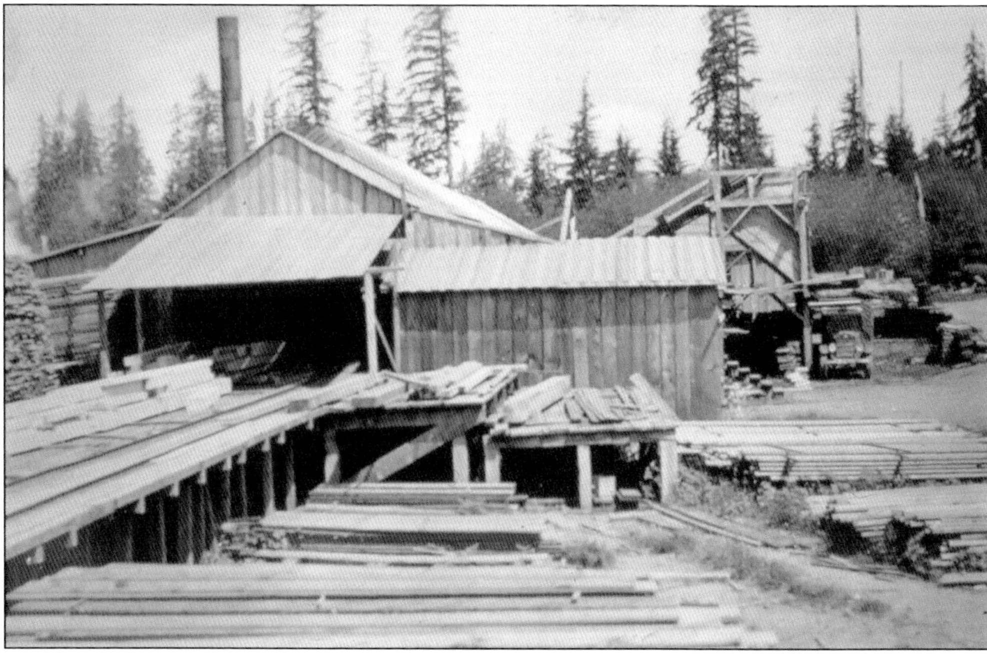

The Al Shearer and Oscar Wahlgren mill, located along Calawah Way, specialized in milling spruce during World War II. Large commercial sawing mills also provided lumber for local building and, more importantly, jobs and an export industry for Forks. Sorting and grading timber and lumber became a skilled occupation. A variety of lumber sizes were cut from the first-growth spruce, Douglas fir, and western red cedar trees.

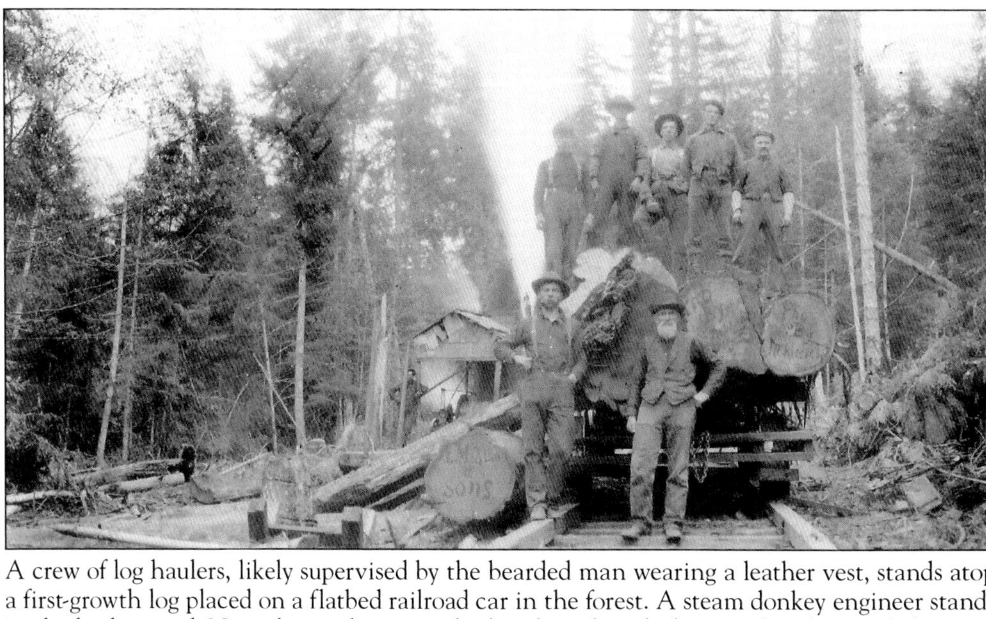

A crew of log haulers, likely supervised by the bearded man wearing a leather vest, stands atop a first-growth log placed on a flatbed railroad car in the forest. A steam donkey engineer stands in the background. Note the markings on the log that identified ownership; here, it belongs to F.M. Madison & Sons.

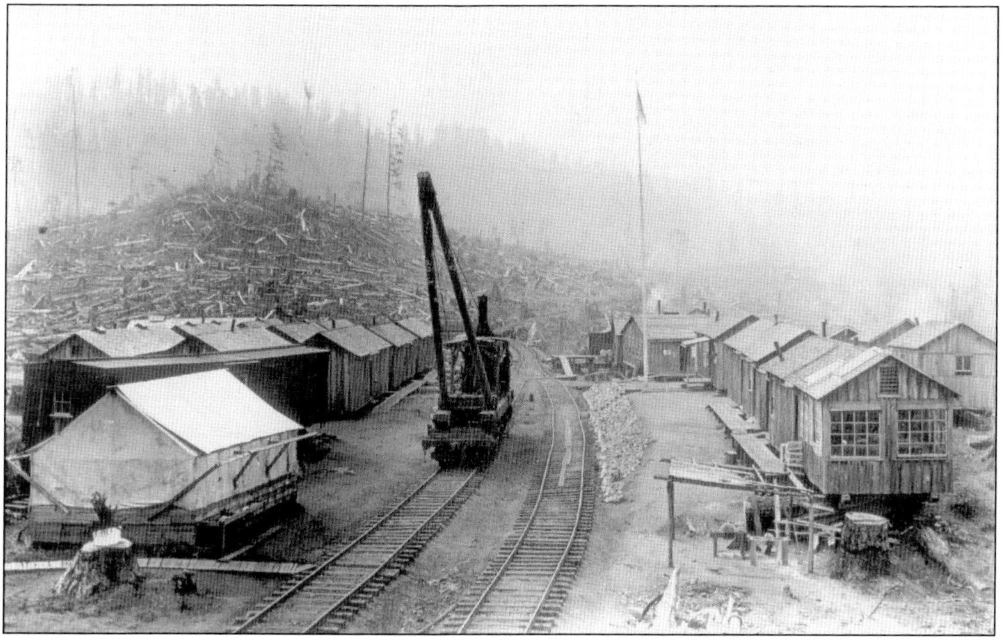

Logs dropped helter-skelter on a rise await transport out of the West End aboard railroad cars. A flagpole marks the railroad camp's office, and a cook tent is in the foreground. Workers would live in the board-and-batten–sided sheds. Parallel tracks are needed: one for flatbed cars and the other for a steam donkey-powered crane to load the logs.

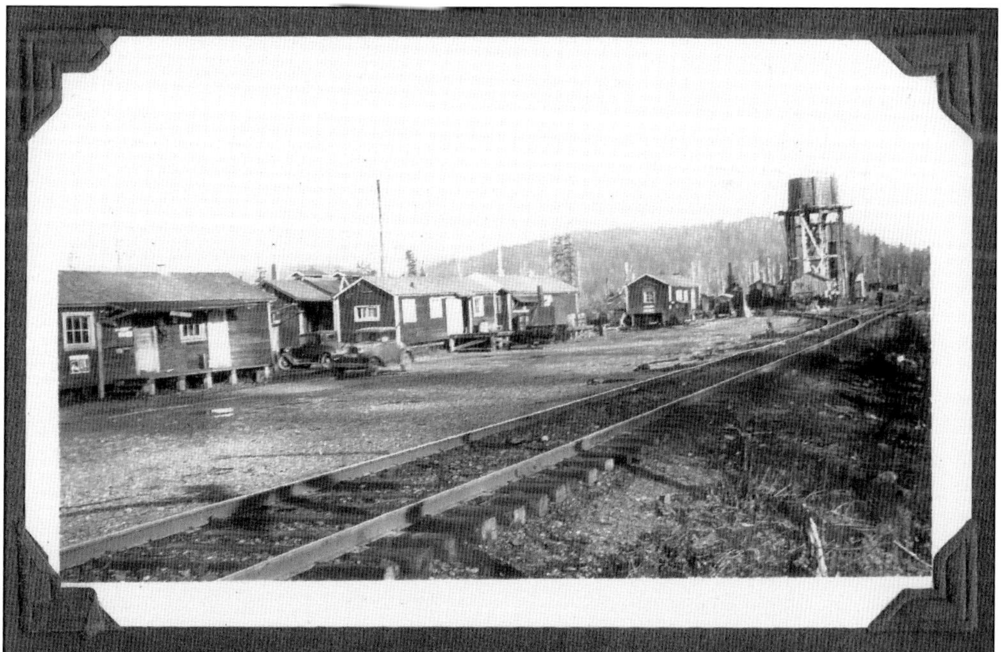

A lumber camp in Beaver in the 1920s was situated at the end of the Spruce Railroad line running out of Port Angeles and around the north shore of Lake Crescent. The water tower would supply steam locomotives and steam donkeys. Supply sheds and offices stood near the locomotive tracks.

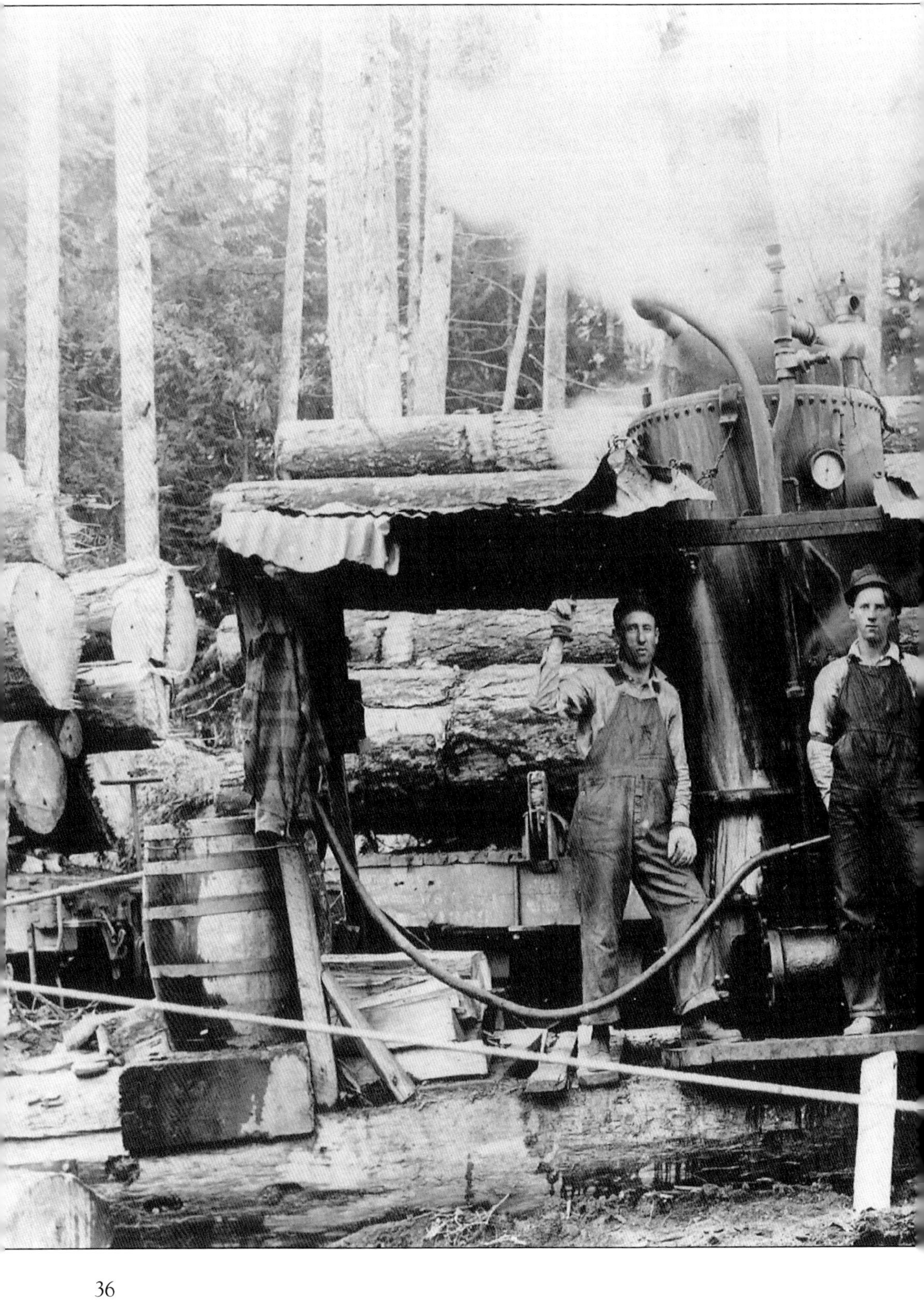

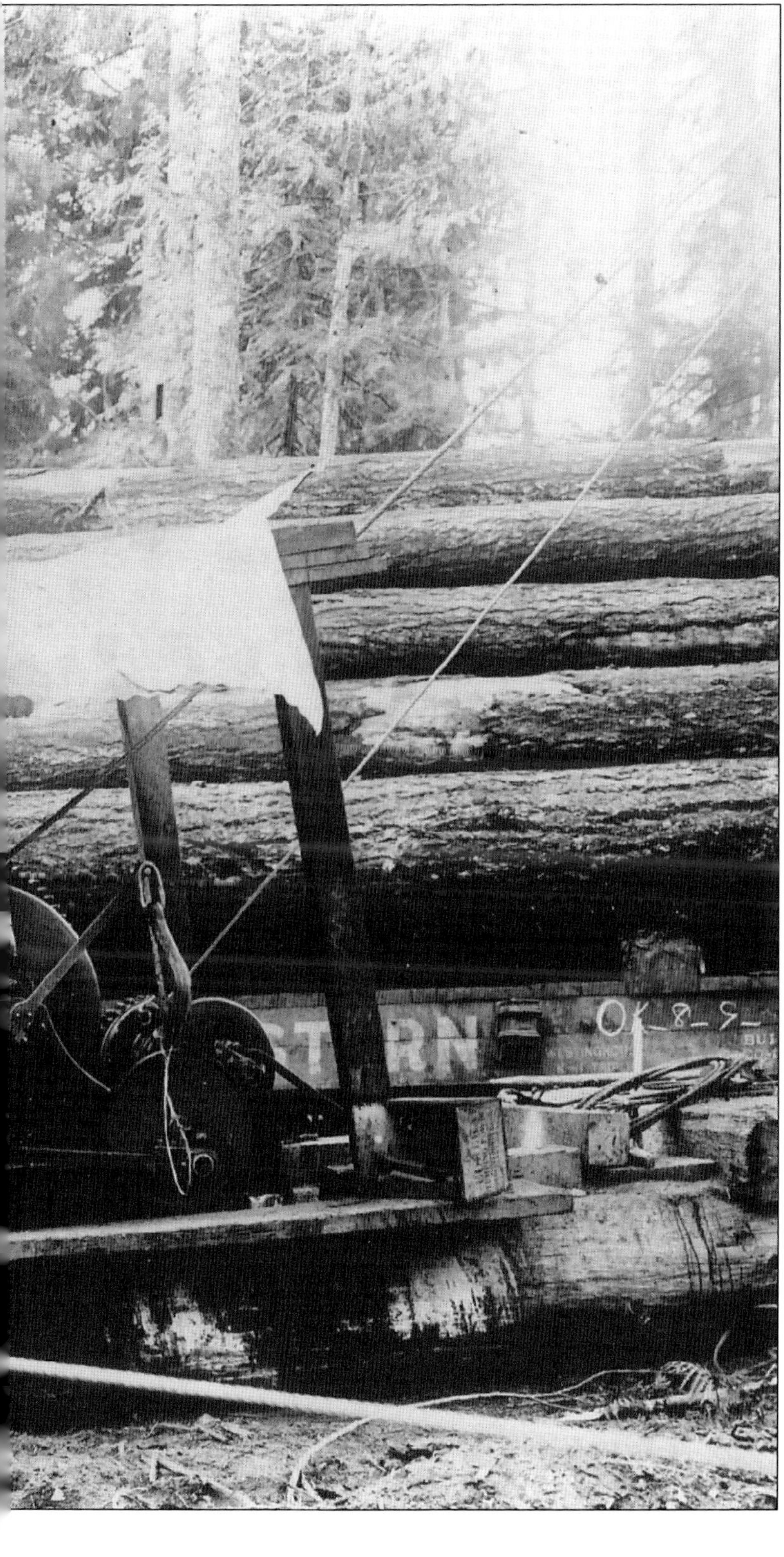

A steam donkey engineer (left) lets off a blast of steam, and his assistant stands by on a loading dock. The steam donkey boiler, originally modeled after the "donkey" capstans used on ships to weigh anchors and load freight, is used here to turn winches attached to cables and chokers for loading logs onto flatbed railroad cars.

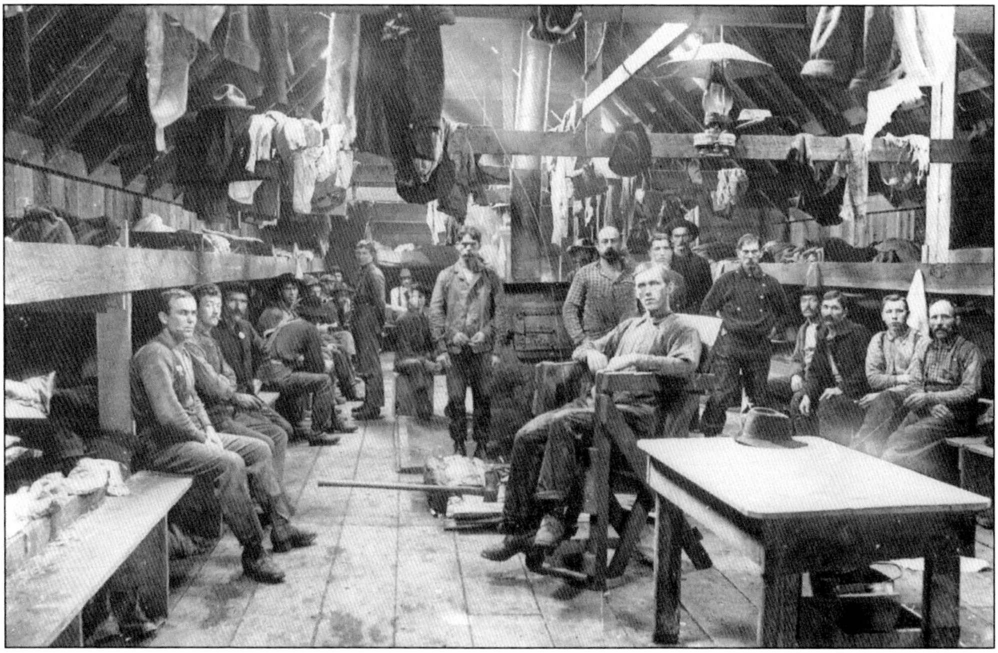

Loggers relax after work in typical logging camp living quarters. The ripe odor of the room was concocted from the sweat of men, who bathed only on Sundays; dirty clothing, which hung from the rafters to dry; wood burning in a stove; chewing tobacco spit into spittoons; and kerosene oil burning in lamps.

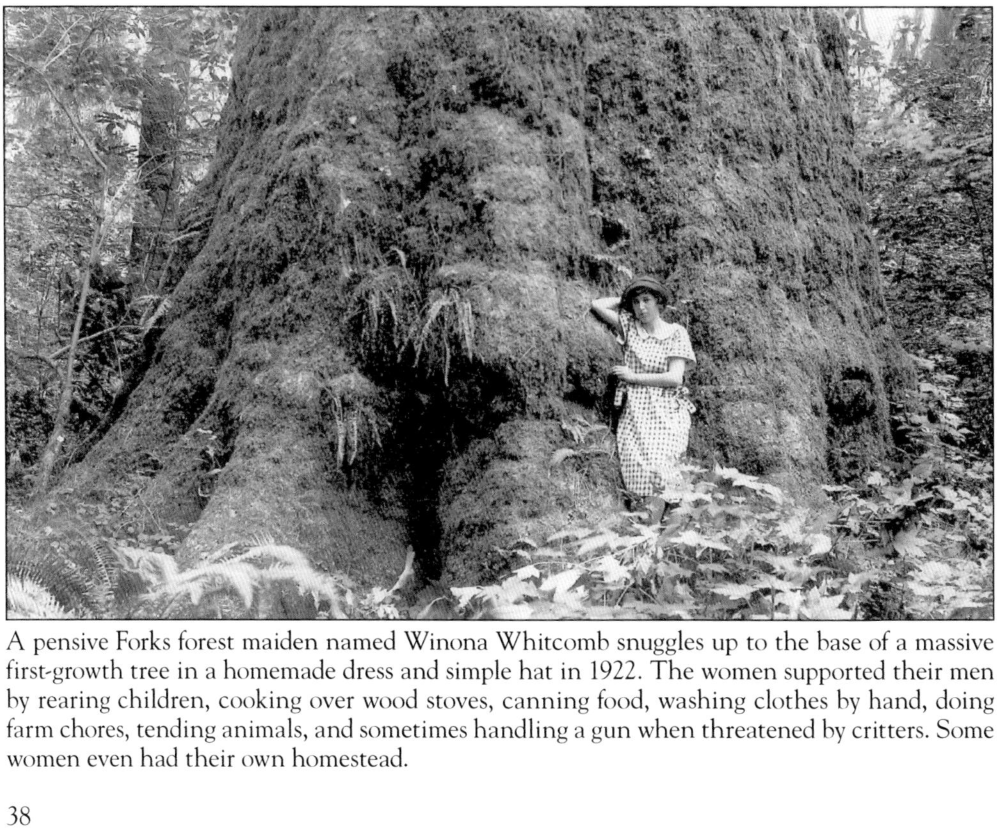

A pensive Forks forest maiden named Winona Whitcomb snuggles up to the base of a massive first-growth tree in a homemade dress and simple hat in 1922. The women supported their men by rearing children, cooking over wood stoves, canning food, washing clothes by hand, doing farm chores, tending animals, and sometimes handling a gun when threatened by critters. Some women even had their own homestead.

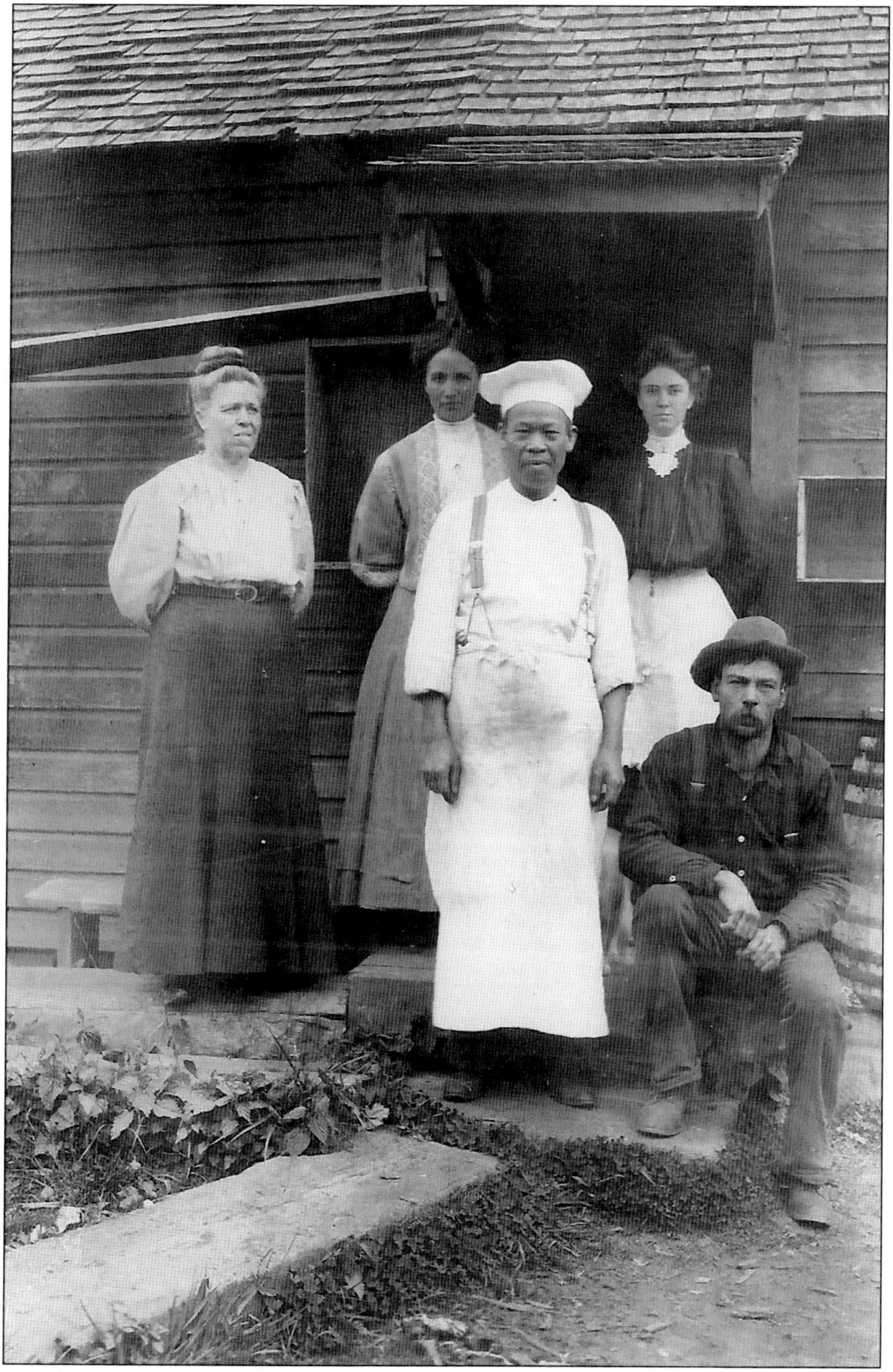

Taking a break outside the backdoor of a cookhouse are a trio of women, who perhaps hurriedly waited and cleared tables for a dining room of hungry loggers; a Chinese cook; and a young man, who quite possibly was biding his time working in the cookhouse while recovering from a logging injury.

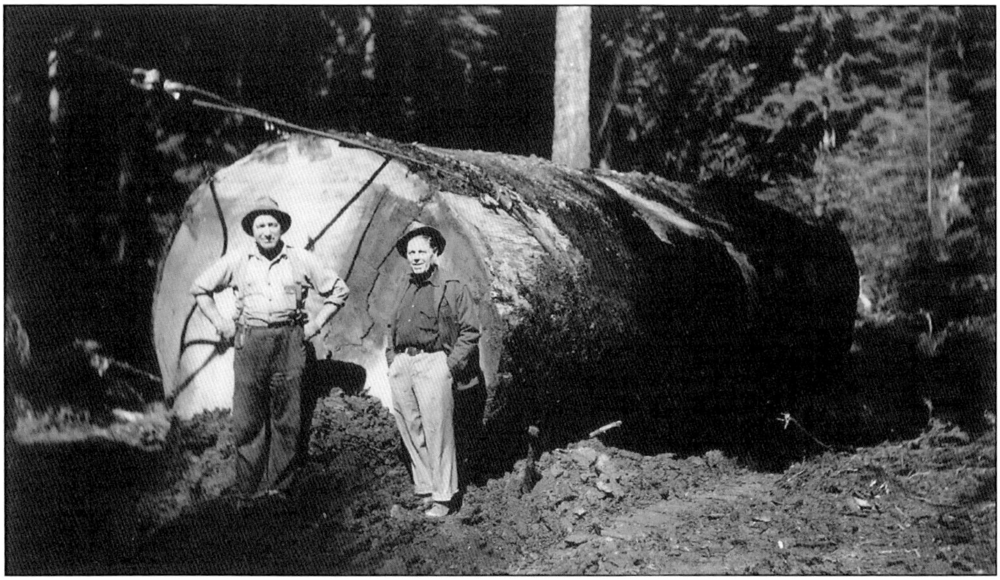

A we're-in-it-together relationship between logging crews and their bosses and timber company owners helped nurture the Forks timber industry. Workers toiled long hours, facing danger each day, while owners raised and invested capital, kept the books, managed spending, contracted for hauling logs to mills, and negotiated and bargained with mill owners for a good price for the logs.

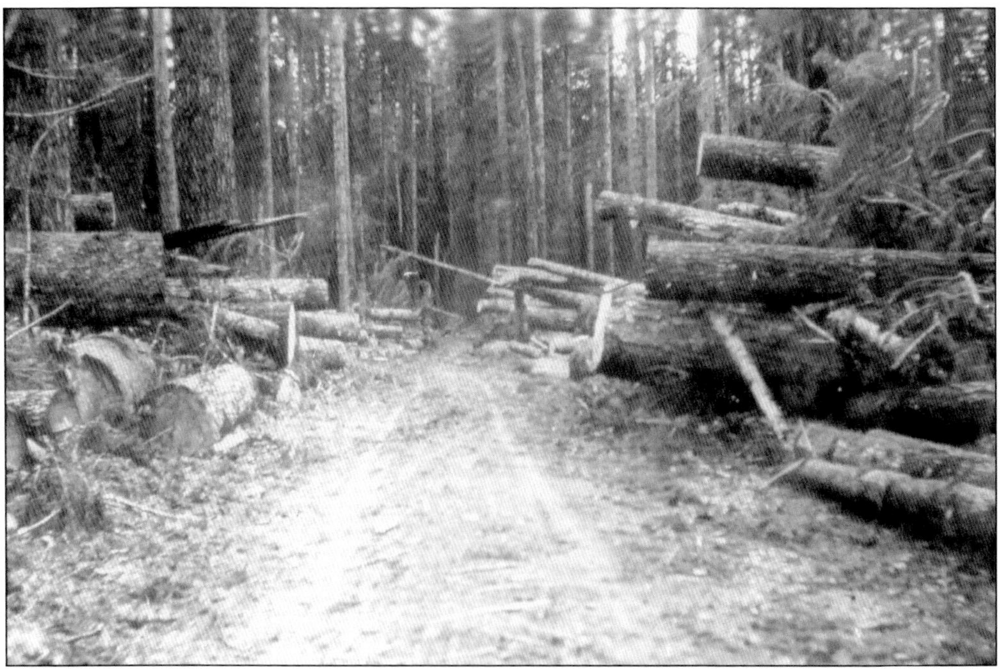

The hurricane-force "Great Blowdown" of timber swept across Forks on January 29, 1921. Millions of board feet of first-growth trees swirled in arcs, broke their roots free, and crashed down along the Washington coast. Forks and West End forests were hit the hardest. Downed trees covered almost the entire Olympic Highway from Forks to Lake Crescent. The landscape was changed in one day, covered with fallen logs, creating a major forest fire danger.

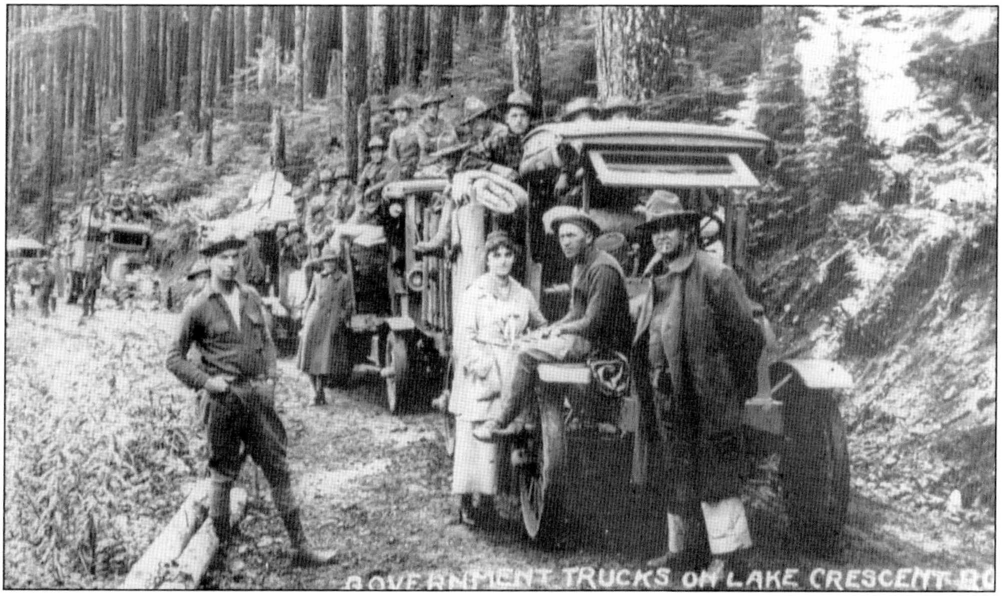

The US Army Signal Corps's Spruce Production Division was a massive movement of men and machinery aimed at gathering a supply of clear-heart spruce for the production of allied airplanes and ships during World War I. This caravan (above) of Spruce Division trucks is making its way along the single-lane dirt road it helped carve out along the south shore of Lake Crescent. The Spruce Division brought hundreds of men to Forks and the West End; some were experienced loggers, and some were there for the experience.

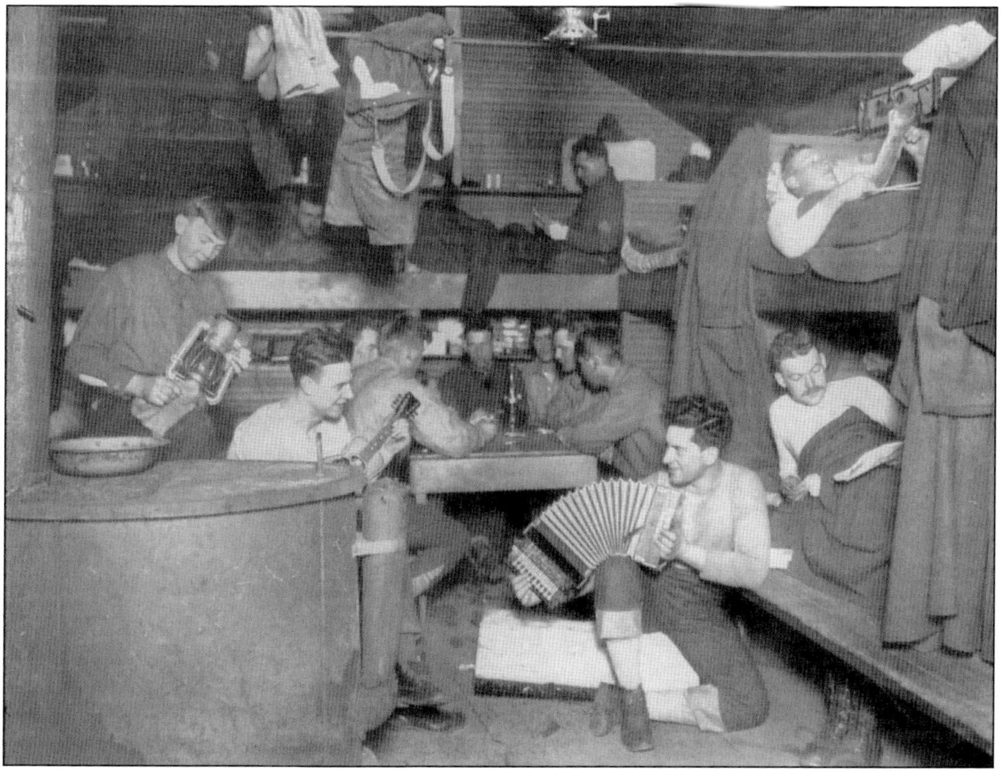

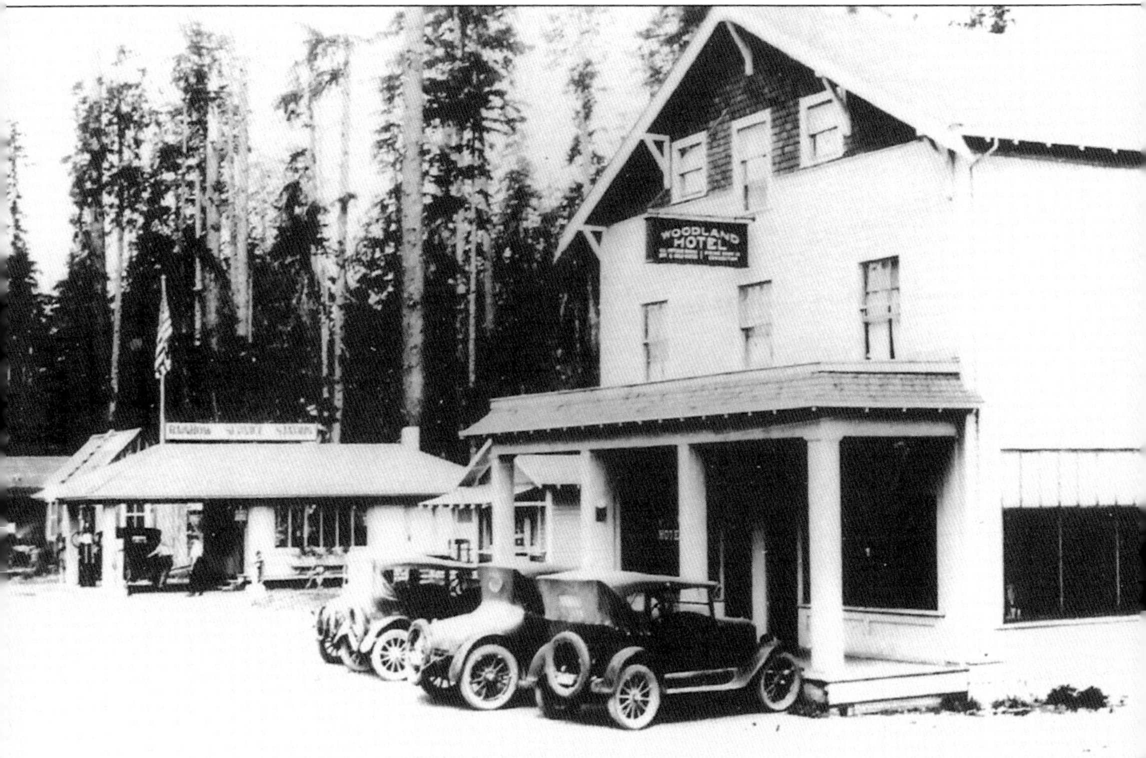

By the 1920s, Forks had begun to gain its title of "logging capital of the world," and logging dollars began to boost the economy. Timberlands still edged close to downtown Forks, a constant reminder of the timber industry.

Three

Forks Becomes a Town

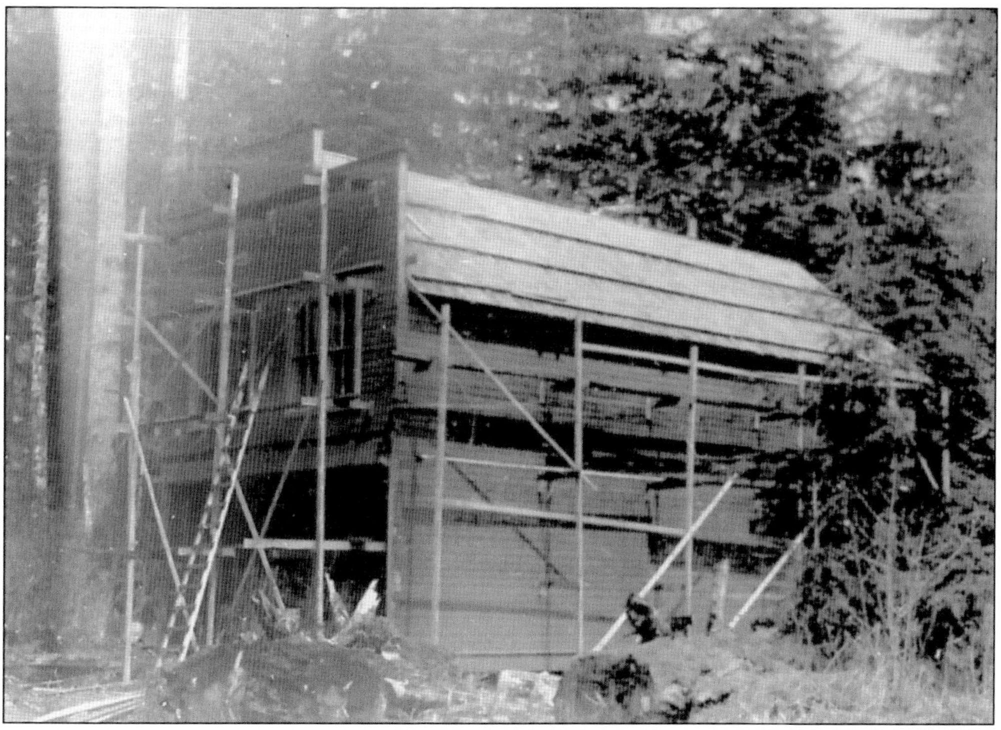

The first International Order of Odd Fellows Hall, with its Western-style false front, is under construction in 1903. The contractor for the job was John Iverson. The hall was one of the first sizable buildings constructed in downtown Forks. A similar structure, perhaps built by the same contractor, was erected in Sappho.

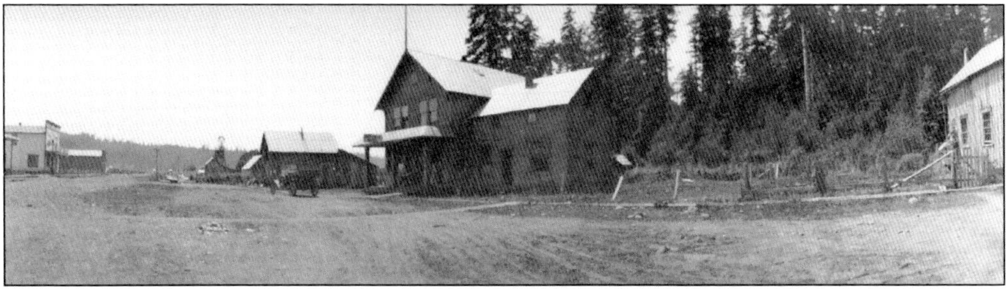

The Cottage Hotel is the building in the center. The building in the distance on the extreme left is the Forks Hotel, where Chinook Pharmacy is presently located.

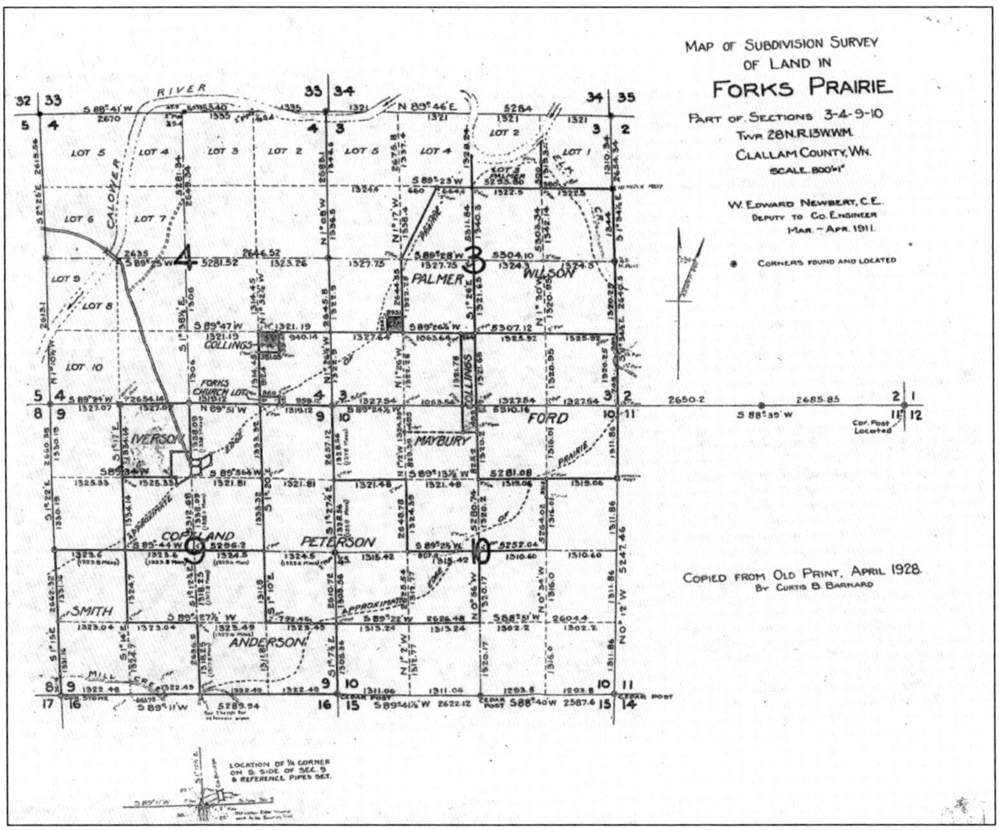

Here is a plat map of Forks taken from a survey that was completed in 1911. The names of pioneer families on the map show where their homesteads were located. The surveyors were likely from out of town, spelling Calawah River as "Calower" River.

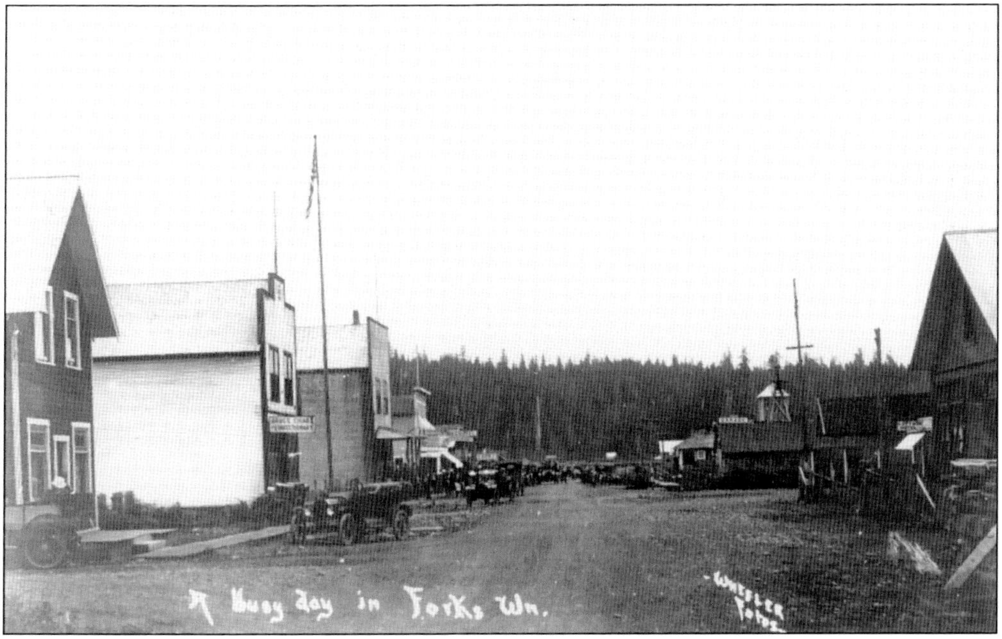

Here, looking south, is a busy day in this c. 1915 photograph of downtown Forks. The Odd Fellows Hall (left-hand side) provides a guide to the location of other buildings.

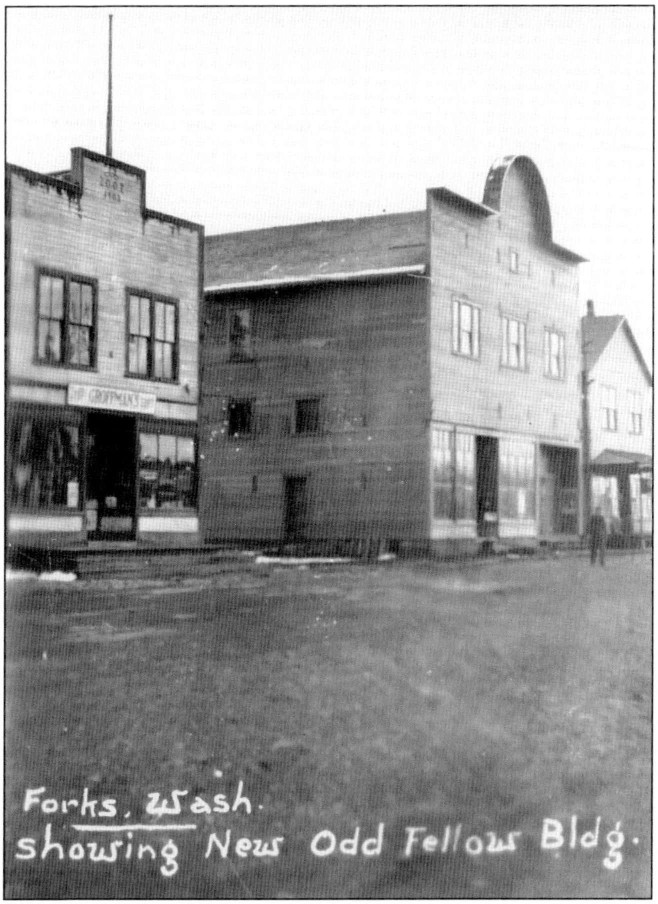

Newly constructed in 1920, the unpainted Odd Fellows Hall is larger than the first hall built in 1903. The devastating downtown Forks fire of 1925 destroyed this building and the 1903 building.

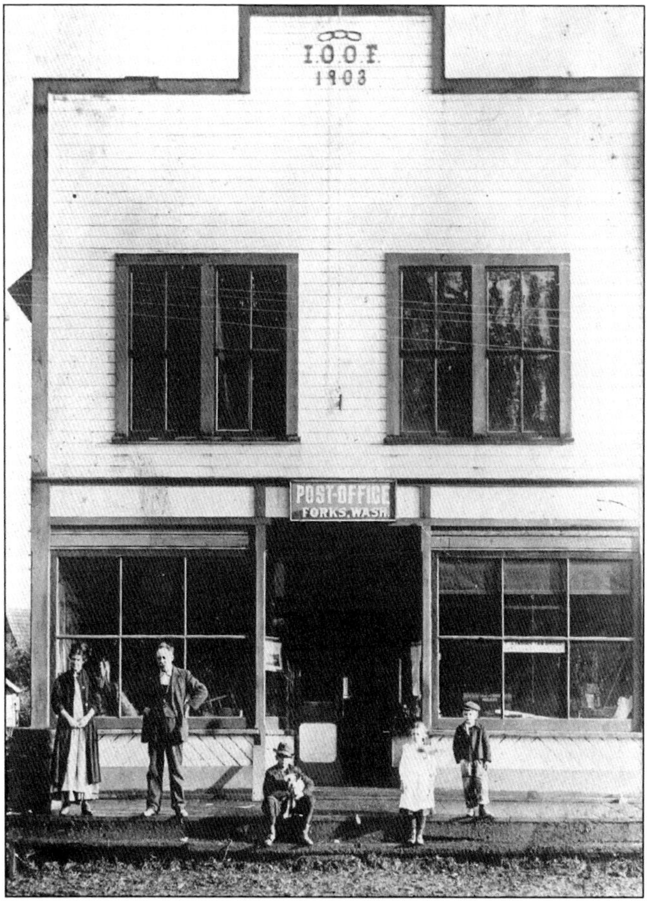

Here is the 1903 Odd Fellows Hall with Forks Post Office located in a store on its lower floor. The mail carrier brought his bags from Clallam Bay twice a week in this era. He also made stops at the post offices on the dirt road that went through Beaver and Sappho while on his way to Forks. With no telegraph or telephone service in place in town until 1909, mail was a vital and much anticipated connection to the world outside the forest.

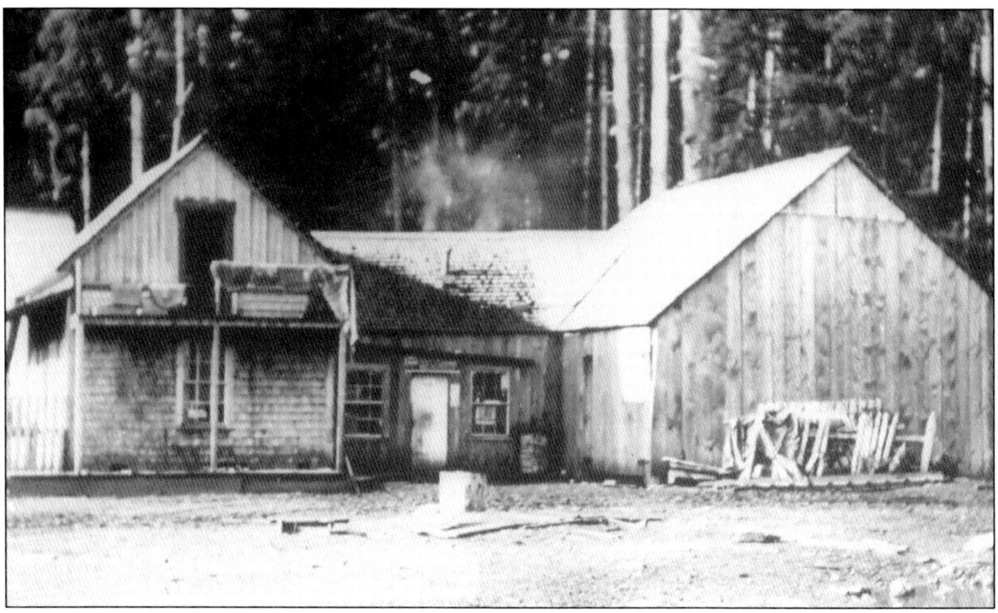

This hotel in Forks shows the rough-hewn construction of early downtown commercial buildings.

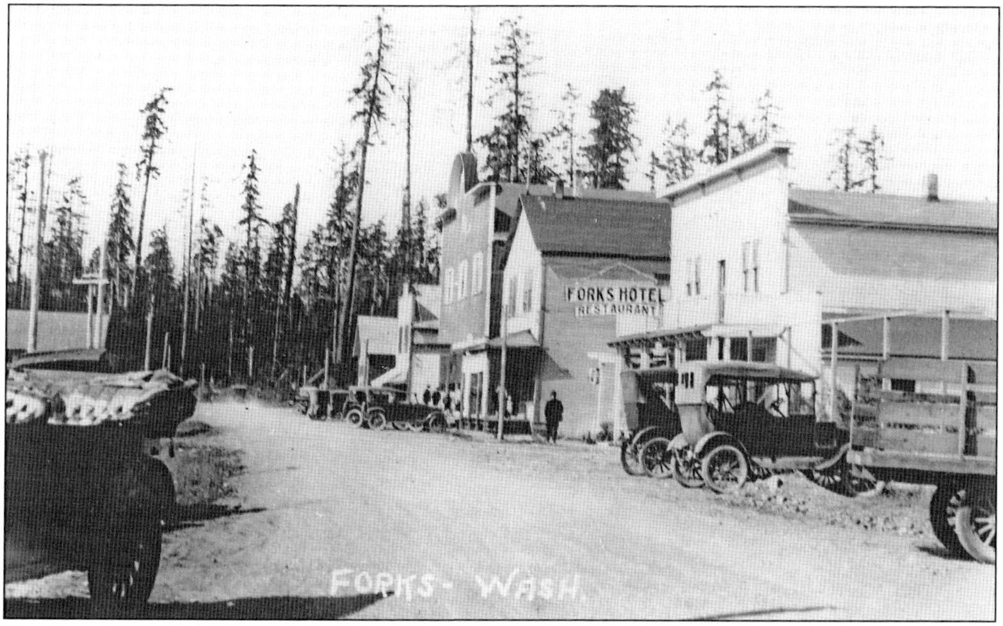

Touring automobiles line Forks's Main Street in the early 1920s, carrying visitors to town and allowing easier transport for local residents to other locations on the West End, Port Angeles in East Clallam County, and points beyond. However, the highway ended in Forks, leaving only horse and foot trails heading south.

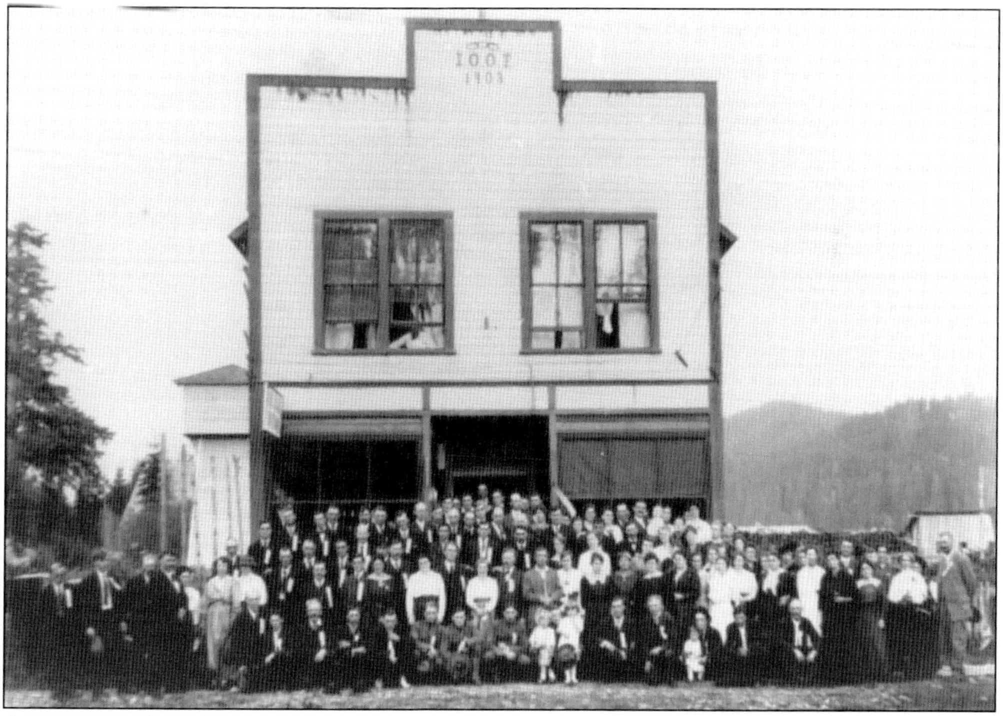

A semiannual gathering held in September 1917 at the Odd Fellows Hall called for a group photograph. The Odd Fellows provided benevolent social services in a time when government aid for families and individuals was limited at best.

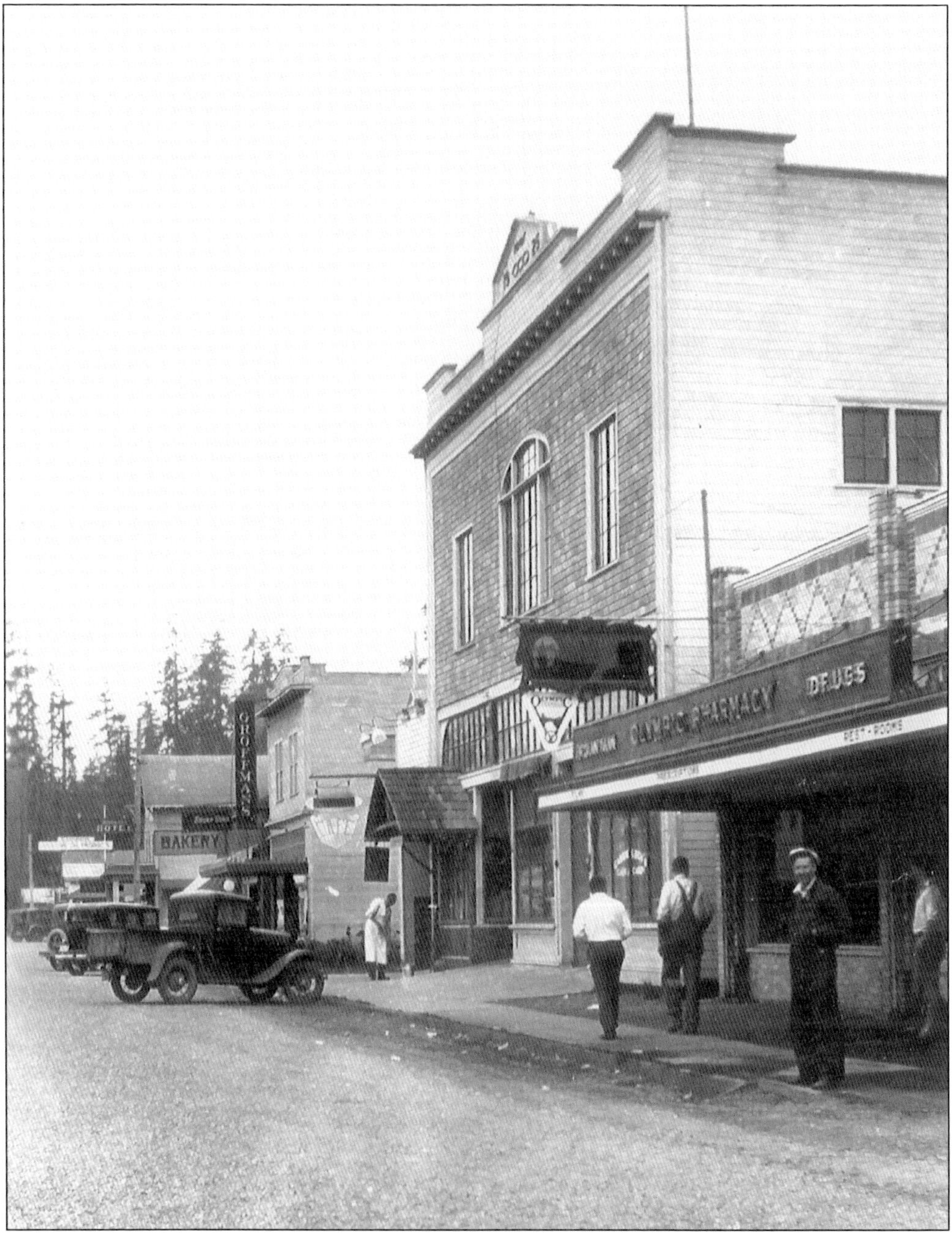

Downtown Forks added concrete sidewalks and renovated buildings, including the Odd Fellows Hall, following the 1925 fire. The Olympic Pharmacy, with its intricate brickwork wall designs, boosted the level of medical care and products available.

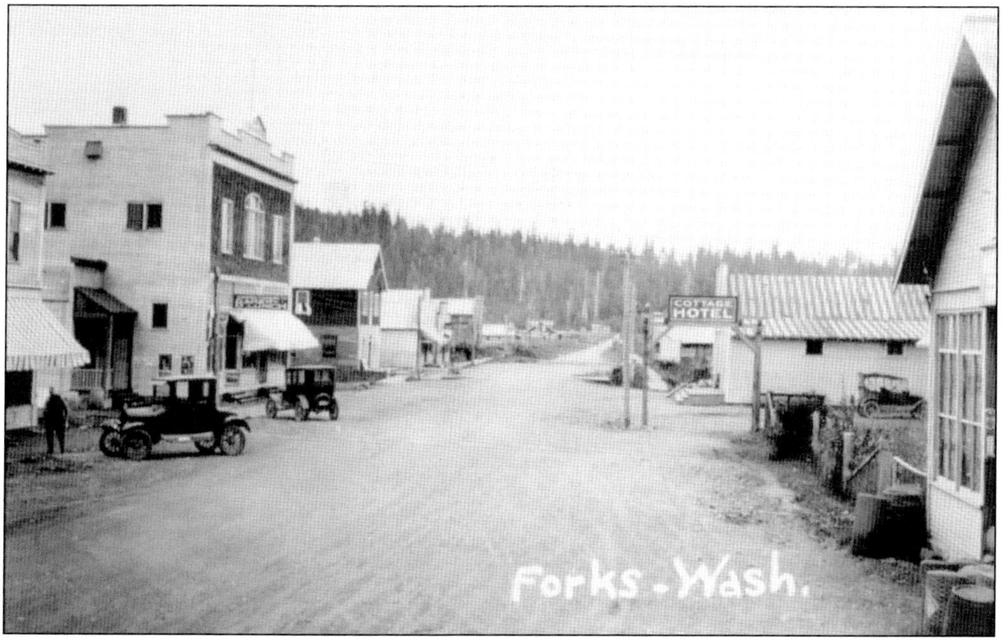

In the late 1920s, most of the south end of Forks remained undeveloped, with the main road continuing on as a trimmed down, path-size route from that point on. A bakery and lunchroom opened on the first floor of the Odd Fellows Hall.

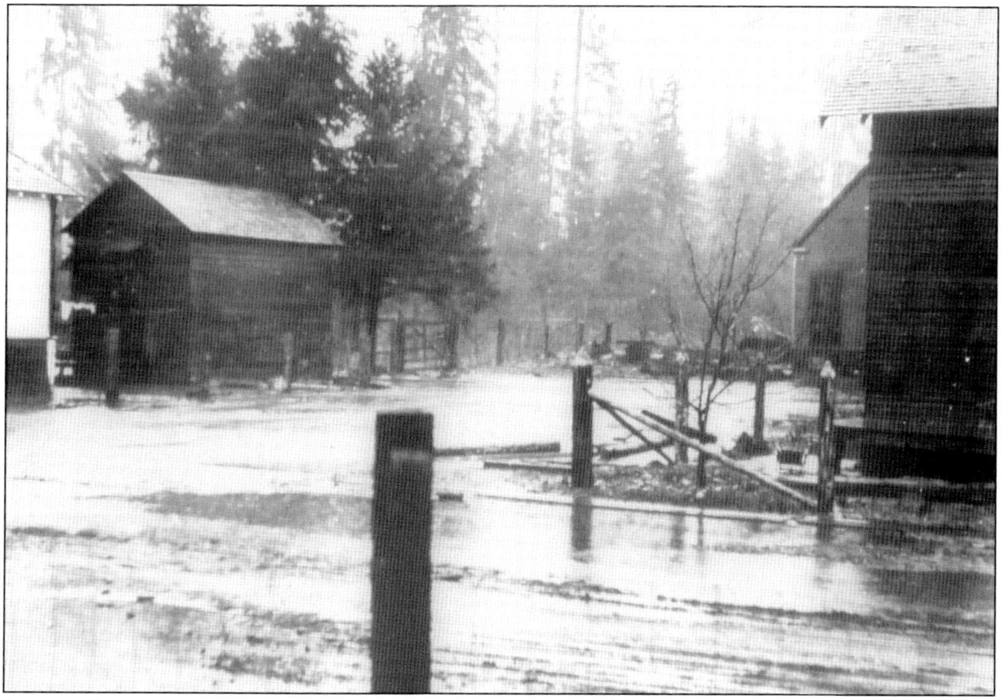

Rain and more rain are a given in Forks. Unpaved roads and walkways made for muddy travel. Residential and commercial buildings were often set off the damp ground with a foundation of rocks and wood. Over eight inches of rain can fall in a 24-hour period, causing loss of power and evacuations of low-lying homes.

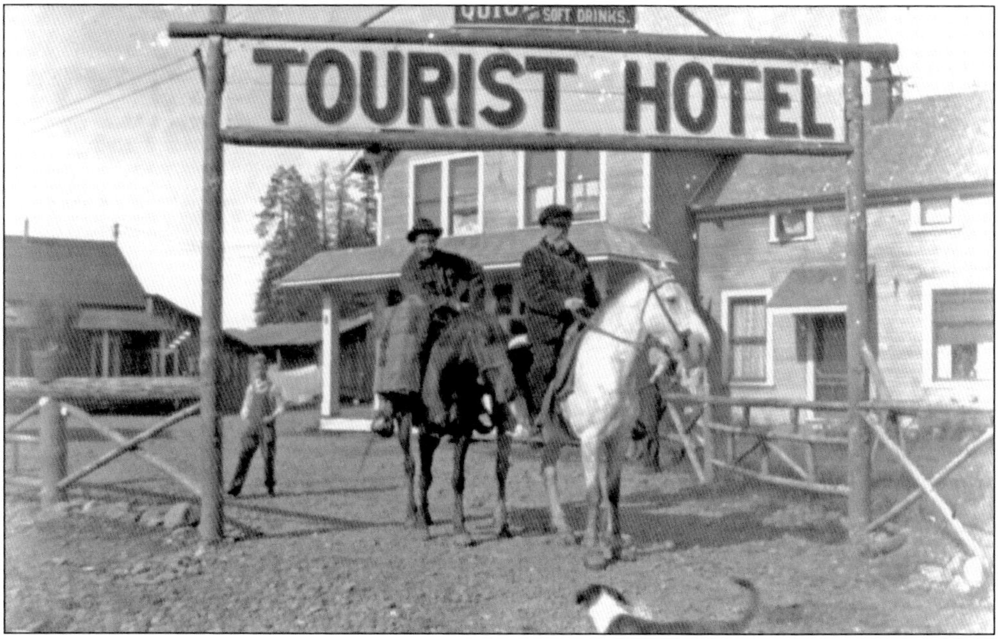

Visitors could not miss this hotel, which was simply named Tourist Hotel, around 1920 in Forks. To see the sights beyond the unpaved highway and settlement in Forks meant either walking or mounting a horse, as these gentlemen did.

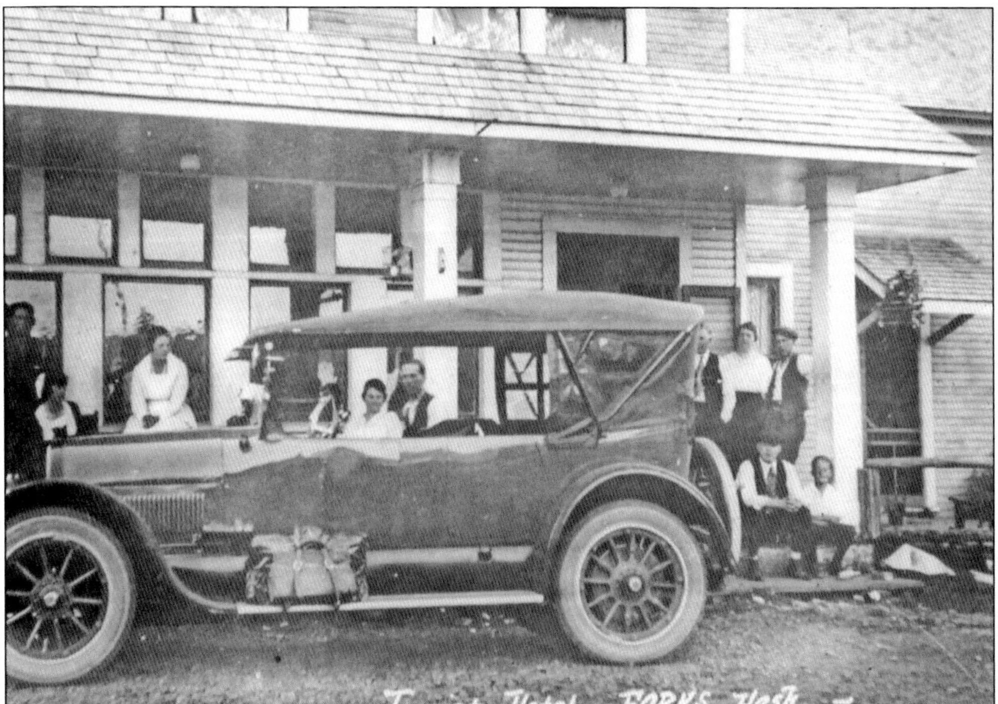

Tourism started up early in the 20th century in Forks. Here, relaxed visitors in their city suits and dresses linger outside the Tourist Hotel. This touring car was the first motorized stage used to transport passengers in Forks.

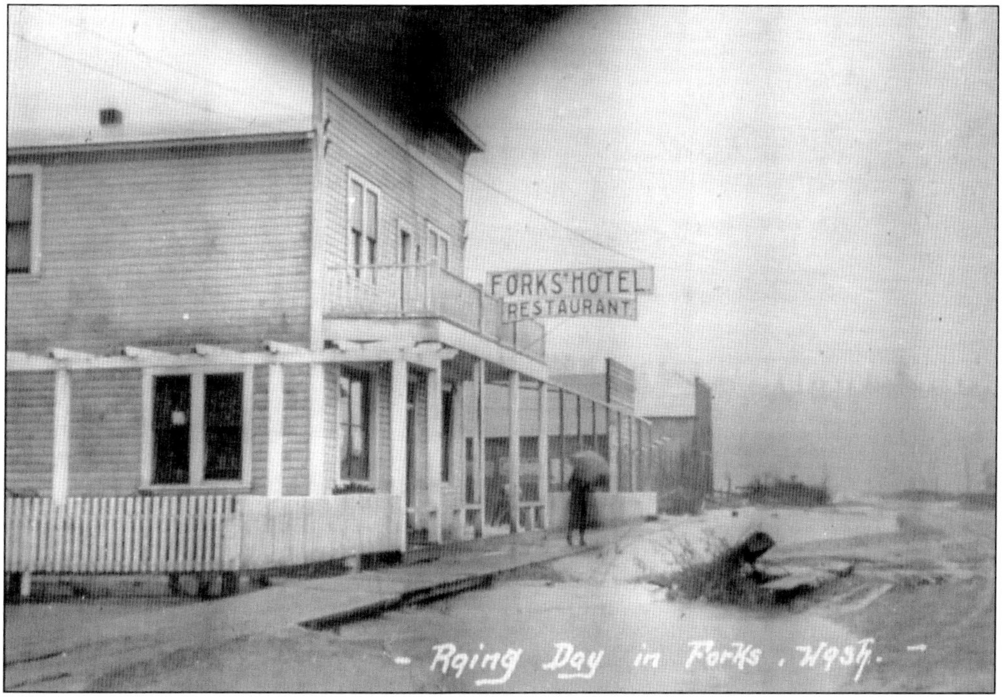

Making her way down the wooden sidewalk past the Forks Hotel in the 1910s, a woman fights the rain and wind under her umbrella—a rare sight in Forks even today, where the Northwest pioneer tradition lives on of appearing oblivious to personal hardships like getting soaked in a rainstorm.

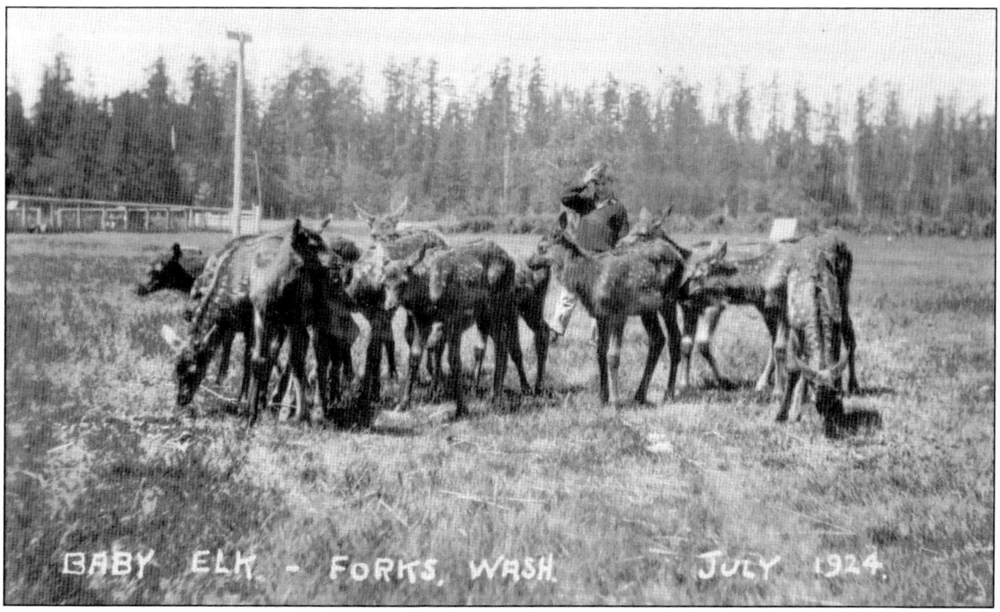

A herd of baby Roosevelt elk grazes in a grassy lot in the summer of 1924. Lena Fletcher and Dora Huelsdonk (Richmond), daughters of pioneering Lower Hoh River families, were among those who walked the elk out of the West End to sell to zoos in the Seattle area, Alaska officials for seeding herds to the north, and elsewhere.

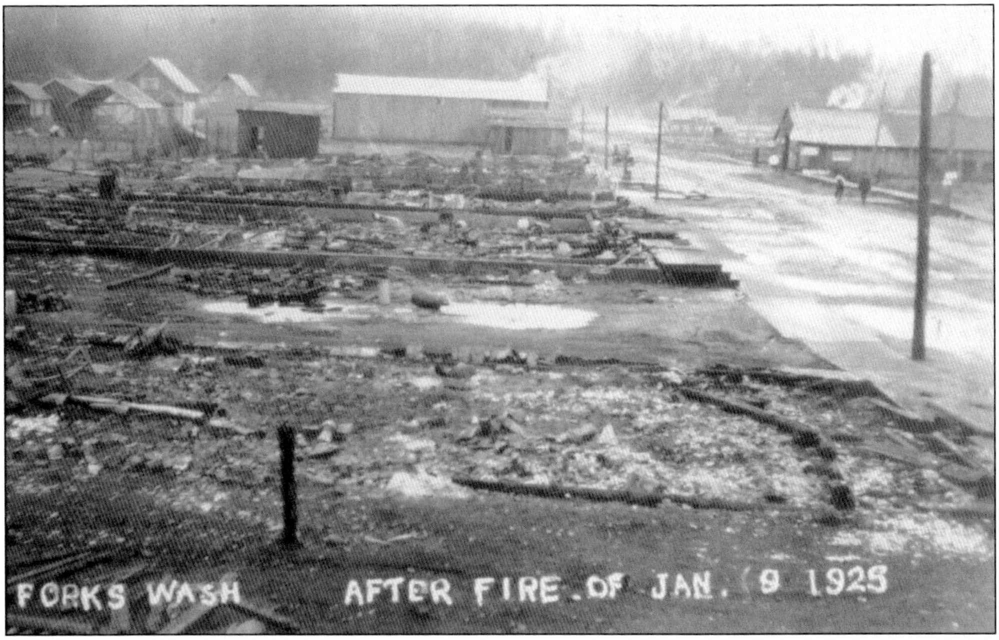

The Forks fire of 1925 leveled half a dozen commercial businesses on the east side of town, including the 1903 Odd Fellows Hall. The fire turned out to be a blessing in disguise. The rebuilding effort revamped downtown Forks, bringing a modern hotel and other new facilities.

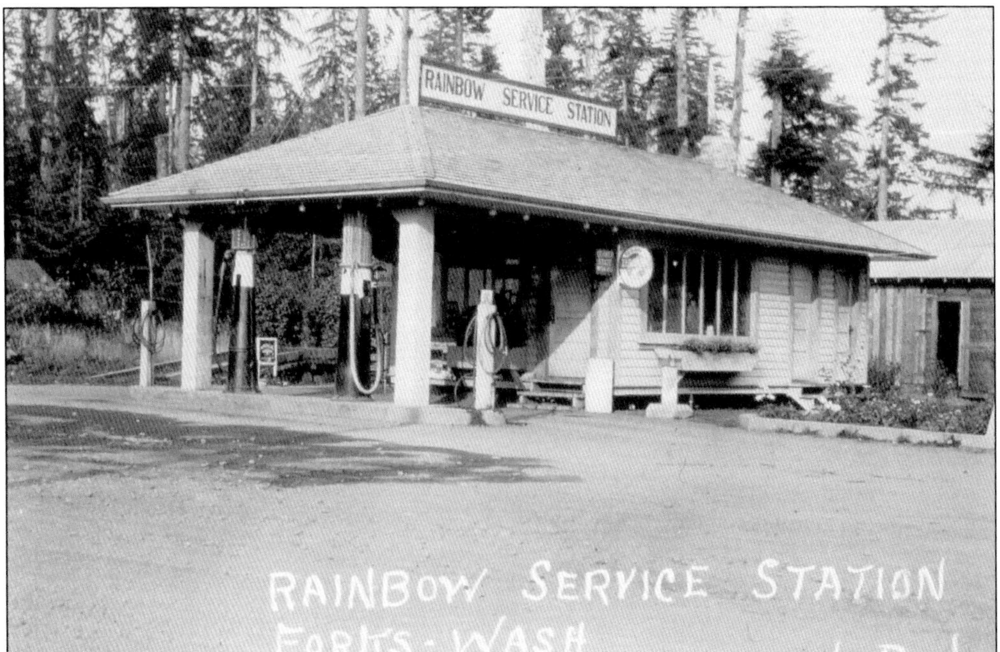

J.B. Hahn brought a stand-alone fueling service to Forks drivers when he opened the Rainbow Service Station. The amount of gas going into tanks was visible in the clear glass tops of the pumps.

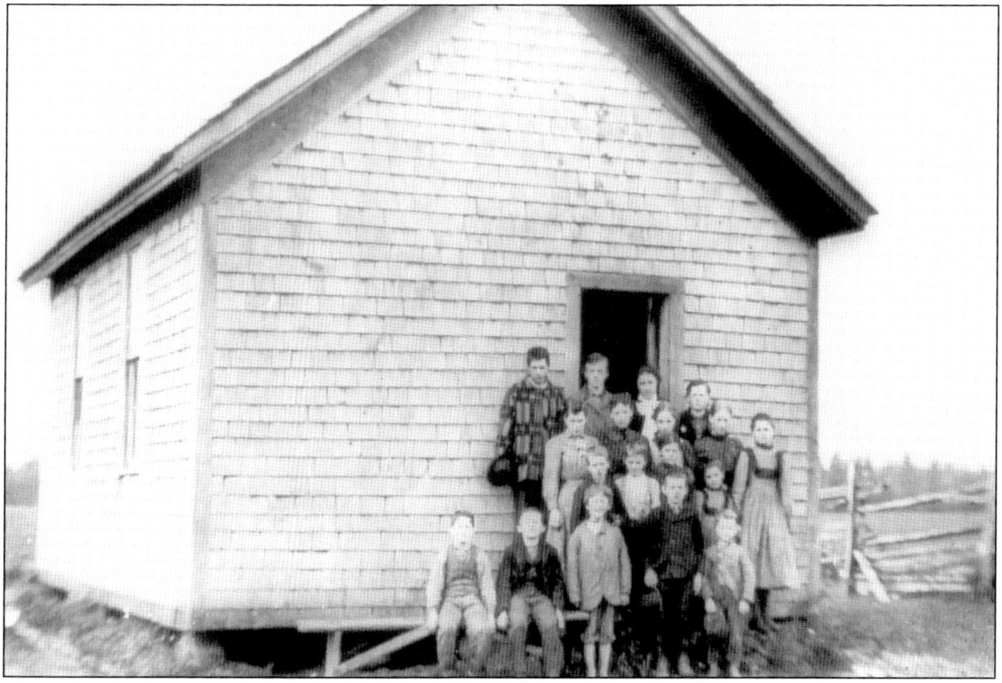

This early-1900s building was typical of the one- and two-room schoolhouses where children from the Forks and Quillayute prairies studied. The community constructed the schools, and parents funded the education.

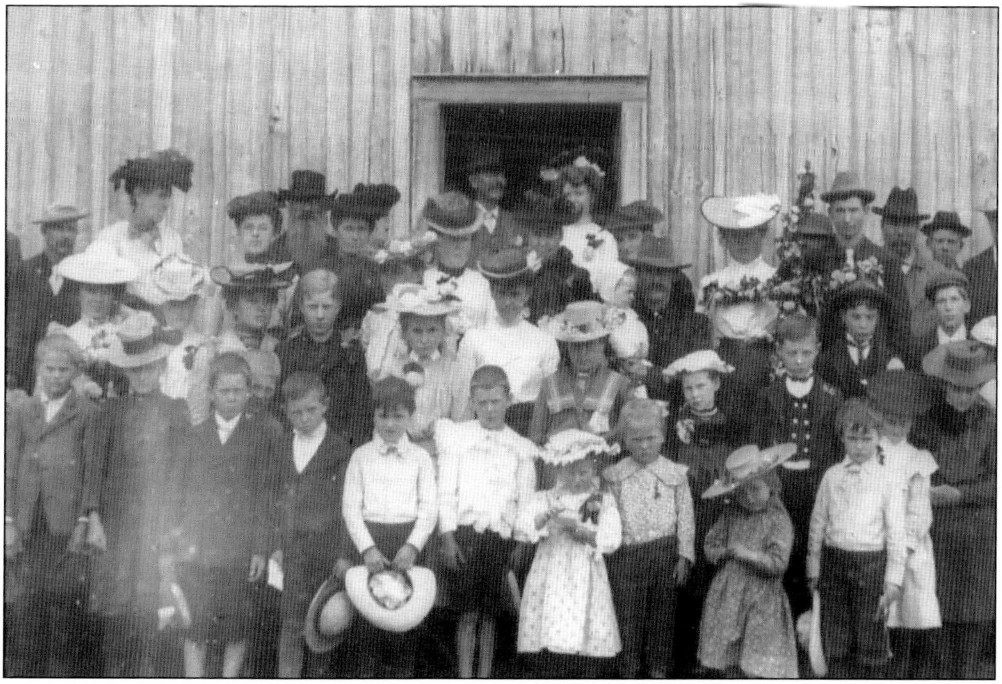

School events, like graduations and concerts, provided parents and children an excuse to dress up. Bonnets—often decorated to match the season with flowers, ribbons, and lace—were a fashion item for women and young ladies.

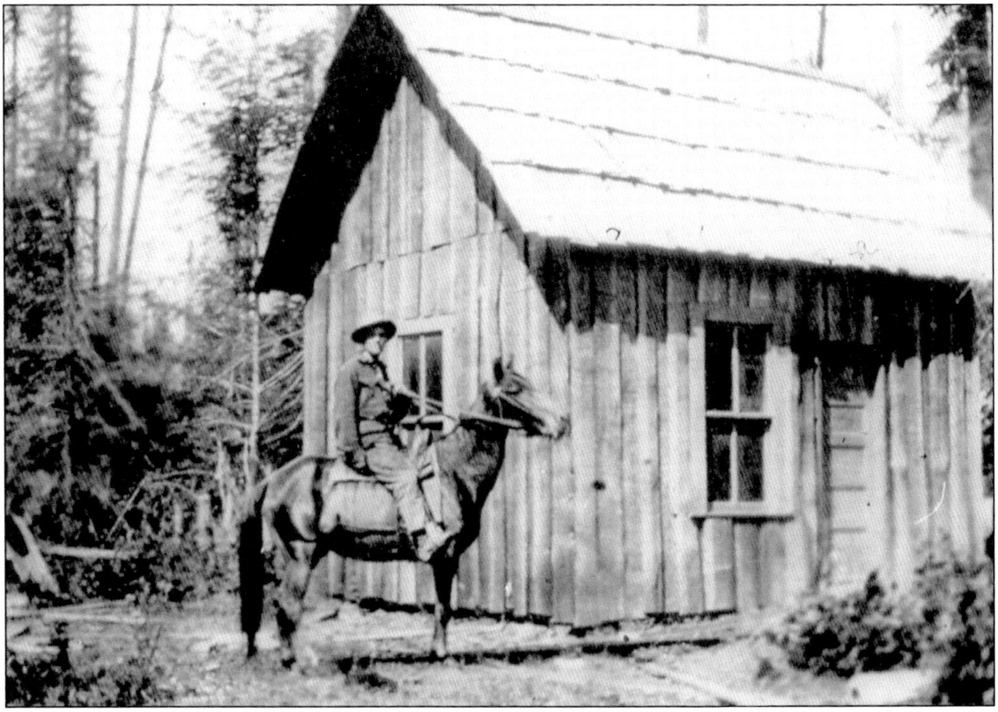

Some schoolhouses served only a few students, such as the Schutz School. West End men served on school boards during the development of local school systems, sometimes posing in Western dress for yearbook photographs. Seen here is Peter Schutz.

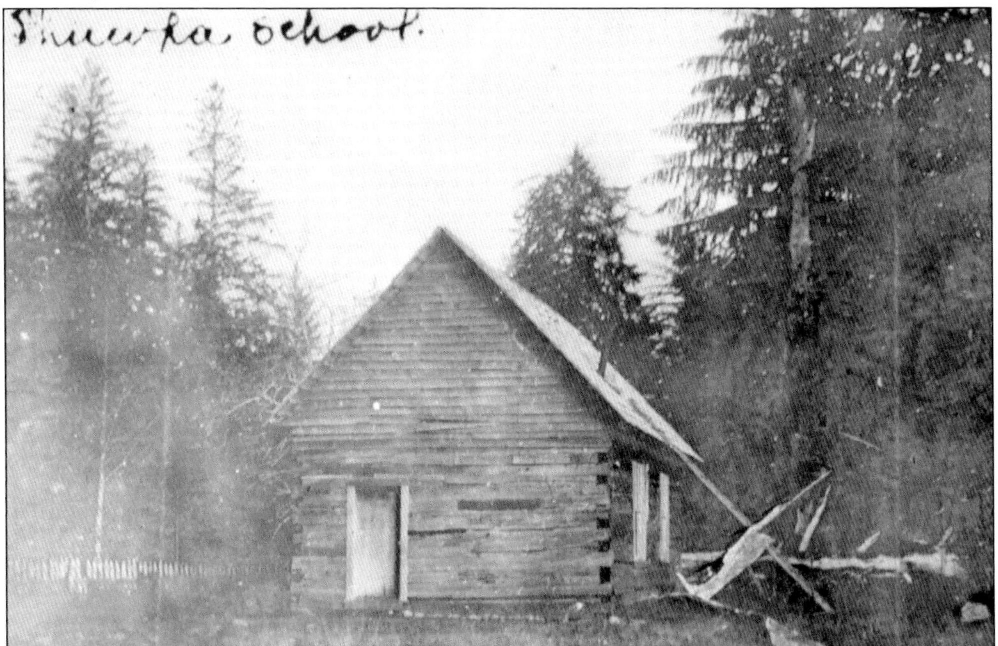

Smaller settlements, such as Shuwha, located west of Forks, built their own schools. The small town had its own post office by the early 1900s.

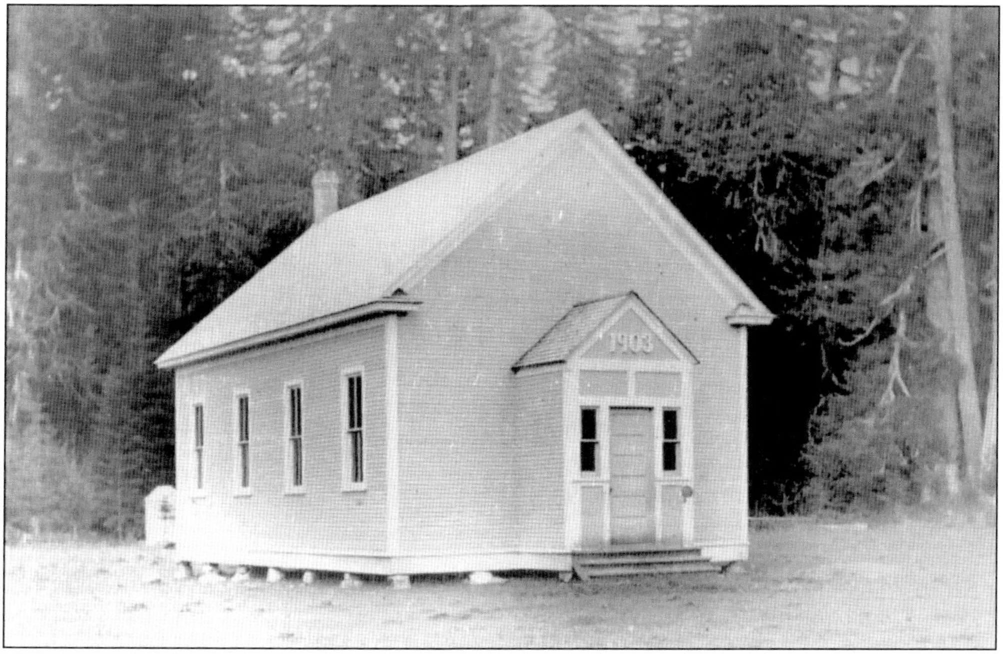

This 1903 schoolhouse in Forks was built to a higher standard than those in outlying communities, thanks to having more students and a commercial center. The schools also served as a gathering place for community meetings; farmers to discuss crop prices, continue endless talk on the weather, and sort out other issues before a Grange was organized in Forks; and church services.

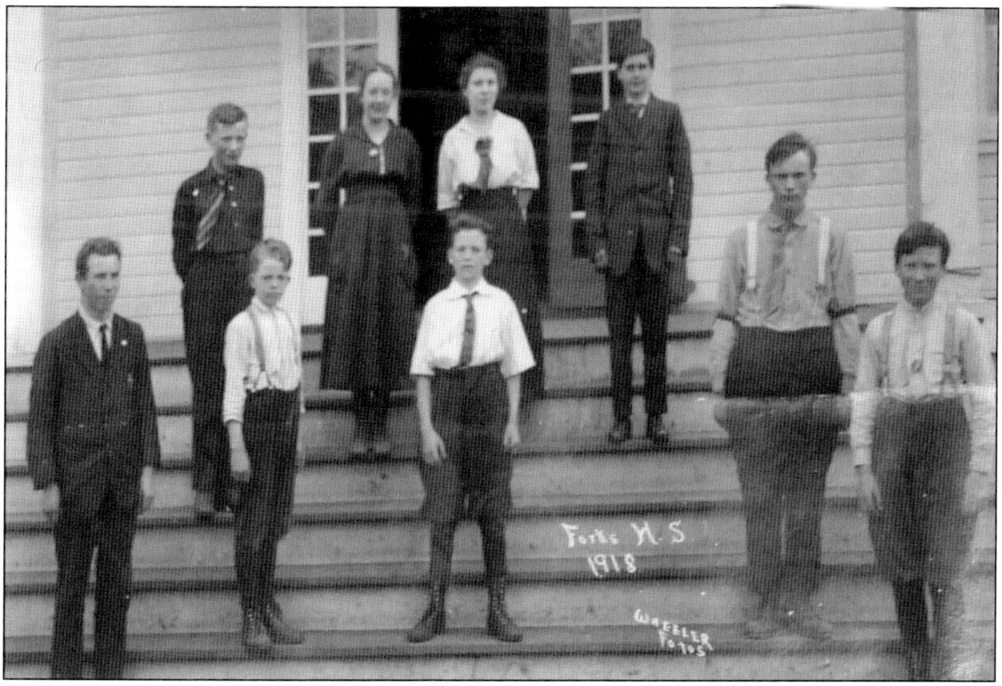

Forks High School students and teachers pose on the steps of their school in 1918. The high school class sometimes included students who had found the means to return to school at an older age.

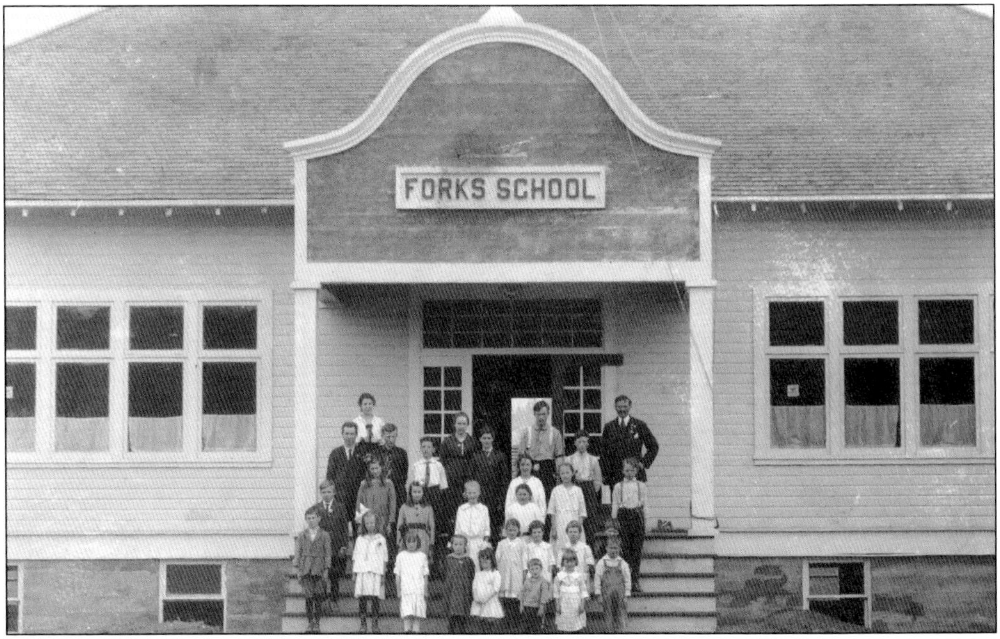

An elementary school class poses on the steps of the Forks School. The building had a basement, an unusual feature that was usually omitted due to Forks's damp soil. Unfortunately, this school burned down, but a structure very similar in design replaced it. The building is still in use today as a Forks High School administration building.

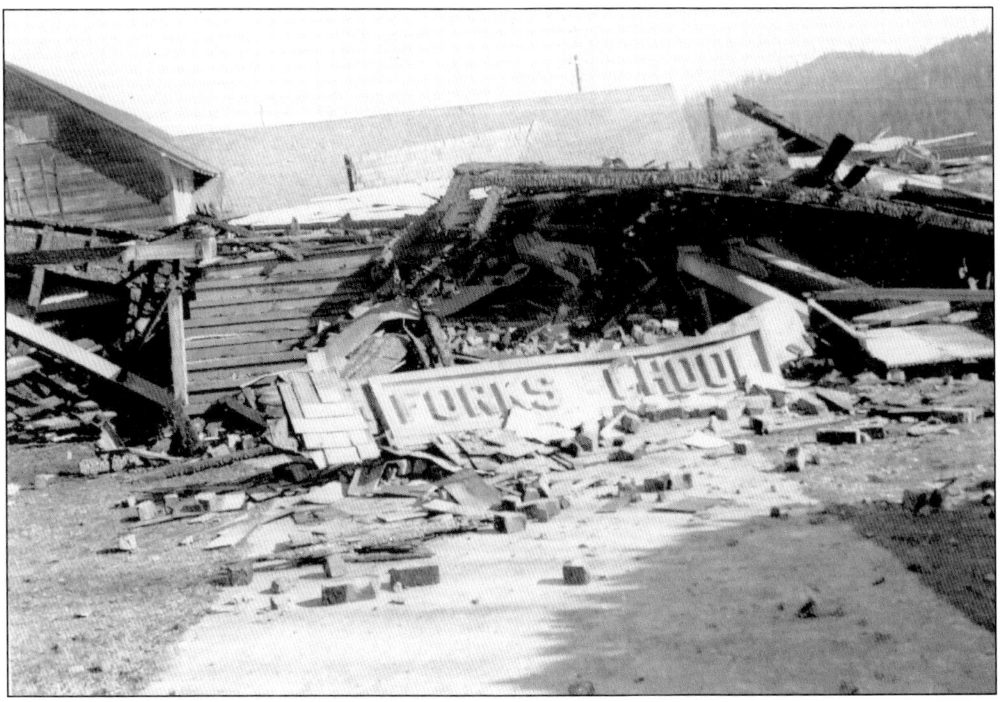

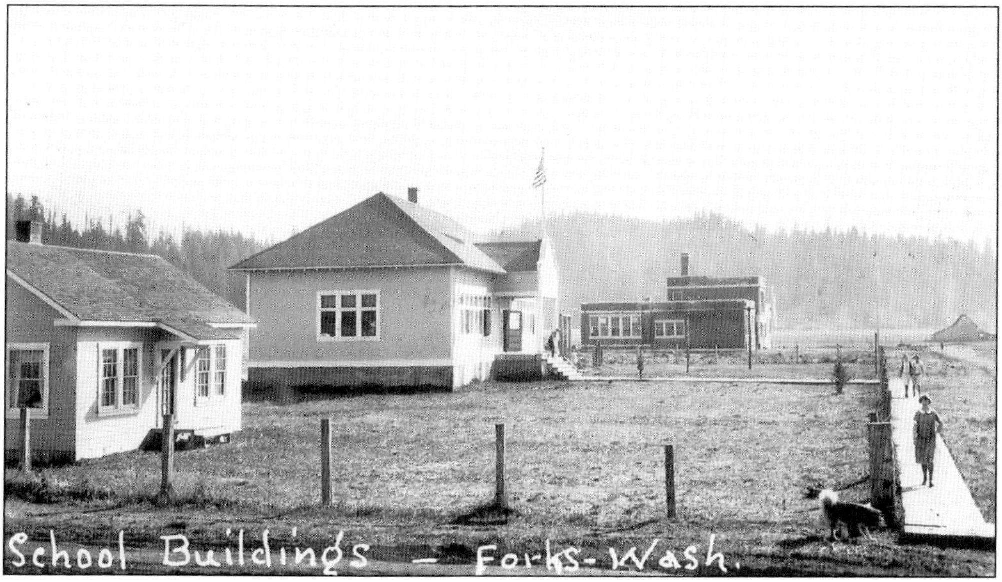

The Quillayute Union High School was constructed in 1925 and brought together high school students from Forks and several outlying schools, thus, the "union" title. The new high school offered an enhanced curriculum and found funding from Clallam County coffers. The small house in the foreground of the photograph above served as a teachers' cottage. The terra-cotta features and classic architecture of the new high school's main entrance added a modern look to the town. A time capsule was tucked away in the cornerstone of the brick school.

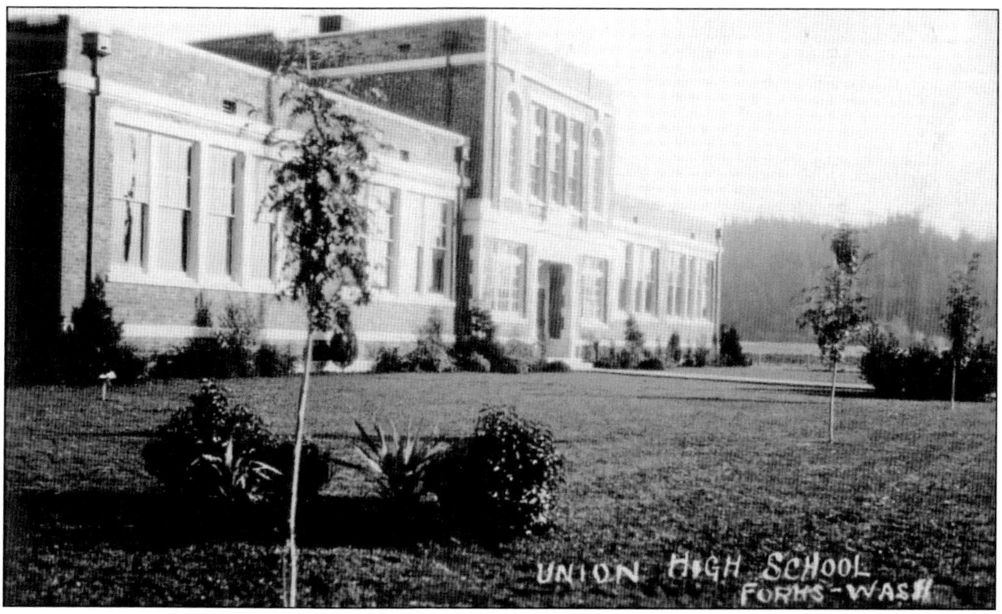

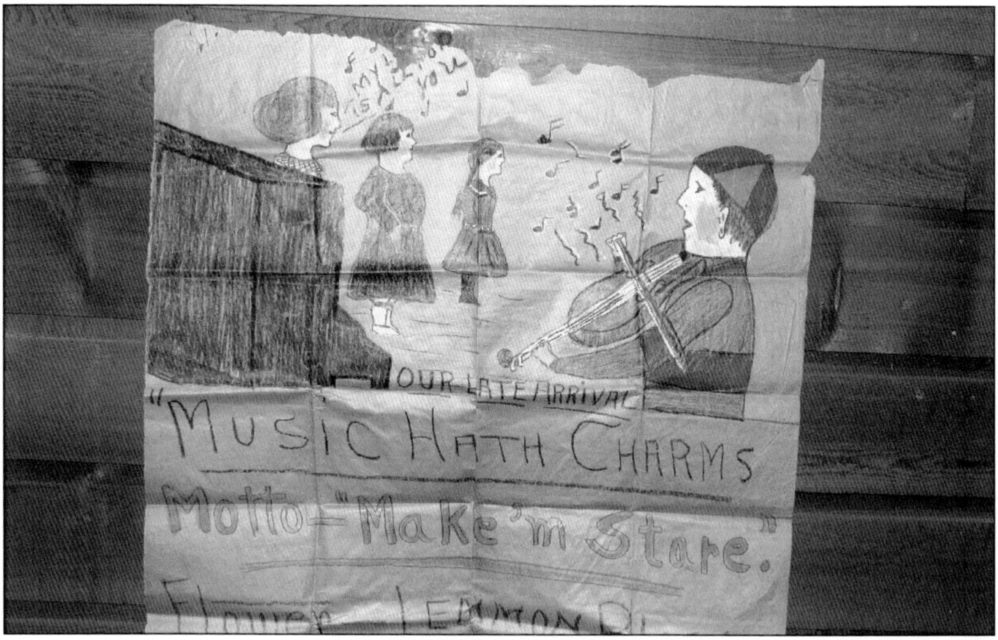

A stylized, late-1920s school concert poster from the elementary school in Forks invited students and parents to the event. The styles of the time depicted in this illustration include a multicolored beanie cap and unique girls' hairdos.

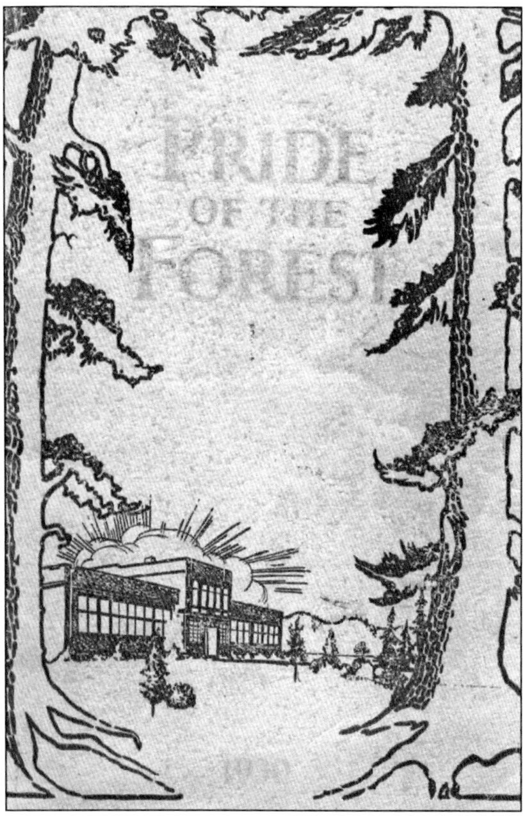

The cover of the 1930 *Pride of the Forest* yearbook encircled the Quillayute Union High School in tree limbs and pictured a bright sunrise, symbolizing the future. Local businesses underwrote the yearbook with advertisements, and humorous pages of student photographs captured Forks's frontier sense of humor.

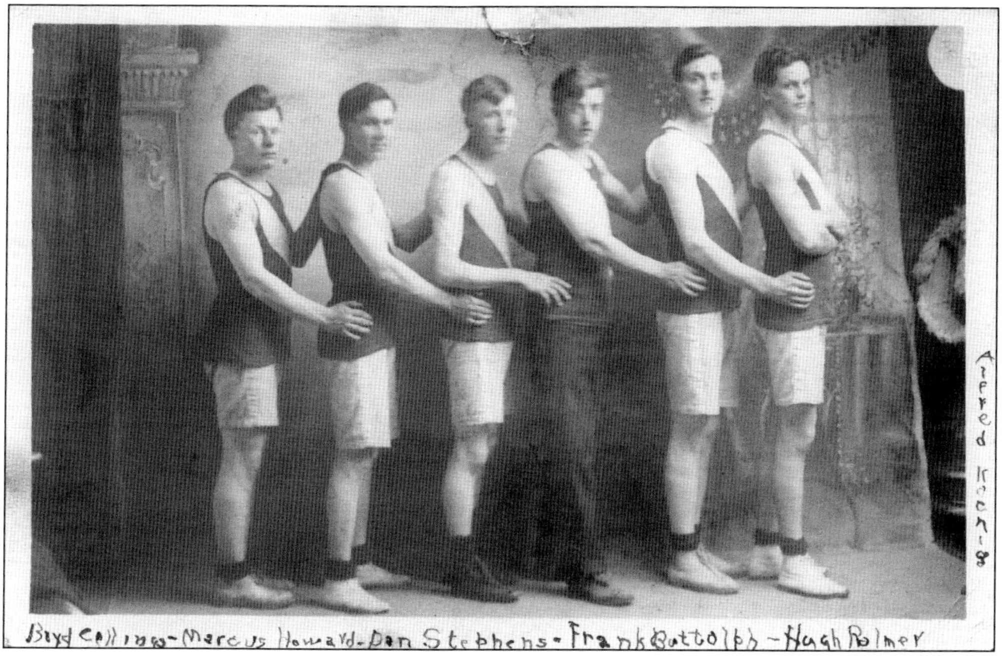

Here is the proud Forks town basketball team of 1913. The team played games around the region. Sports, then and now, play significant roles in rural, isolated communities like Forks. Games brought the community out and gave team members the opportunity to travel to compete in Joyce, Port Angeles, and other East Clallam County towns.

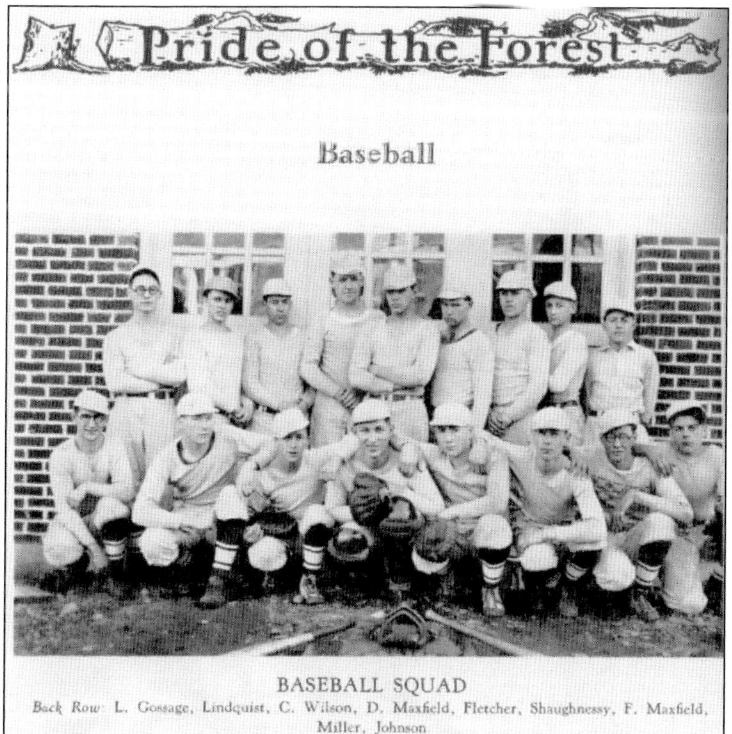

The Quillayute Union High School baseball team from 1930 included sons of pioneer families, such as the Maxfields, Klahns, Wilsons, and Lindquists.

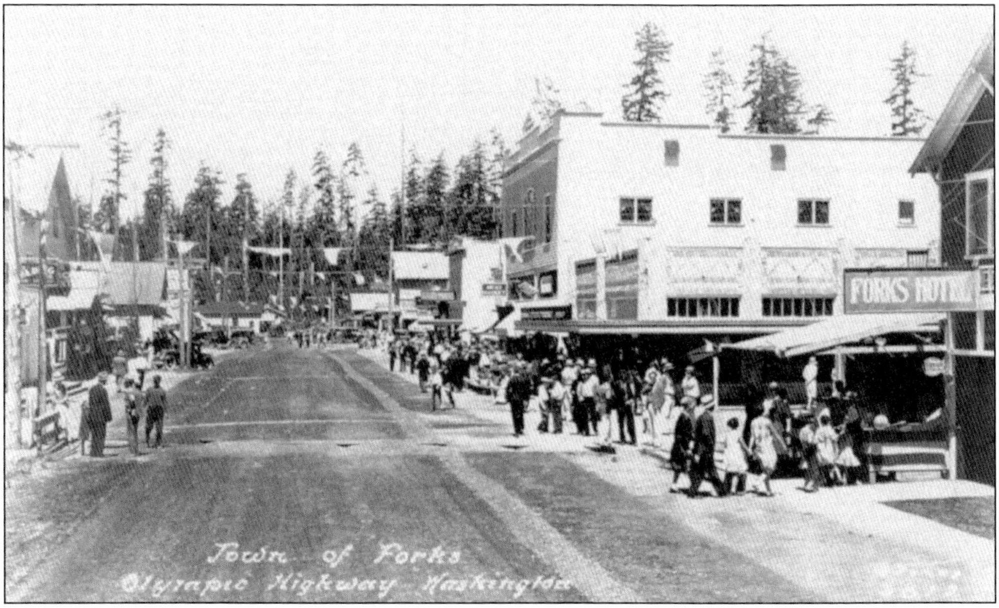

A sunny summer day brings out American flags and crowds to downtown Forks on the Fourth of July in the 1920s. Vendors with red, white, and blue decorations draw the holiday crowd to booths set along the sidewalk, on what is traditionally the busiest day of the year.

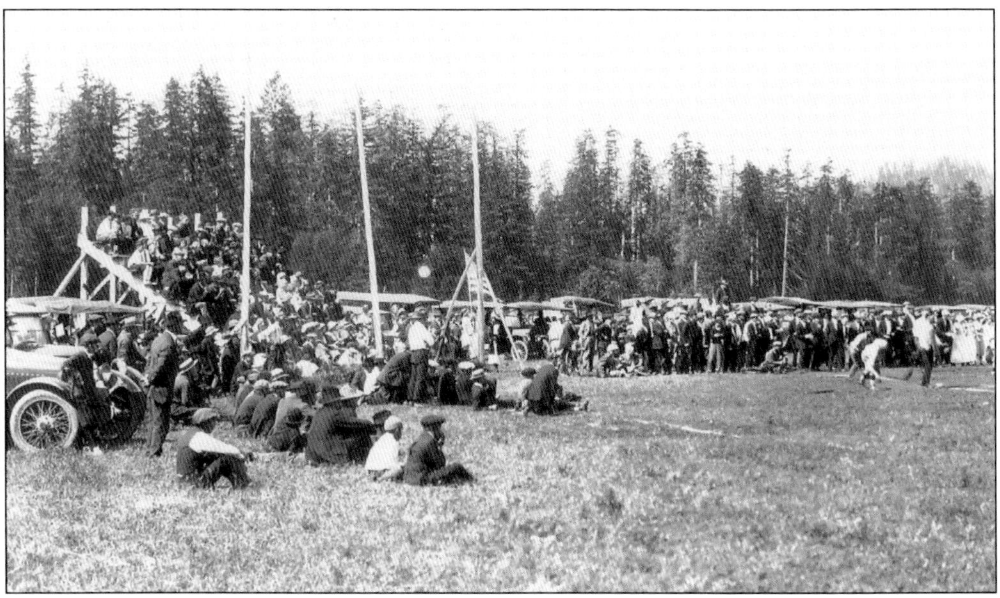

A c. 1920 Fourth of July crowd cheers on baseball teams at a ball field located in the Merchant Road area on the south side of Forks in the Calawah Valley.

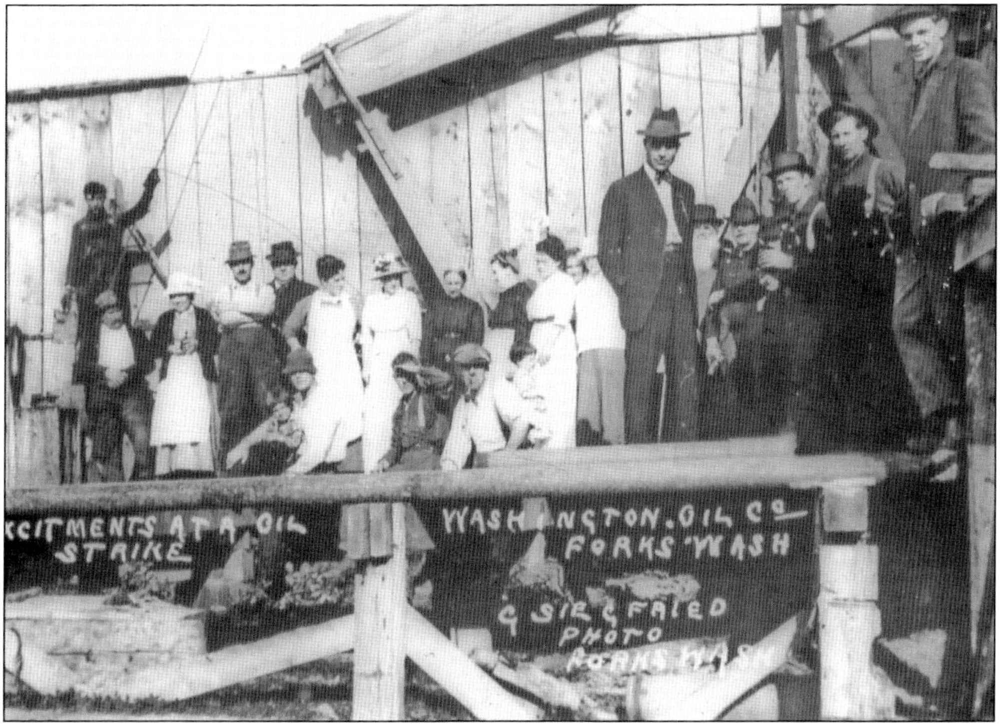

A scene at the strike of oil by the Washington Oil Company draws oil rig workers, speculators, and parents with children—all hopeful of a big payout. Oil fields dotted the land outside of downtown Forks and along the coast, ranging from LaPush to Oil City on the north bank of the Hoh River and down to Ruby Beach. Some pools of clear, almost pure oil were found and could be used unfiltered to provide fuel for an automobile.

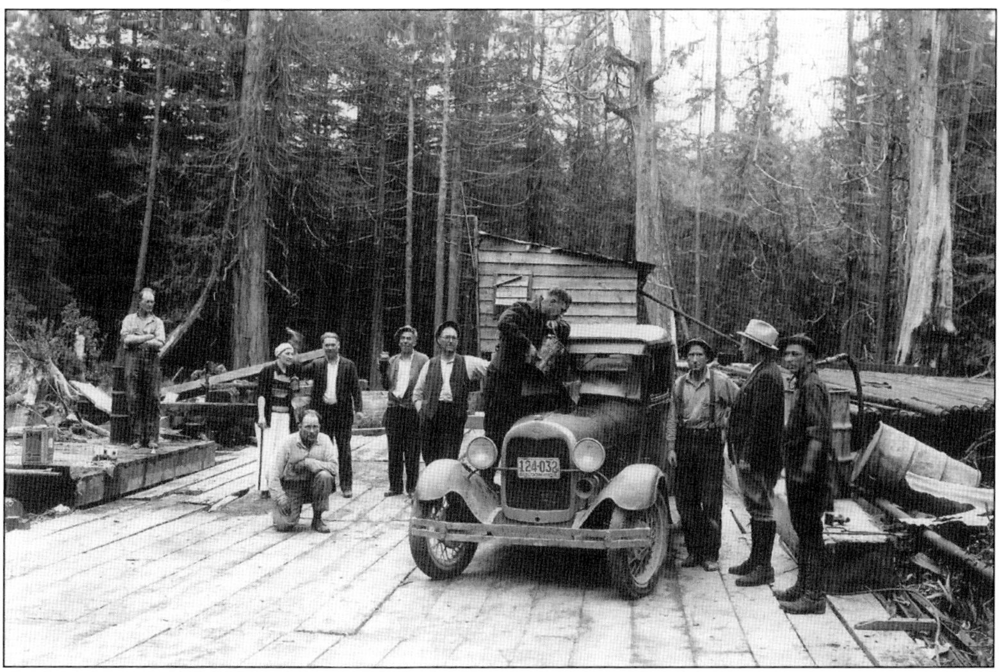

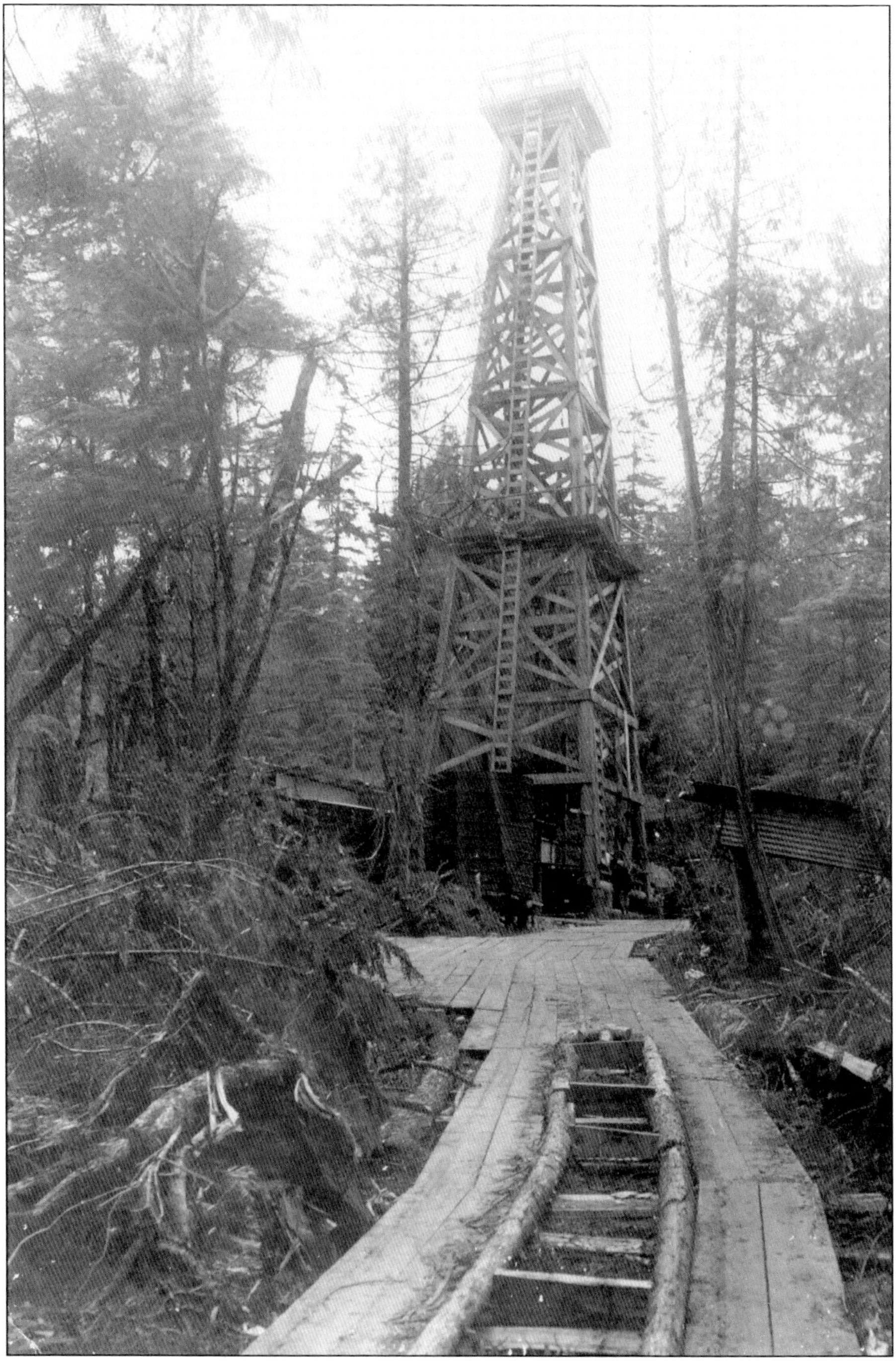

The Sol Duc Oil Company was based in Port Angeles, with a field office in Forks. The wooden well towers, erected alongside tall firs and spruce trees, were built in the Bogachiel Valley area on land owned by the Wilson brothers. The Forks Commercial Club, a forerunner to the Forks Chamber of Commerce, promoted the burgeoning oil and natural-gas drilling industry. Geologists from Standard Oil, who made a survey in the late 1890s, declared the area worth exploring for oil and announced the possibility of a major oil strike in the area.

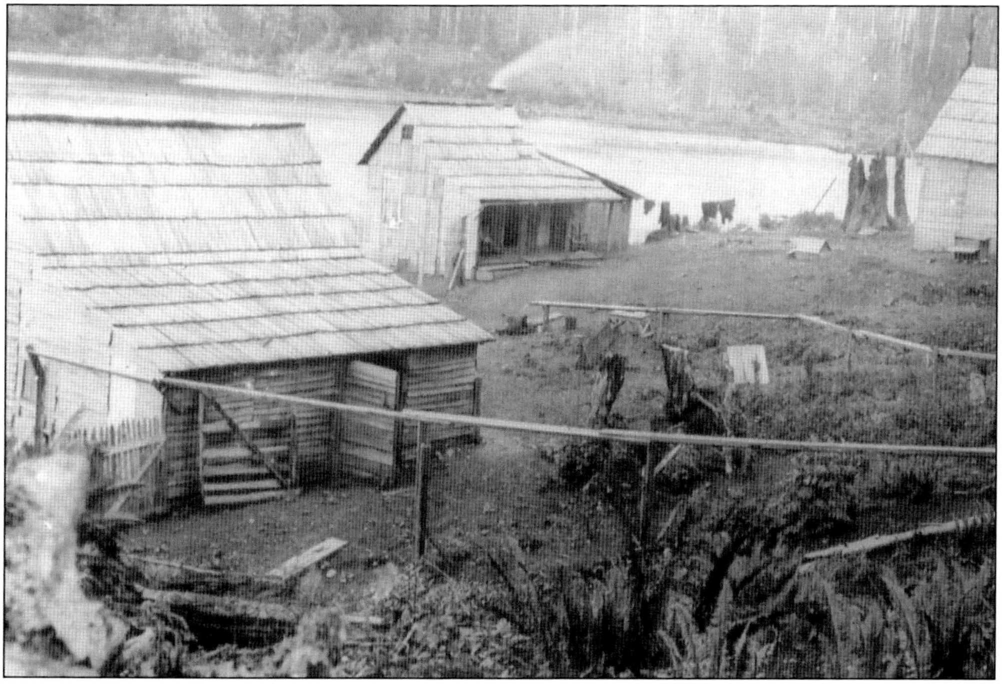

The first sparks of electricity came to Forks when electrical engineer and inventor Elton Floyd Ross of Indiana started up a generator at his home on the east bank of Lake Pleasant. By 1920, Ross and partner Frank Ackerly had launched the Forks Lighting Association, illuminating streets, homes, and businesses. The generator likely used steam turbines fueled with firewood. Ackerly also invented the gasoline-powered Ross Pump that gave forest firefighters a boost in hosing down blazes.

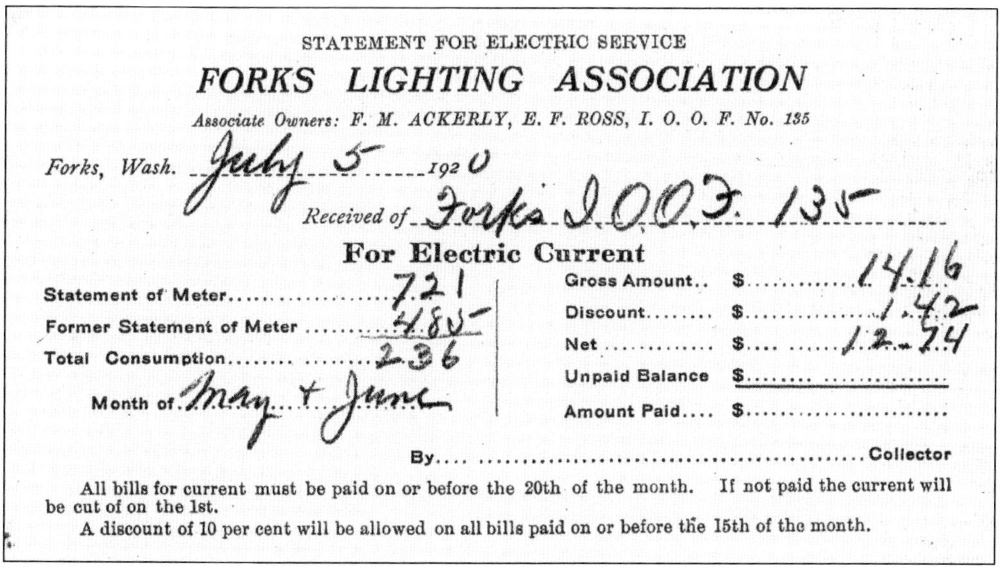

STATEMENT FOR ELECTRIC SERVICE

FORKS LIGHTING ASSOCIATION

Associate Owners: F. M. ACKERLY, E. F. ROSS, I. O. O. F. No. 135

Forks, Wash. July 5 1920

Received of Forks I.O.O.F. 135

For Electric Current

Statement of Meter	721	Gross Amount	$ 14.16
Former Statement of Meter	485	Discount	$ 1.42
Total Consumption	236	Net	$ 12.74
Month of May + June		Unpaid Balance	$
		Amount Paid	$

By.... Collector

All bills for current must be paid on or before the 20th of the month. If not paid the current will be cut of on the 1st.

A discount of 10 per cent will be allowed on all bills paid on or before the 15th of the month.

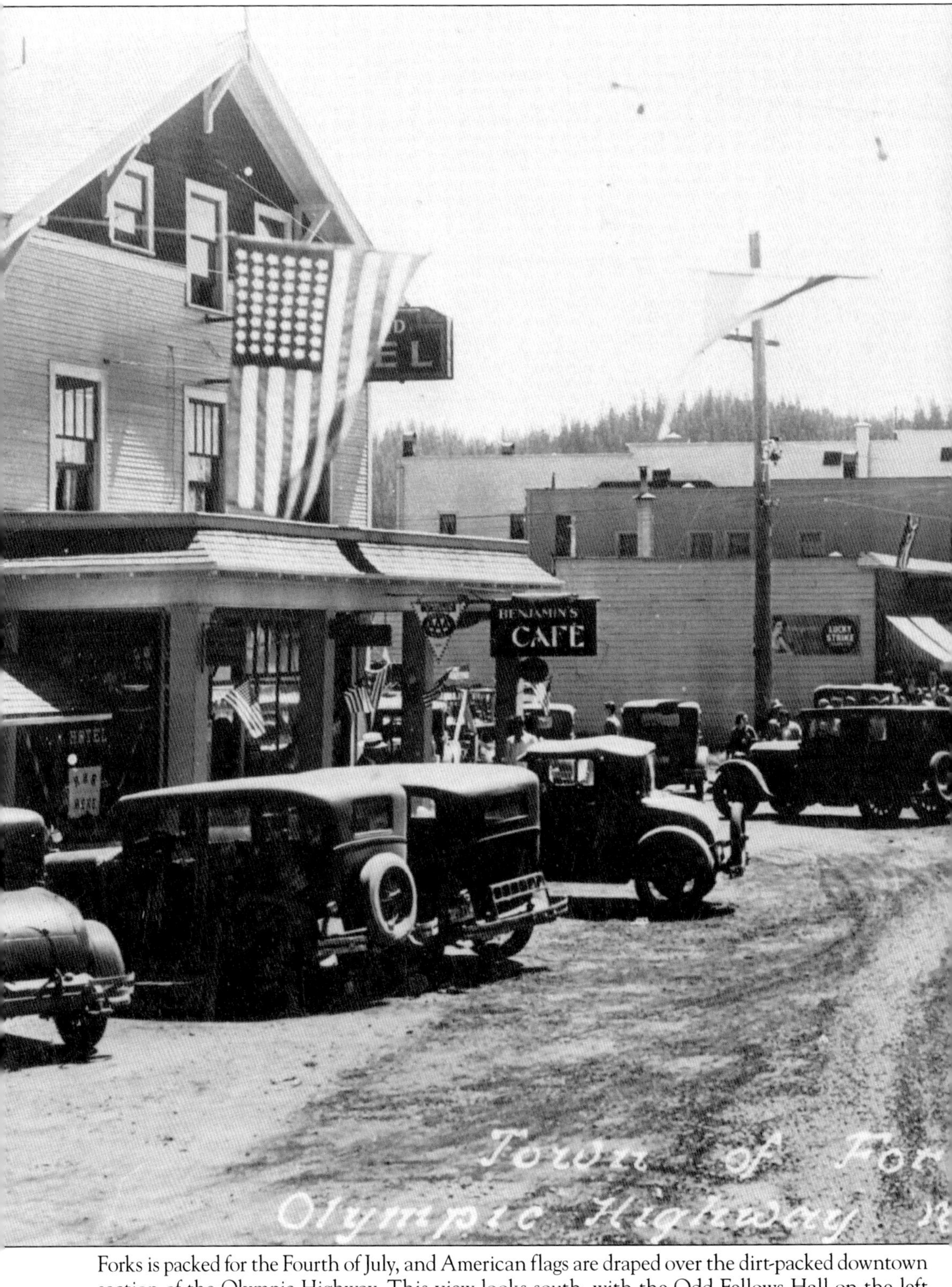

Forks is packed for the Fourth of July, and American flags are draped over the dirt-packed downtown section of the Olympic Highway. This view looks south, with the Odd Fellows Hall on the left

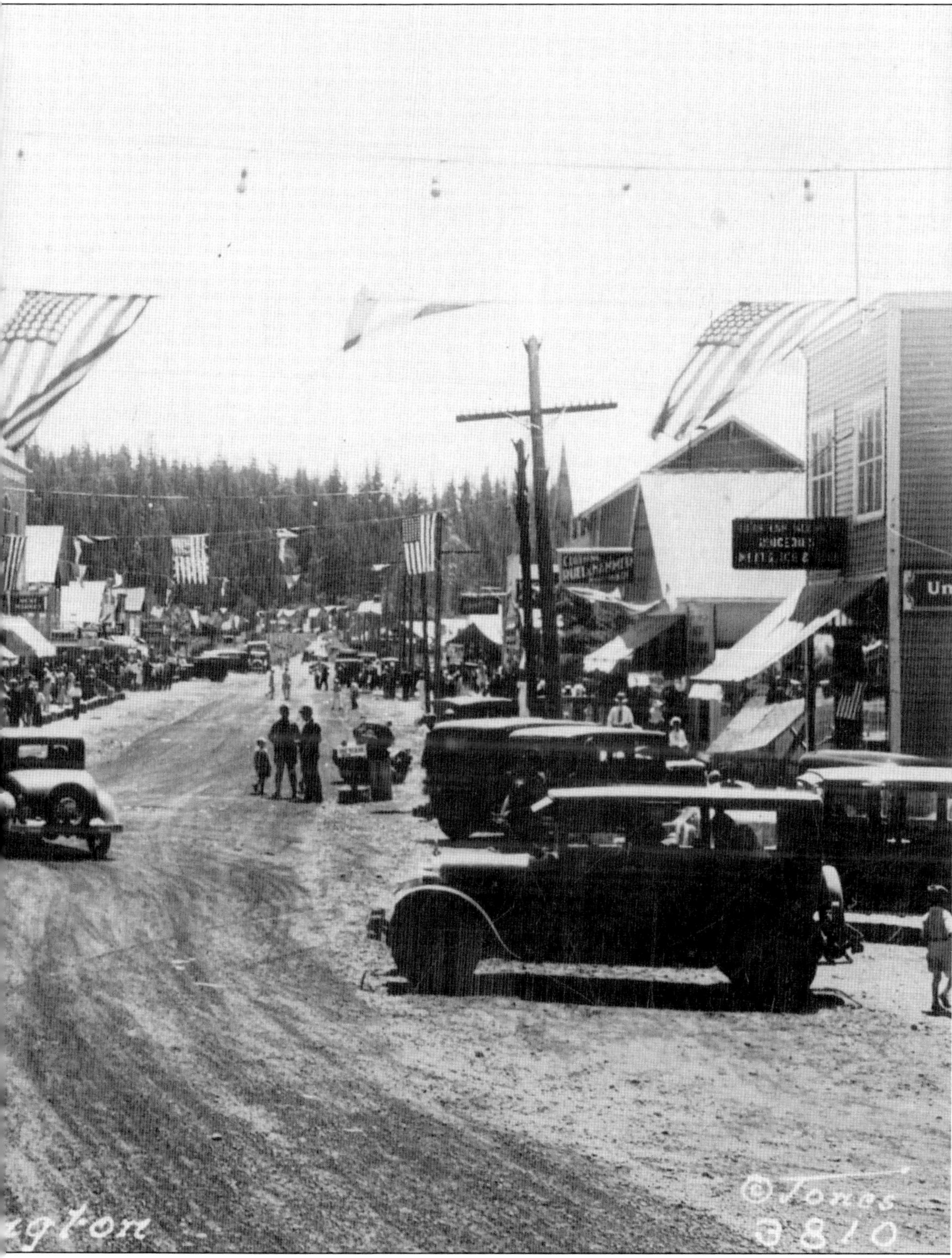

in the middle of the photograph and Woodland Hotel in the foreground.

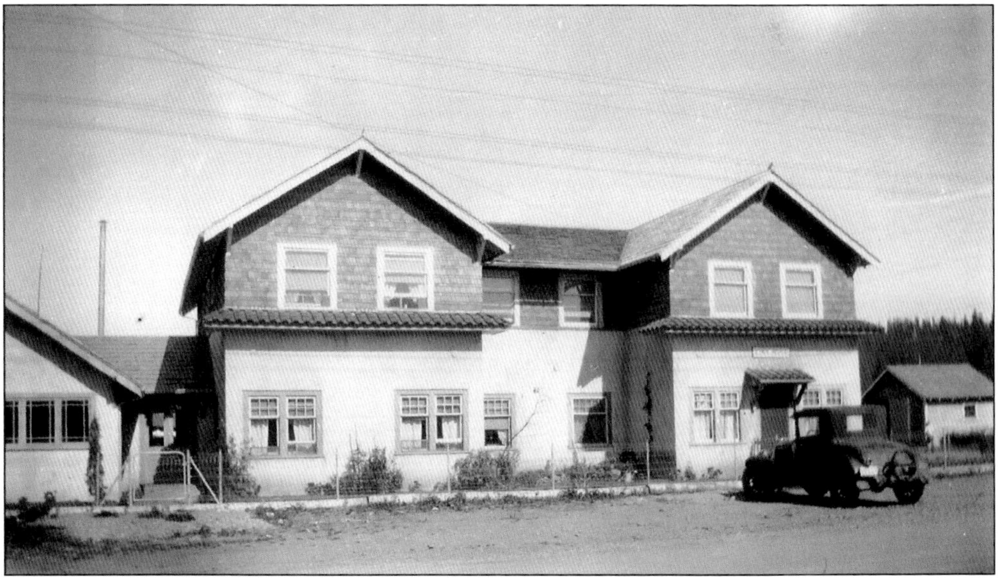

The tiled-roof Olympic Hospital brought modern medical services to Forks. Pioneers knowledgeable in setting bones and stitching wounds and other medical skills took care of early emergencies. Doctors Ford and Meyer, and others with office clinics in town, opened their doors beginning in the 1910s, becoming highly needed and well known in the community.

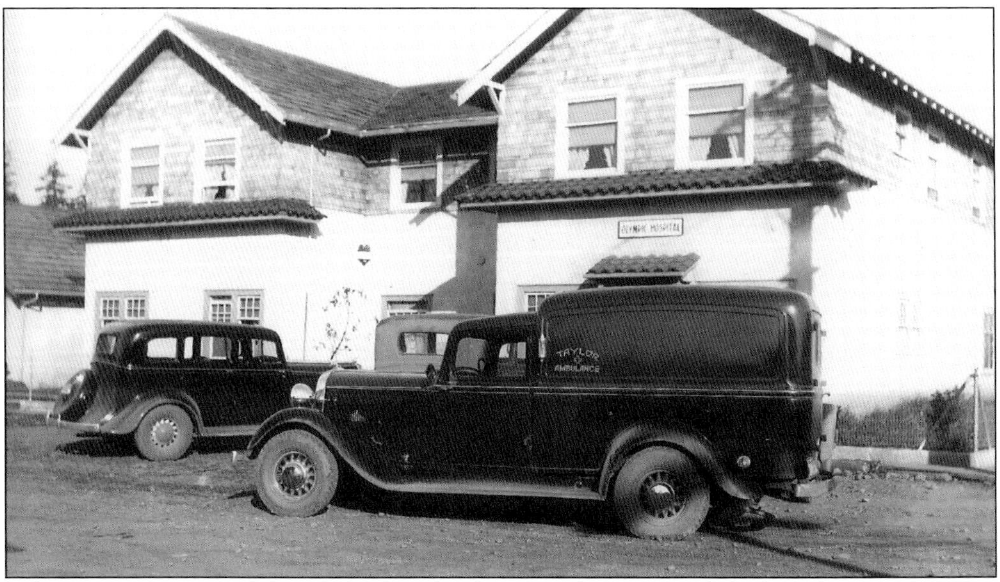

The Olympic Hospital, with a privately owned ambulance out front, was located where the Forks Post Office and Clallam County Fire District No. 1 Station are today. Sending patients off for specialized surgeries to Port Angeles and Seattle hospitals became possible with highway improvements.

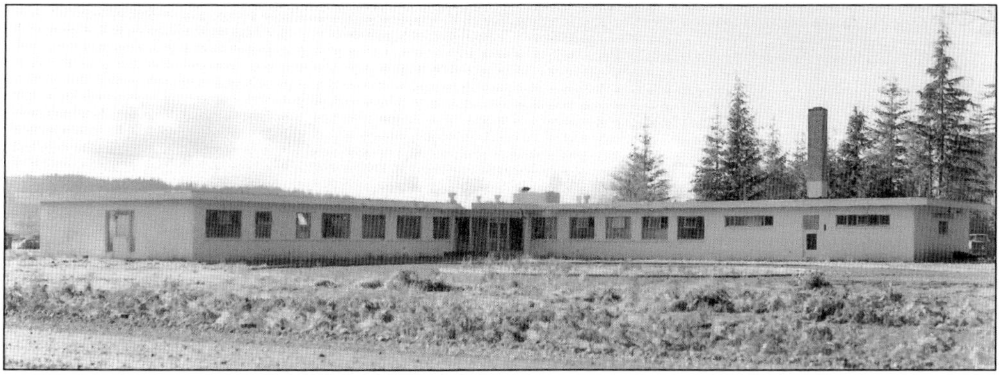

The Forks hospital was relocated to a block of land off Bogachiel Way. Two sections of the hospital were completed by the early 1960s, forming the core of today's Forks Community Hospital.

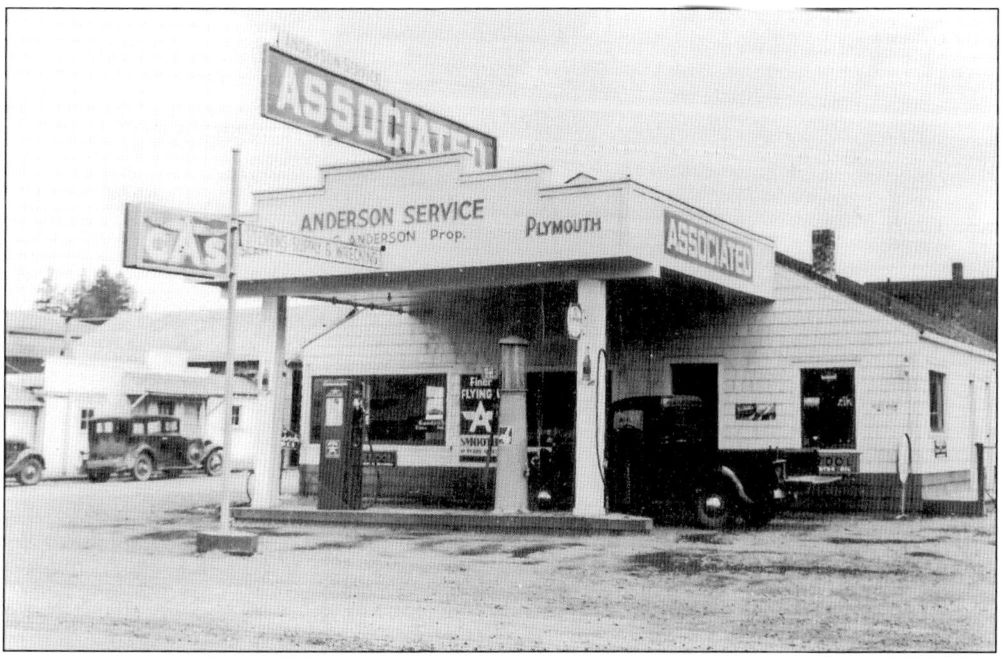

As in many rural towns of the Northwest, gas stations, such as Anderson Service (shown here in the 1940s), provided the following services: pumping National brand gasoline, wiping windows, checking oil, towing, and, sometimes, wrecking yard operations. Occasionally, these stations served as new car dealerships and hangouts for their communities.

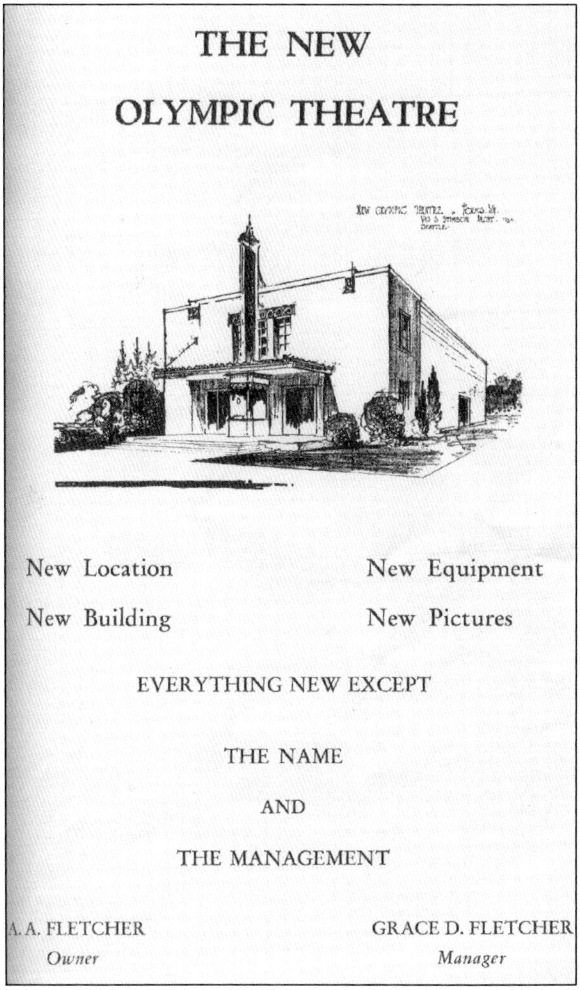

A.A. and Grace Fletcher opened the modern Olympic Theatre in the late 1930s on Division Street, a short walk east from Forks Avenue. The movie house played first-run Hollywood films on a circuit that moved the reels around the North Olympic Peninsula theaters. Being the only picture show in town, it served as a key socializing site; previews for films were even published on the front page of the *Forks Forum* newspaper. The cedar-shingled walls of the theater and its wooden interior beams provided a Forks touch to the building.

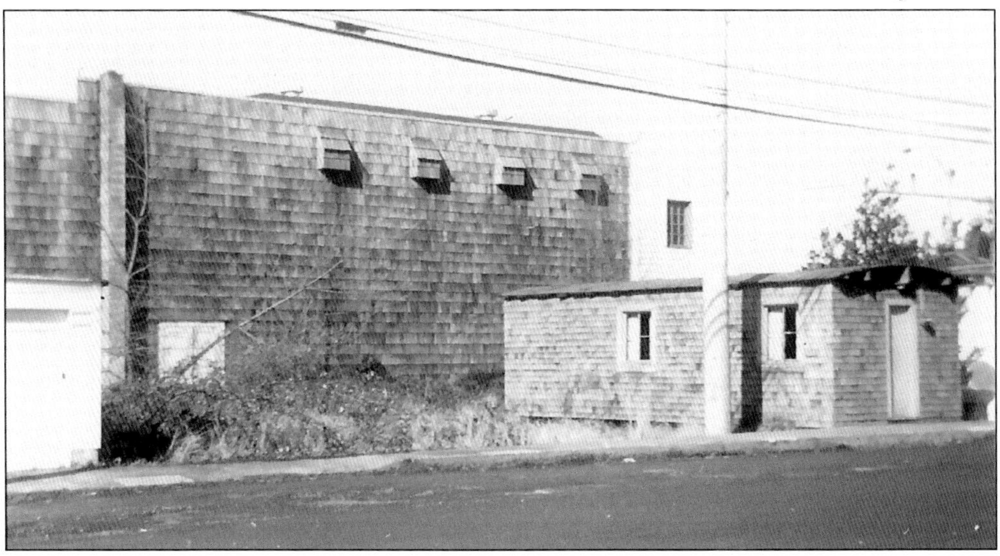

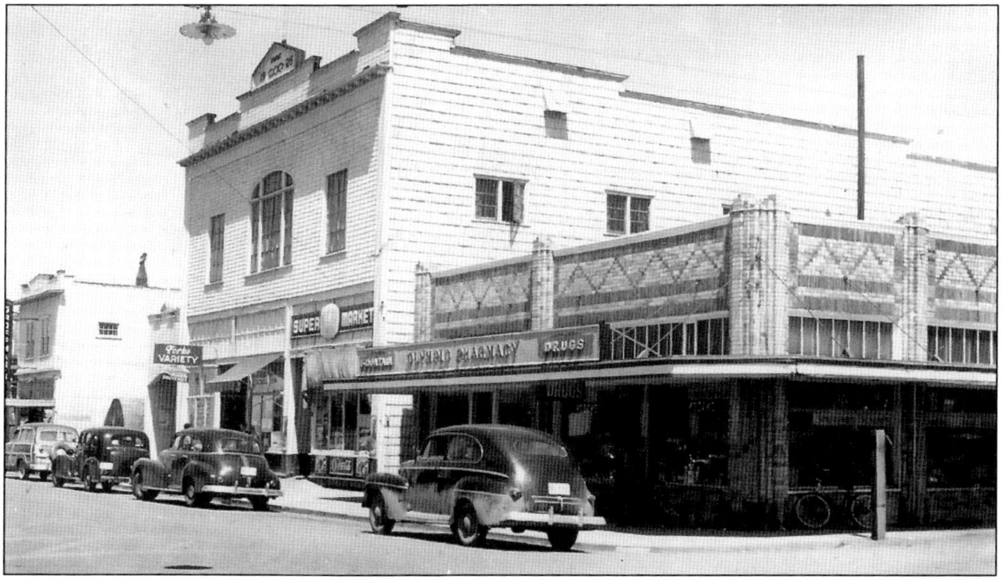

By the late 1940s, the row of merchants along Forks Avenue gave downtown a prosperous look. A souvenir-selling variety store and a supermarket filled the first floor of the Odd Fellows Hall. Olympic Pharmacy's soda fountain served milk shakes and cokes, while the camera department sold rolls of Kodak film. Kids on Schwinn bicycles cruised the downtown area, and families in woody station wagons shopped in town. A streetlight hung over the intersection of Forks Avenue and Division Street, a forerunner to what would be the only traffic light between Port Angeles and Aberdeen along Highway 101.

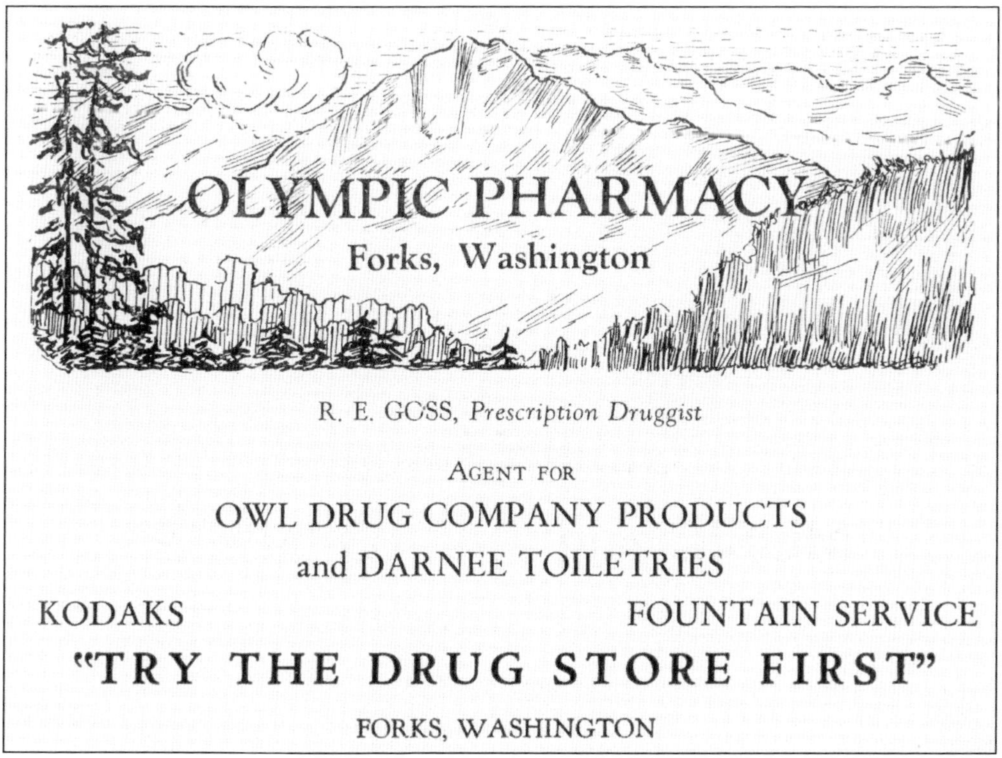

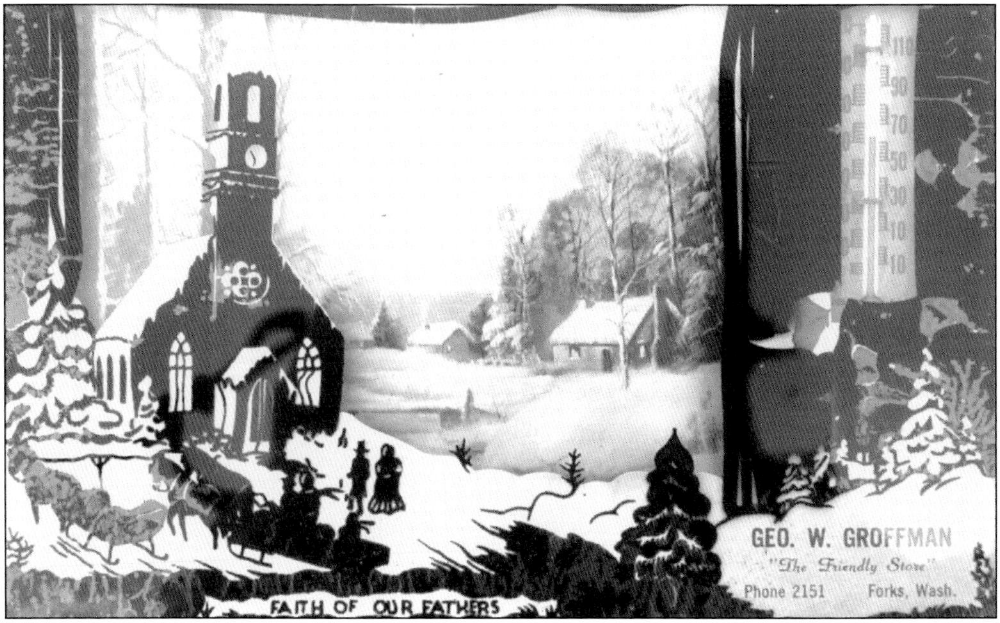

This Christmastime customer giveaway from the long-established Groffman's clothing and variety store captures the dichotomy of the lifestyle of Forks's families. The snowy Christmas scene cutout recalls the idealized Midwestern and New England foundational roots of the pioneers, while the snow-covered, woodstove heated cabins in the forest captured the challenges, adventure, and independence of the frontier life that they led in the Northwest.

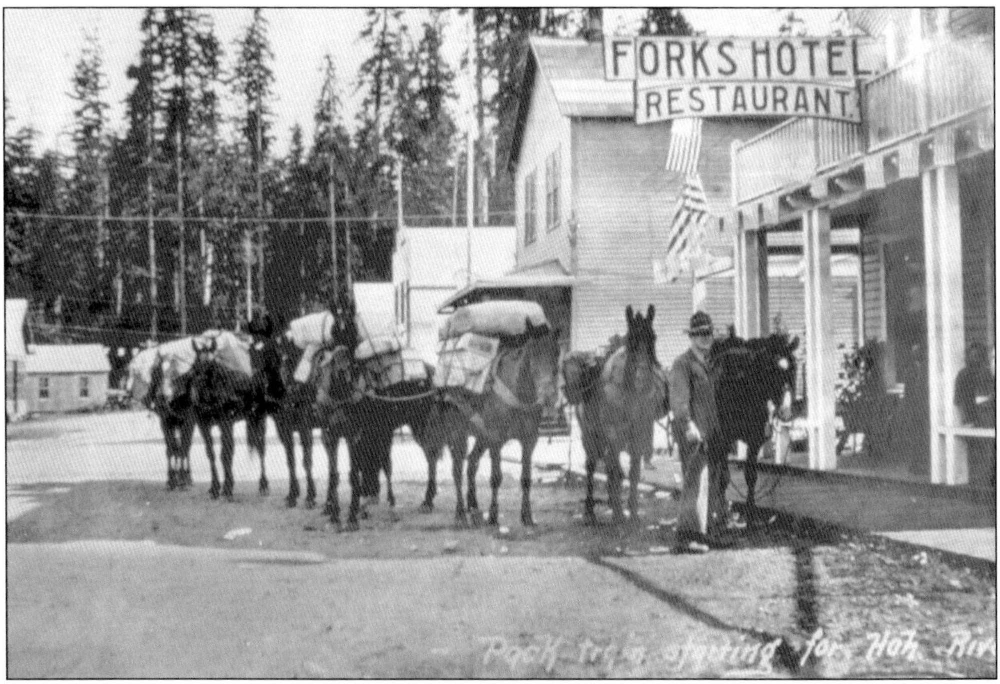

Pack trains headed south from Forks to supply homesteads along the Bogachiel and Hoh Rivers and points in between. The deliveries included foodstuffs, mail, parcels, clothing, tools, and more. The packers followed trails well traveled by the homesteaders on foot and horseback.

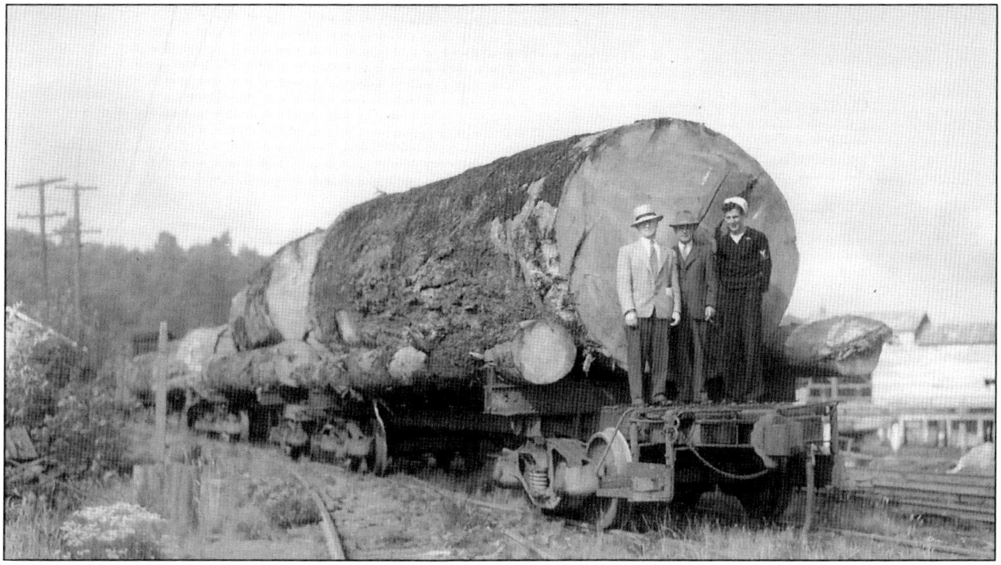

Civic pride in the advancements of the timber industry, as well as of Forks and outlying towns, is apparent here. Two well-dressed men pose with a sailor, perhaps a local youth on leave, atop a railcar with a first-growth log.

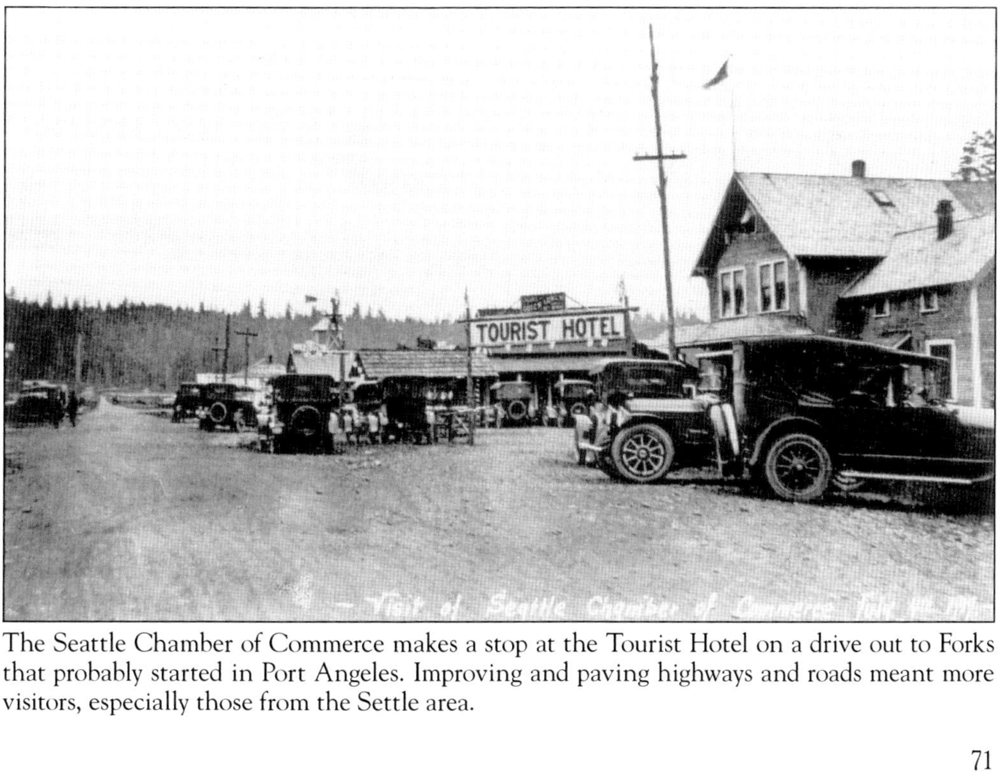

The Seattle Chamber of Commerce makes a stop at the Tourist Hotel on a drive out to Forks that probably started in Port Angeles. Improving and paving highways and roads meant more visitors, especially those from the Settle area.

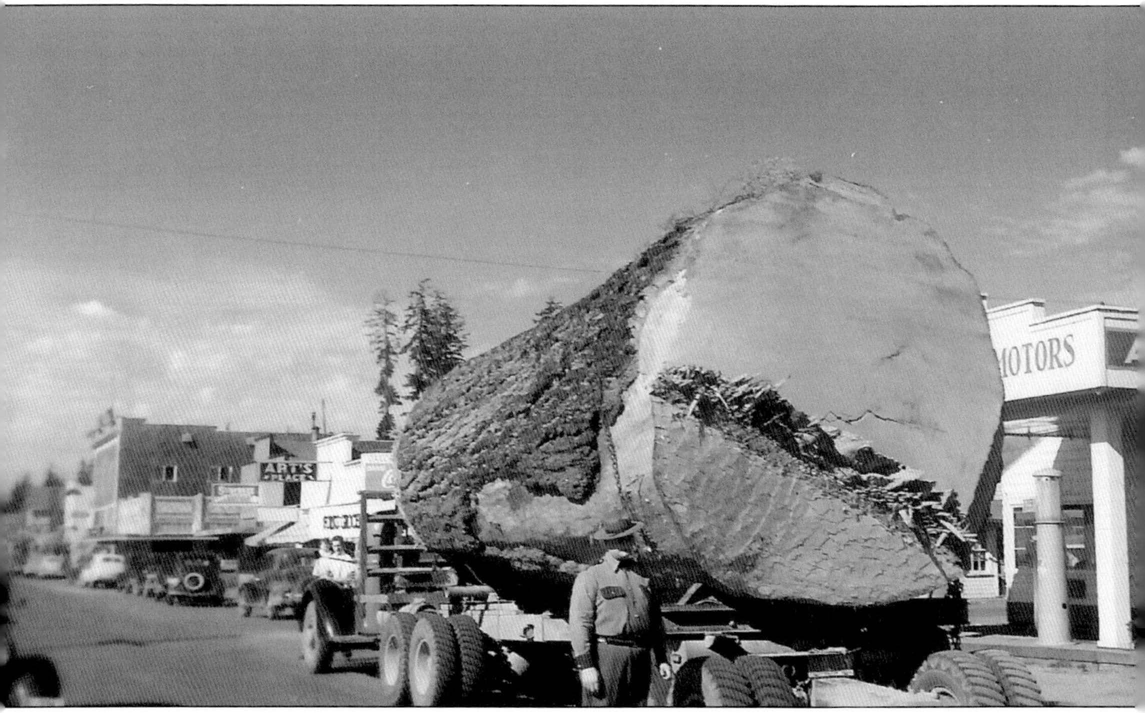

A Washington State Patrol trooper eyes traffic as a logging truck hauls a huge first-growth log through downtown Forks in this postwar scene captured on a busy summer day. Washington State Patrol trooper Boyd Rupp spent World War II in Forks. His duties included patrolling the coast for Japanese army invaders.

Four

TRANSPORTATION

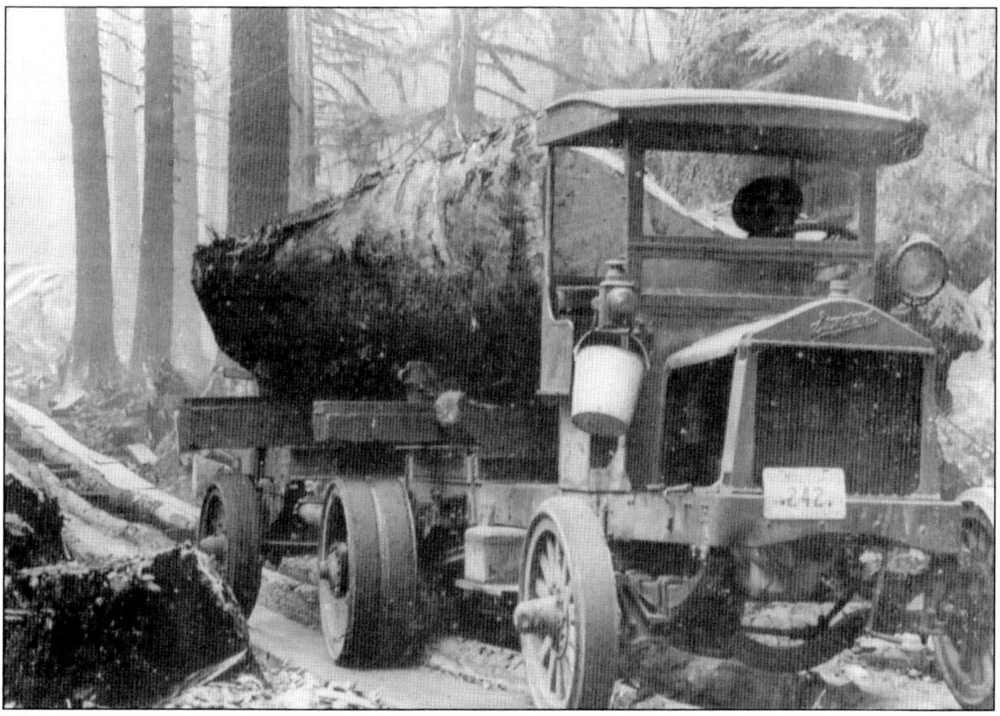

The 1910s saw the arrival of motorized logging trucks (like this Spruce Division vehicle), which were driven on puncheon roads and used in swampy and steep road sections. The truck's wooden wheels are wrapped in slick rubber, and a cable connected under the truck body added boost up grades and braking power on downhill portions.

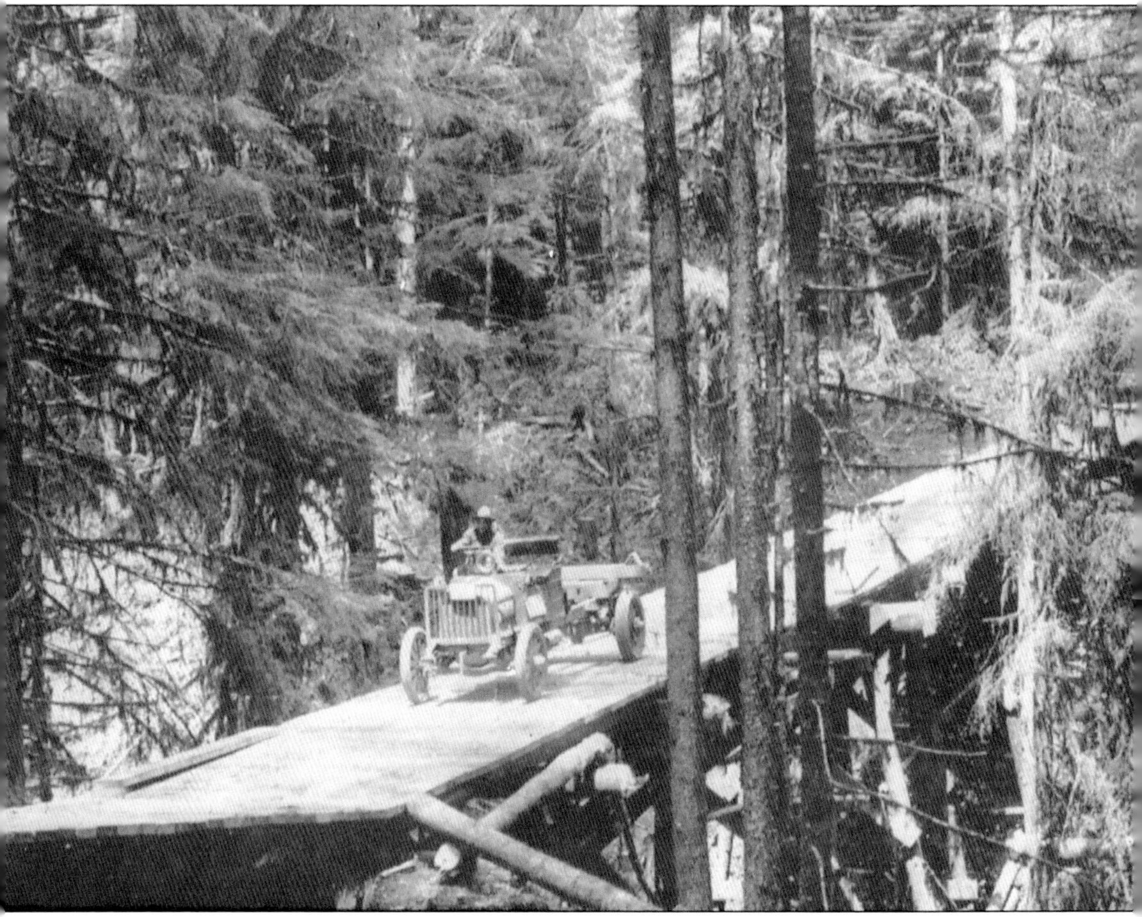

A primitive logging truck hauls lumber to the edge of the logging trestle in the West End forest. Elaborate trestle construction projects were built of local lumber and logs. Engineering logs into the damp stream banks and hillsides was considerably cost effective compared to erecting metal trestles. Sending a trestle across a river or valley opened up new acreage to logging.

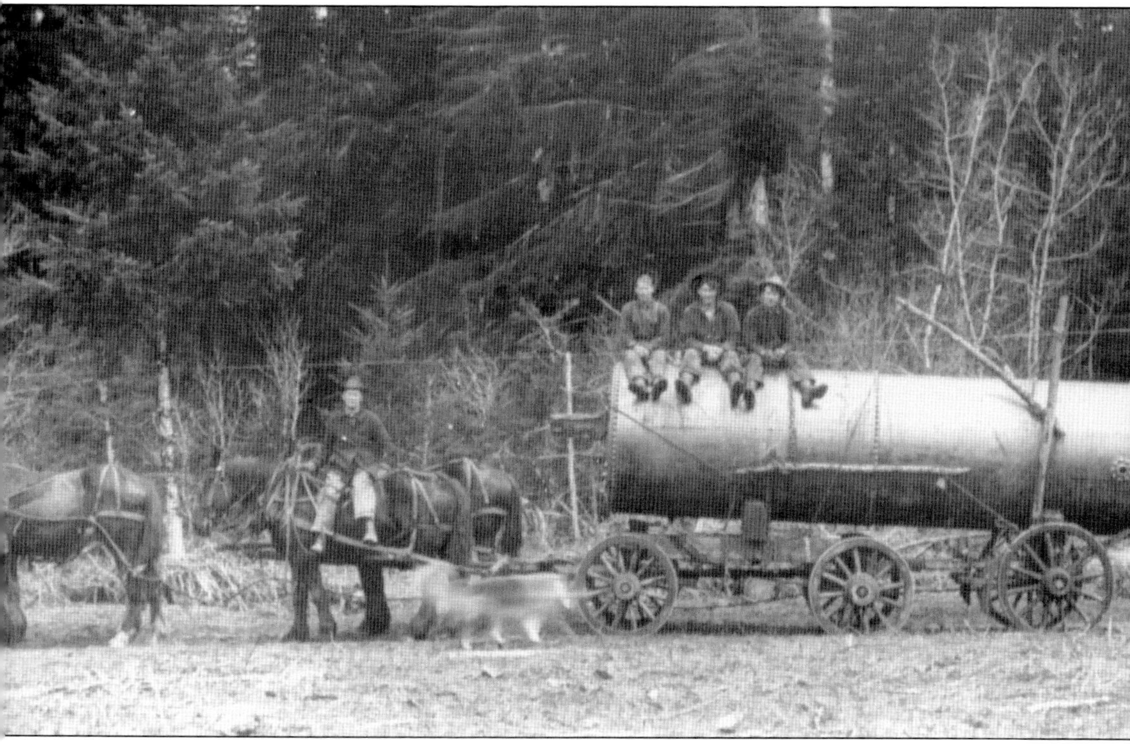

From left to right, Albin Wahlgren, Frank Oberg, and Don Wilson sit atop a big boiler being hauled to the site of the first sawmill built in Forks, which Wilson established at his place at Elk Creek. John Grader is pictured astride one of his four horses used to pull the boiler.

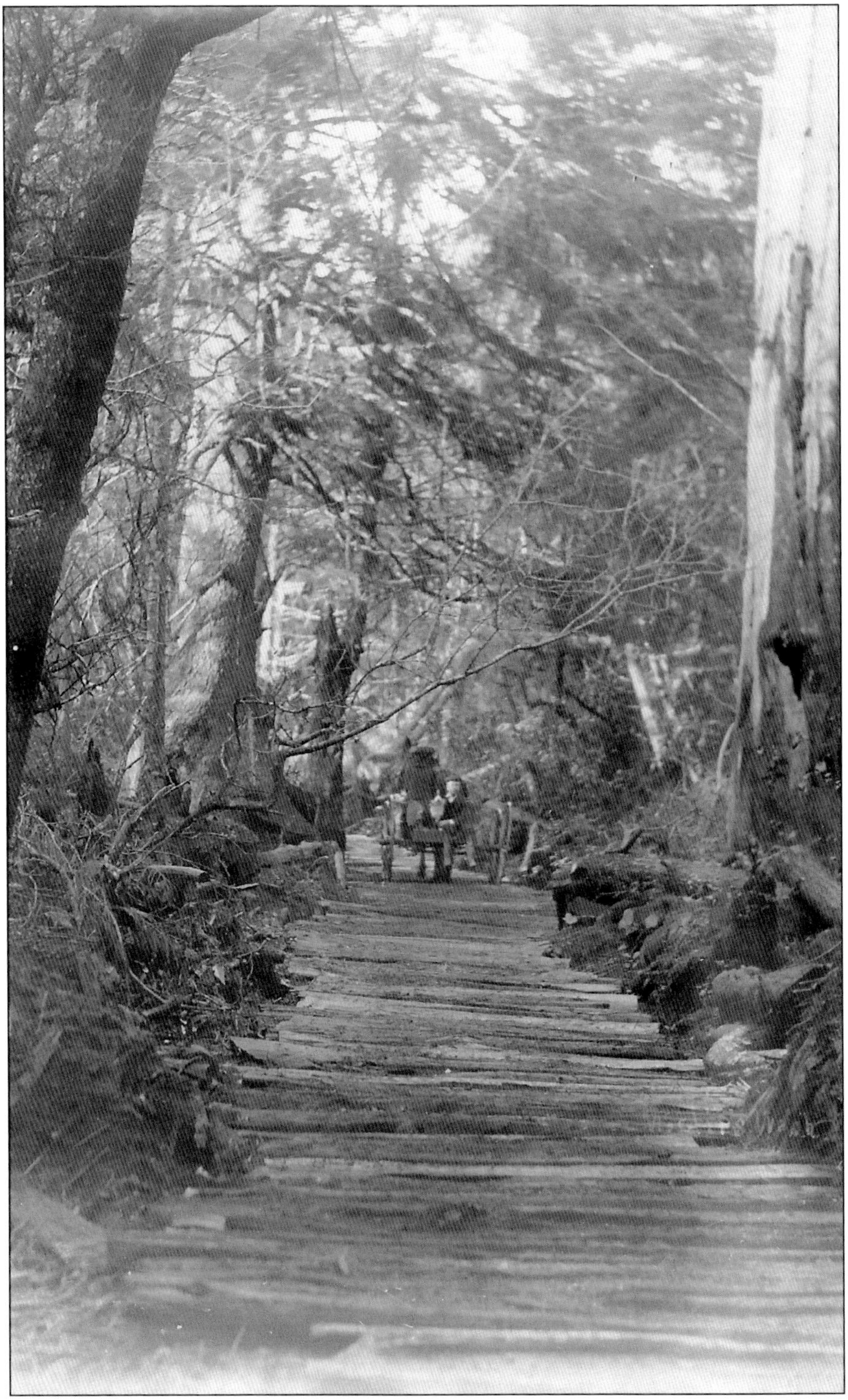

Roads cut in the West End forest outside of Forks were narrow ribbons amidst tall stands of Douglas firs and spruce trees. Muddy conditions failed to deter adventurous drivers who cranked up their Model Ts and other early cars for a drive out to Forks.

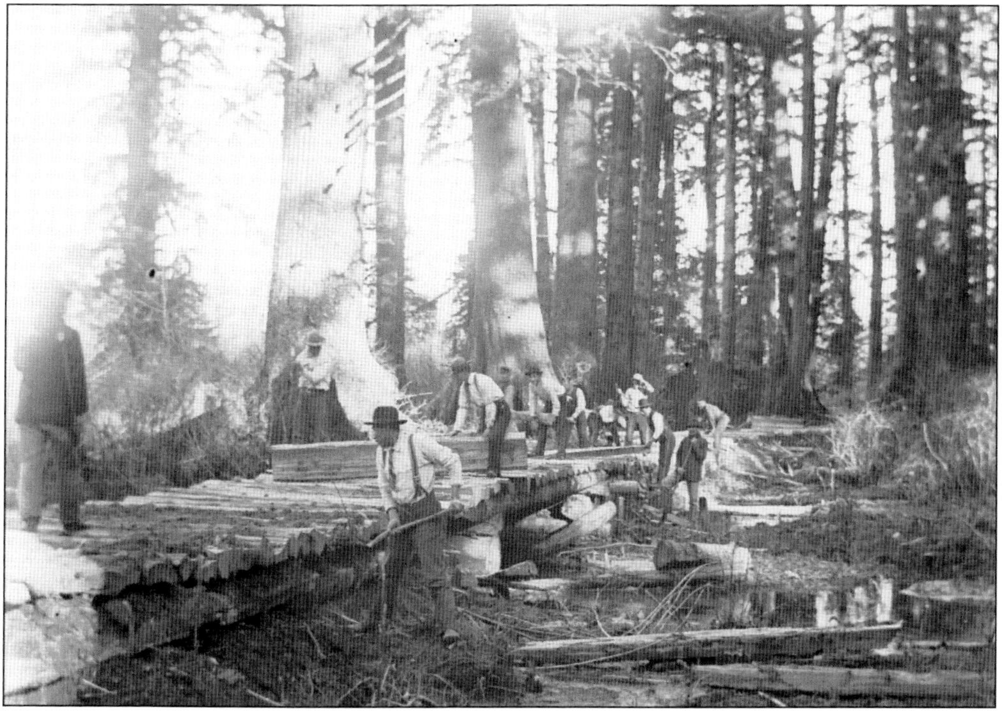

Workmen construct a puncheon road near Mora around 1905. The workmen were conscripted to labor to pay for fines accrued from minor offenses.

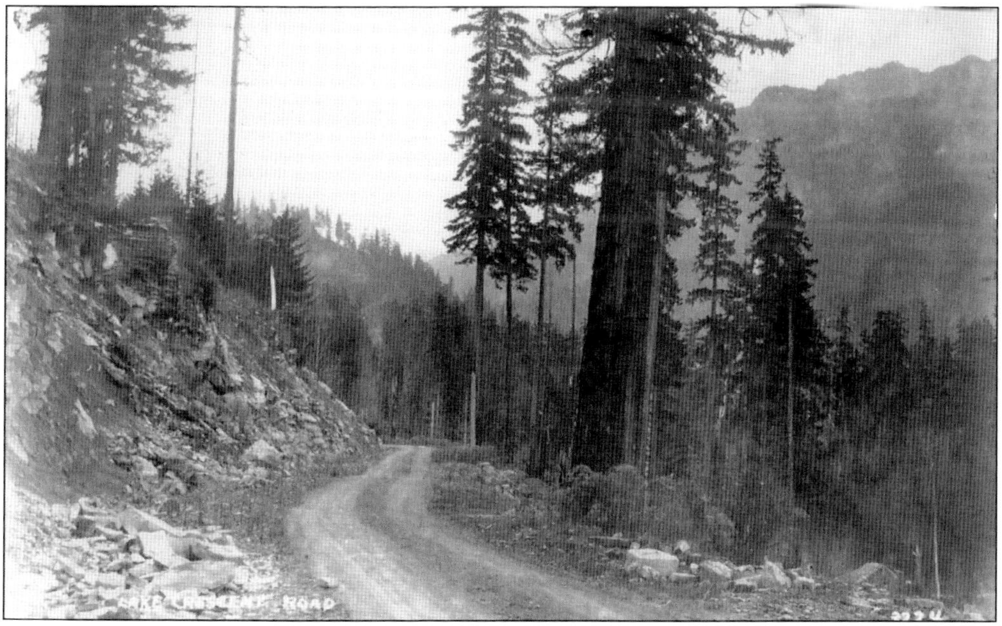

Linking the valleys between the Elwha River and the east shore of Lake Crescent with the road from Fairholm (on the west shoreline) to Forks opened up travel for Forks residents. The federal funding of the Spruce Division and the US Spruce Production Company in World War I to procure spruce logs for wartime biplane production underwrote the construction of a rail line on the north shore and the beginnings of a lakeside road on the south side.

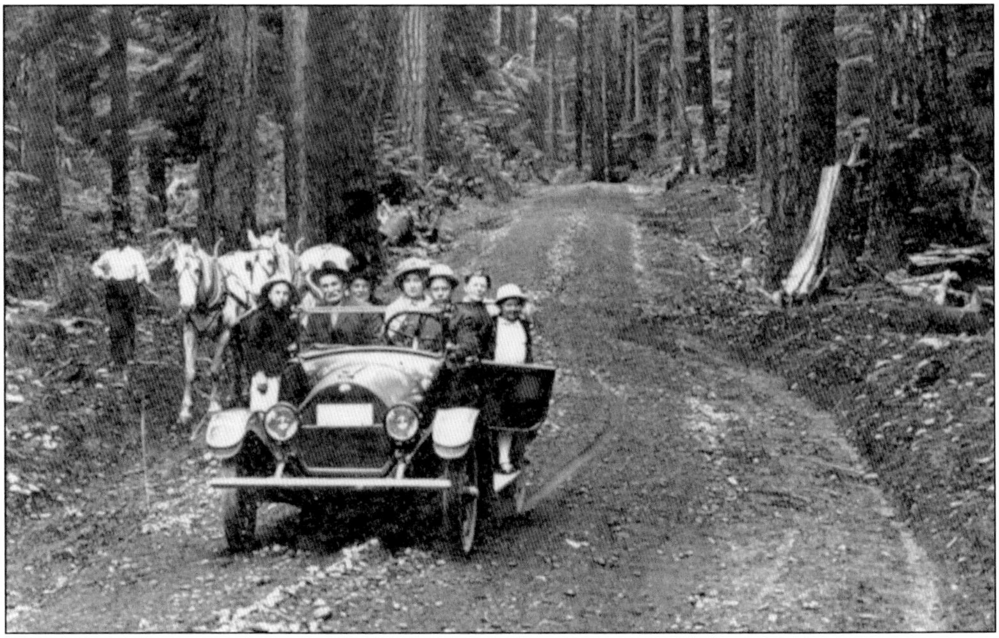

While a drover reins in a team of horses, a family out for a drive motors by in an open car down an unpaved forest road. The automobile cut down on the isolation of Forks to other West End towns and dramatically reduced the amount of time it took to travel elsewhere. The automobile was a novelty in the 1910s and 1920s, but it became a practicality for Forks residents in coming decades. Crossing a wooden trestle, a young beau doubles up in his crank-started Model T. Note the open-air flagon horn and side lamp accessories.

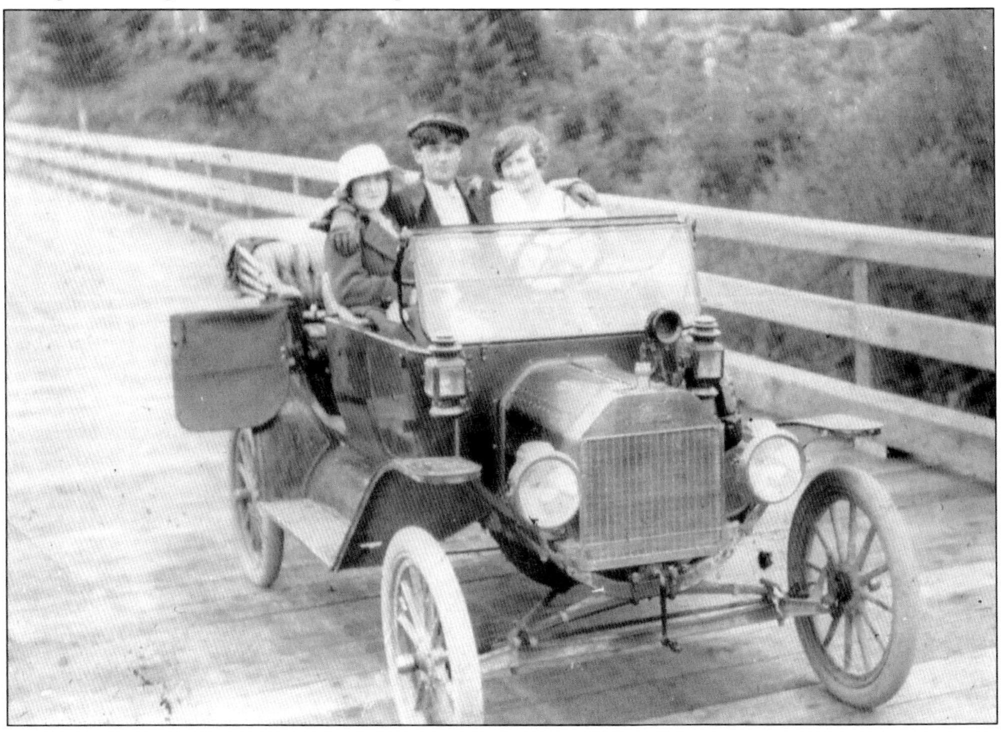

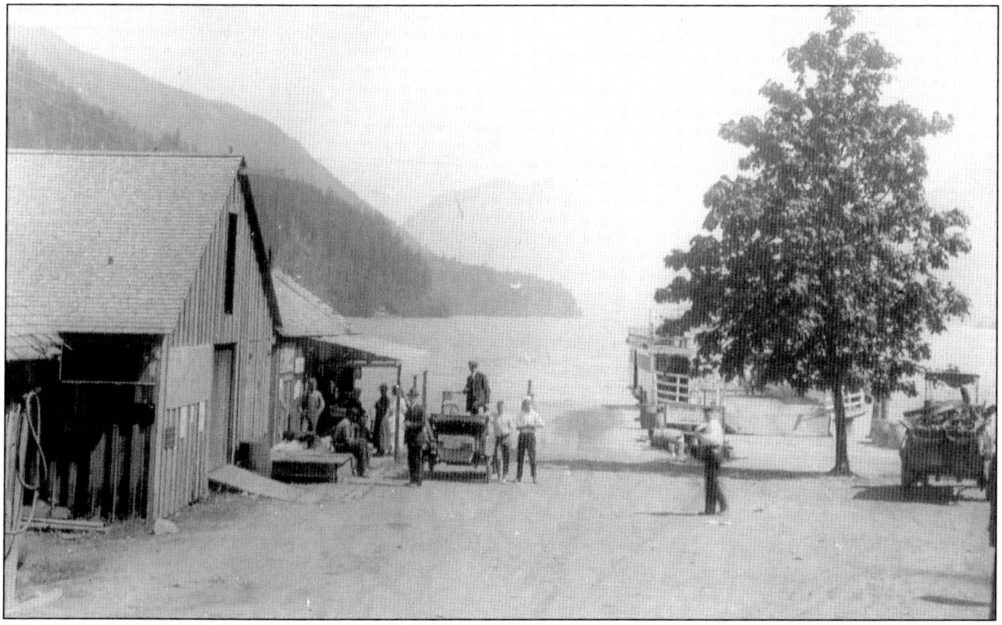

The side-wheel–powered Clallam County ferry *Storm King* brought passengers and vehicles from the East Beach ferry dock on the Lake Sutherland side of Lake Crescent to this ferry dock at Fairholm on the lake's West End. The ferry was taken off the lake in 1922 when the Olympic Highway opened along the south shore, allowing motor vehicles to drive the lakeside rather than cross aboard a ferry. Spruce Division construction engineers began the highway section during World War I.

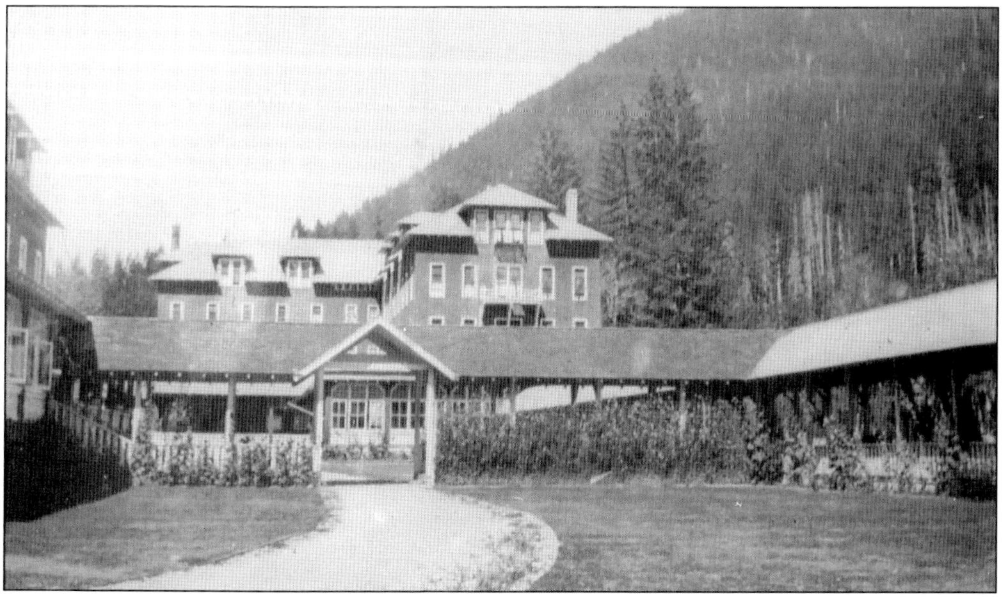

A stop on the way to Forks for many travelers in the early years of automobile tourism was the Sol Duc Hot Springs Resort built by timber magnate Michael Earles. The resort opened in the spring of 1912. The resort's warm mineral water pools were touted as a healthy restorative. Tens of thousands of visitors made the trek out to the upscale 165-room hotel-sanatorium before it burned down in 1916.

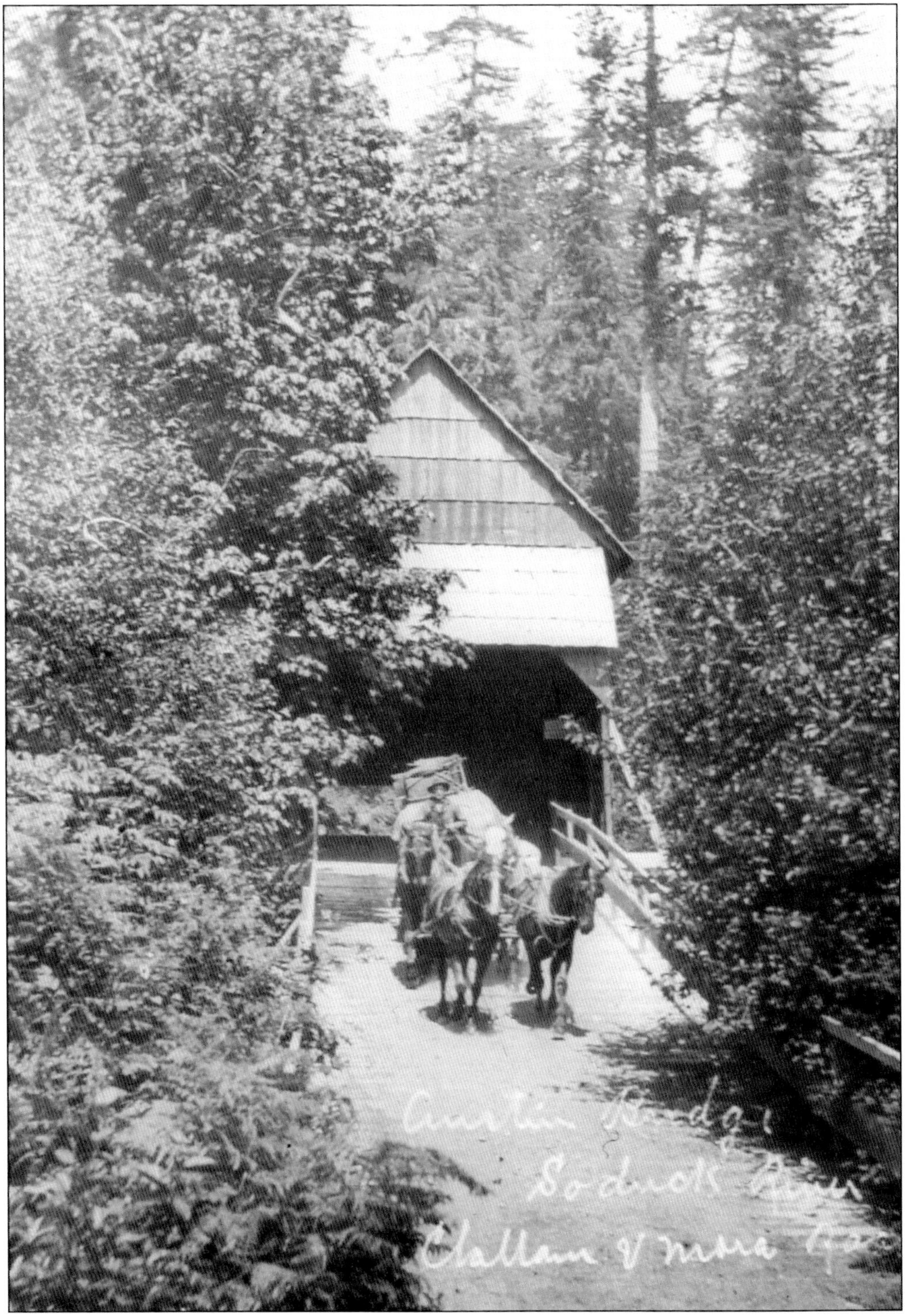

A New England–style covered bridge, sided and roofed with cedar shakes, crosses the Sol Duc River east of Forks in the 1910s. The horse-drawn wagon continued to serve as a means of hauling and transportation well into the 20th century in Forks and surrounding villages.

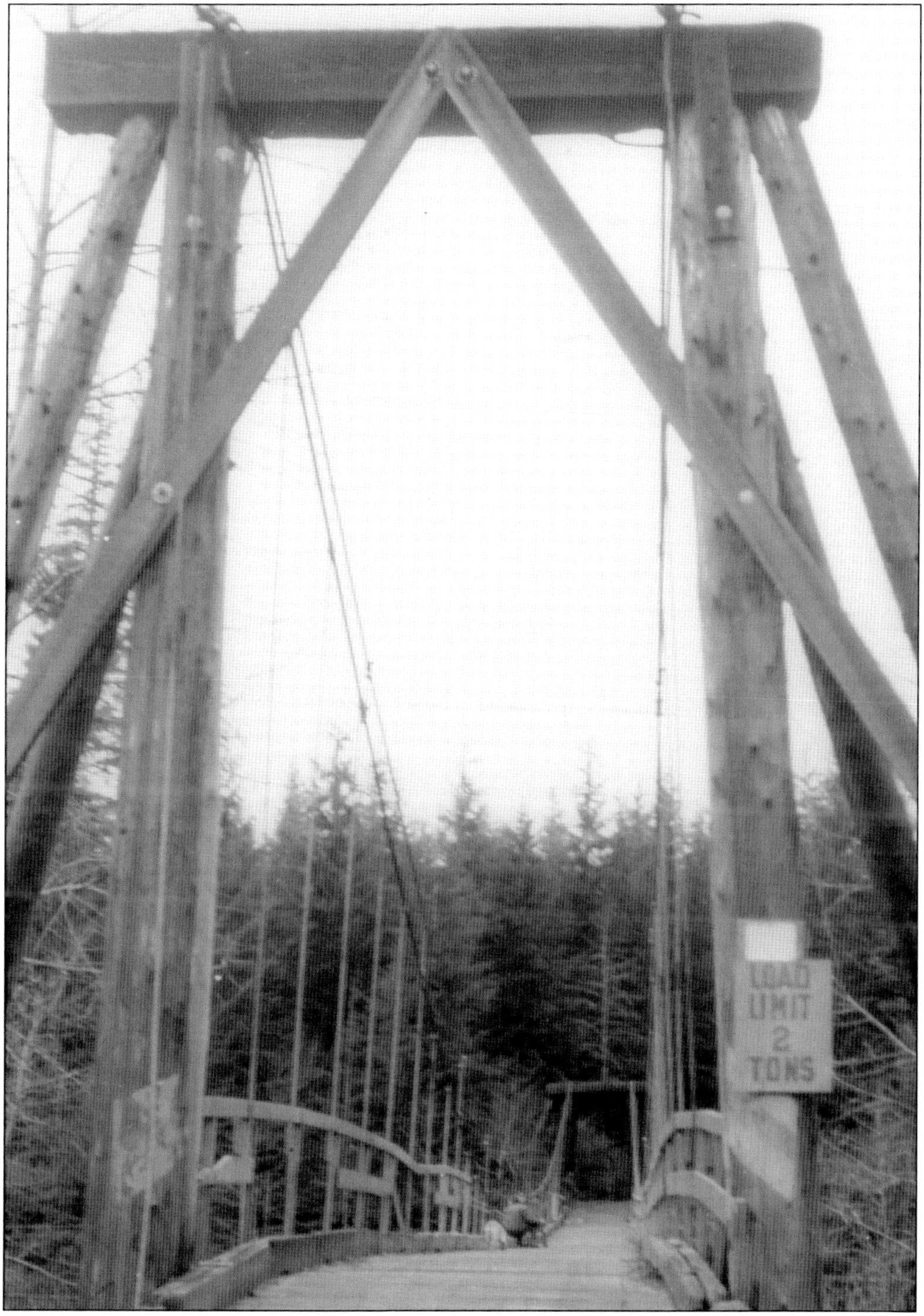

A man and his dog stop for a spell midway along a wooden suspension bridge. With a two-ton limit, the bridge could not handle large loads. Such bridges were made of steel cables and locally cut logs and milled lumber. No matter what materials were used, every bridge enhanced the growing network of roads in the wilderness outside of Forks.

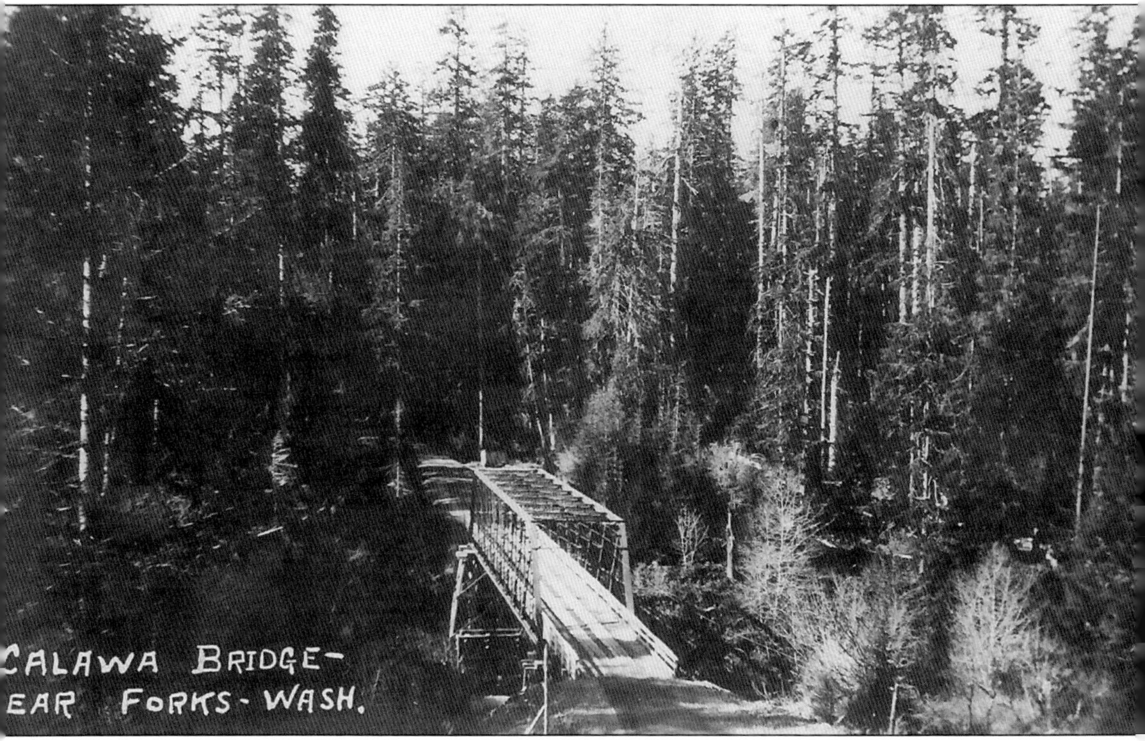

The Calawah Bridge at the northern entrance to Forks is pictured in a souvenir photograph. Tall forest trees line the Calawah River, shadowing what would become the Olympic Highway in Forks.

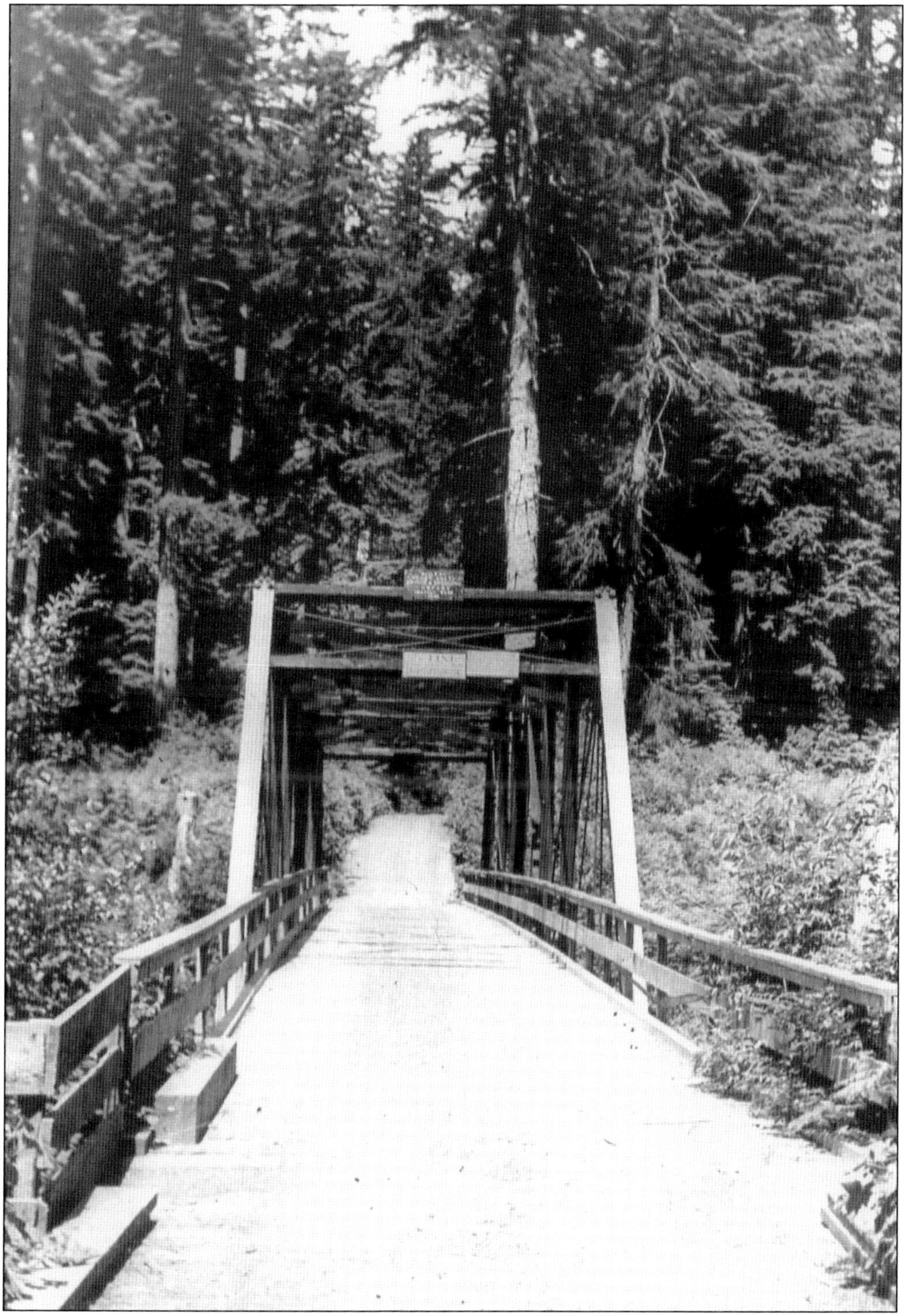

A classic steel truss bridge braced by metal framework was placed over the Calawah River, which meant easy movement into Forks for passenger cars, logging trucks, and the bus that ran to Clallam Bay.

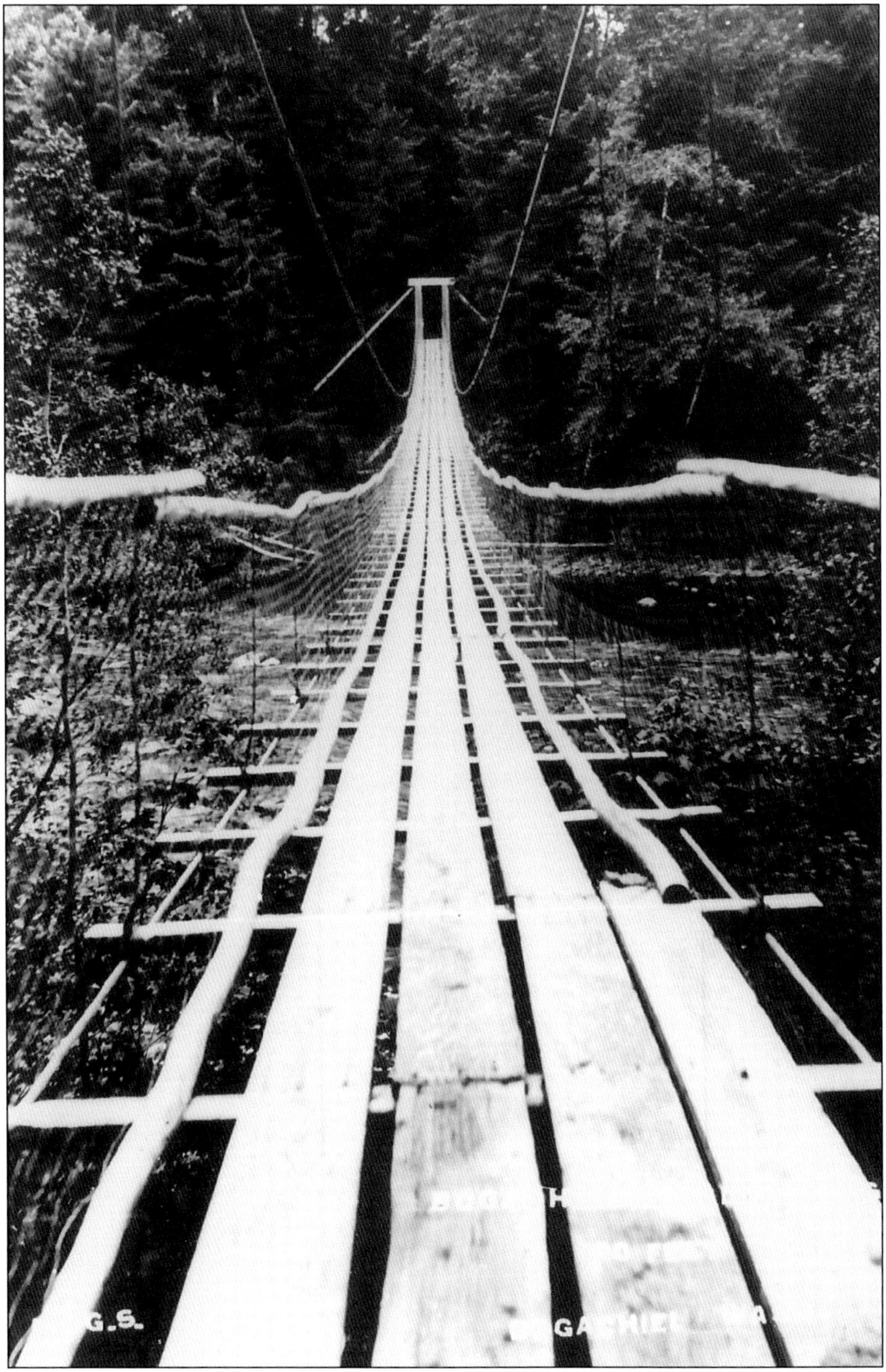

Pedestrian suspension bridges linked isolated homesteads and communities outside Forks with roads and other communities in places where a steel truss bridge or a complex wooden trestle was impractical, mostly due to cost. Suspended from cables, the wood-handled swinging bridges swayed when walked across.

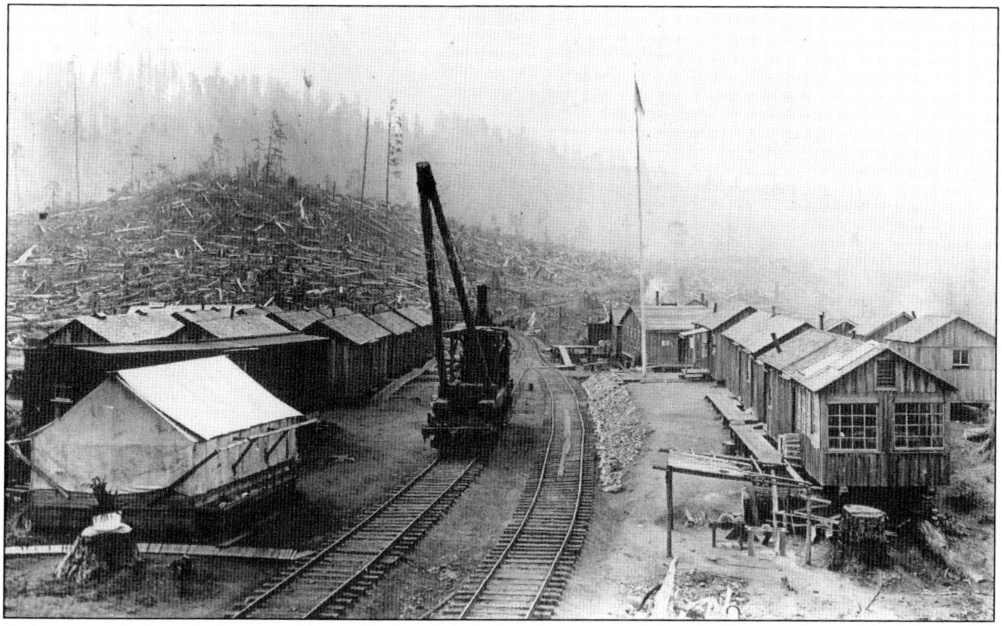

A logging railroad camp at the end of a rail line is shown with a supply of felled logs waiting for shipment on flatbed railcars. Tents and one-room shacks housed workers. A steam-powered utility railcar with a crane loaded the logs. Laying track and building trestles in order to have trains took large amounts of capital, and the train systems needed highly qualified engineers and brakemen to operate.

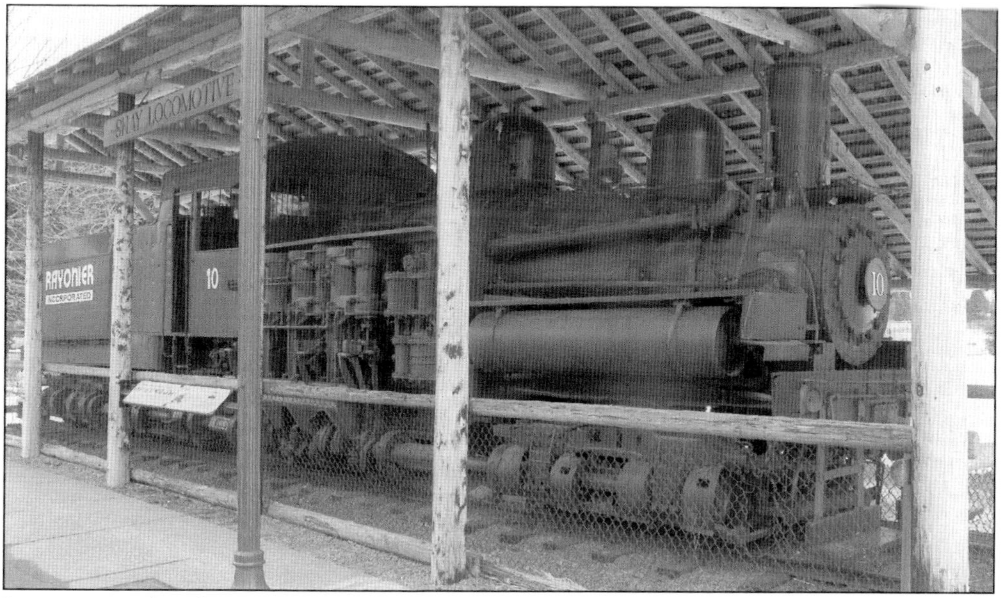

Locomotives played an important part in timber history for decades. They allowed huge quantities of large logs to be moved rapidly out of the dense West End forest to be shipped for milling. This coal-black Rayonier Shay locomotive No. 10 display was dedicated in 1960. The Rayonier Shay locomotive, built in Lima, Ohio, brought power and traction to logging railroading. The locomotives could pull heavy loads of logs up steep grades. Rayonier Shay used this Pacific Coast type of locomotive in the Ozette area.

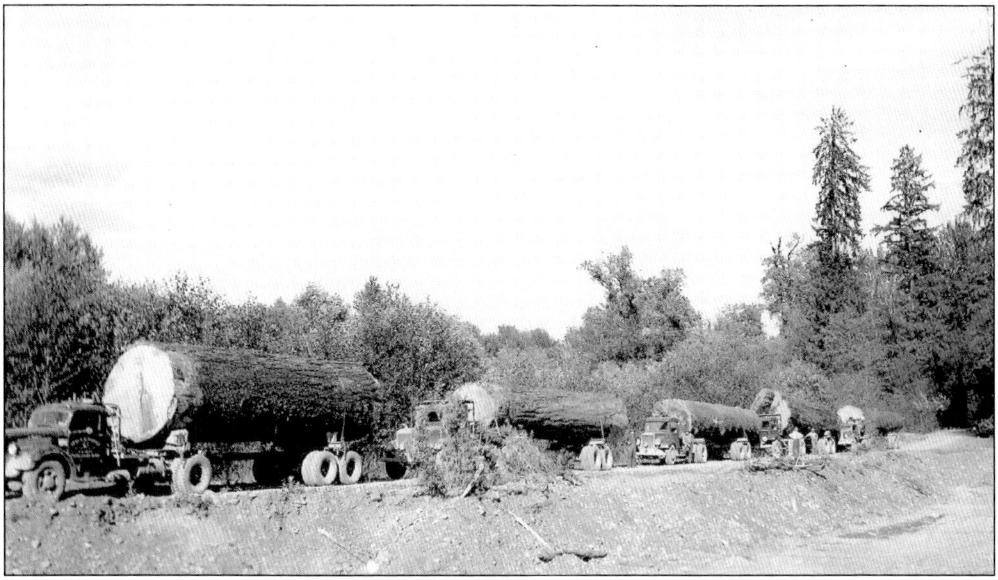

The post–World War II era saw the decline of railroads when modern logging trucks became affordable and more powerful. At first, the trucks hauled logs from sections located away from train lines. Gradually, the flexibility, safety, and cost savings of using a logging truck supplanted the train. By the 1960s, the roar of passing locomotives was gone from the West End.

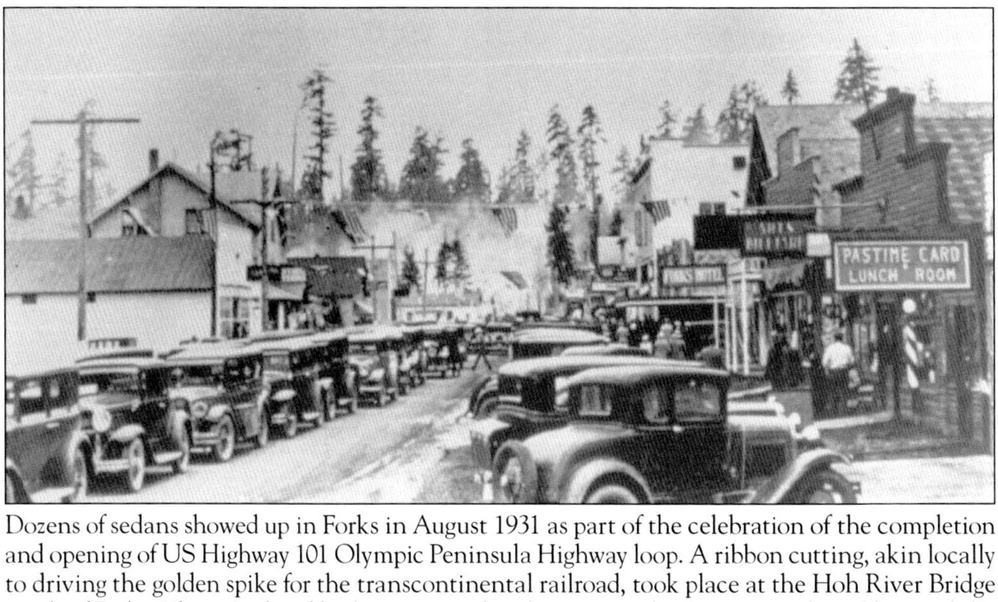

Dozens of sedans showed up in Forks in August 1931 as part of the celebration of the completion and opening of US Highway 101 Olympic Peninsula Highway loop. A ribbon cutting, akin locally to driving the golden spike for the transcontinental railroad, took place at the Hoh River Bridge south of Forks. The completed highway opened up logging trucks to areas south and boosted the tourism industry.

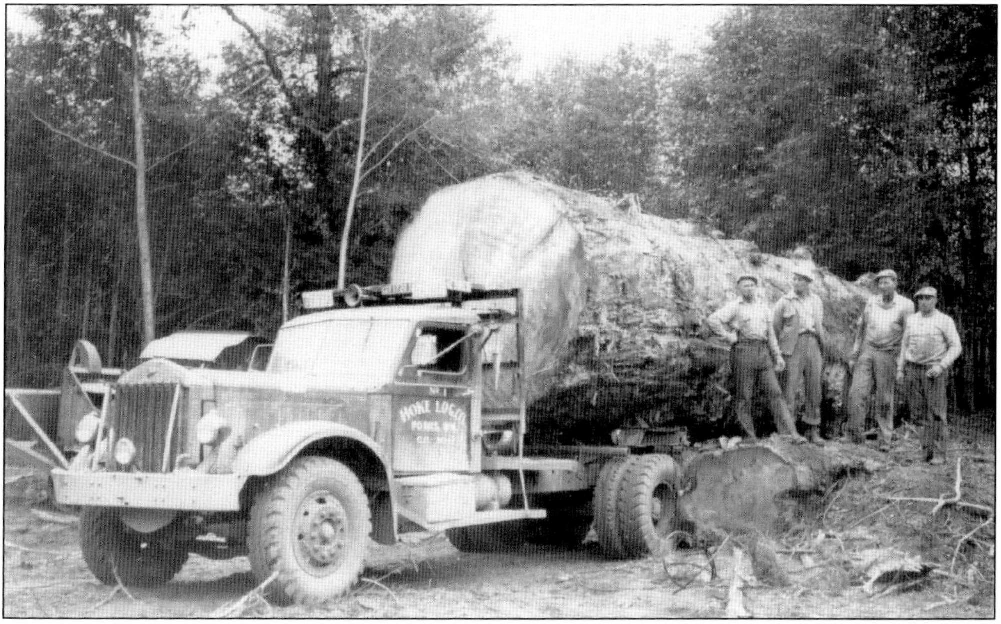

The men of the Hoke Log Company of Forks stand atop a felled tree, posing before their air horn–equipped truck. Such companies would keep offices and oversized garages in Forks while working logging sections across the West End, sometimes transporting logs far south and east. The huge logs were sometimes positioned on hillsides and rolled onto the beds of logging trucks. Maneuvering the trees into position with heavy equipment was an art.

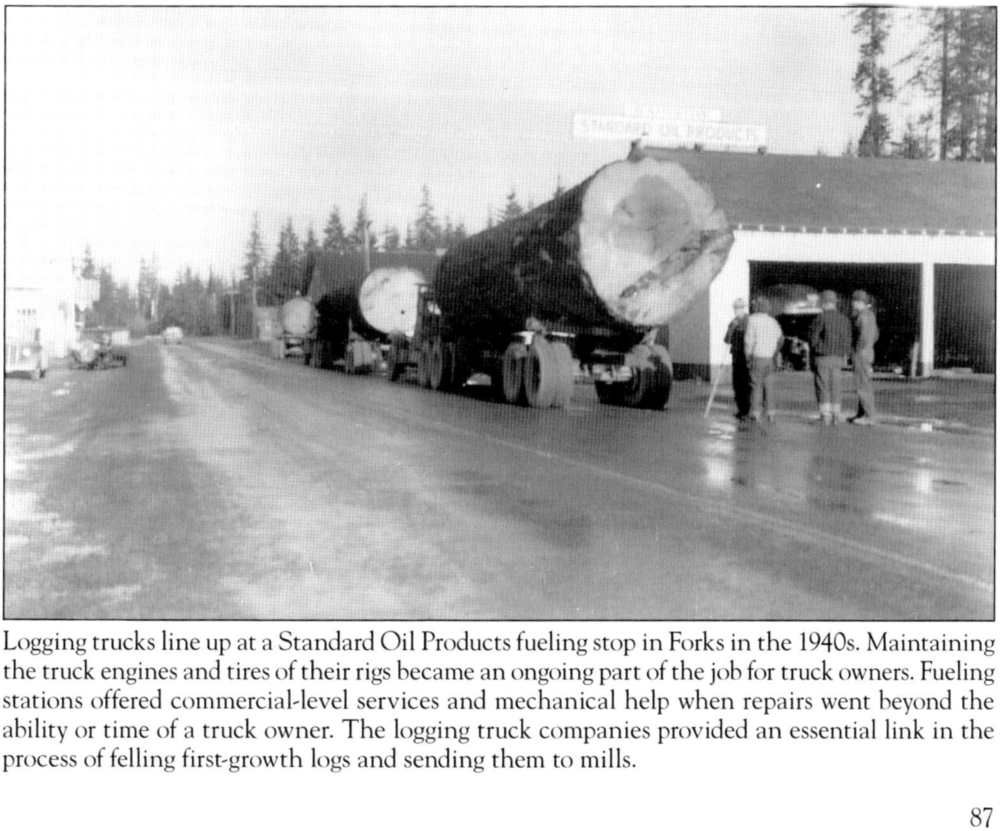

Logging trucks line up at a Standard Oil Products fueling stop in Forks in the 1940s. Maintaining the truck engines and tires of their rigs became an ongoing part of the job for truck owners. Fueling stations offered commercial-level services and mechanical help when repairs went beyond the ability or time of a truck owner. The logging truck companies provided an essential link in the process of felling first-growth logs and sending them to mills.

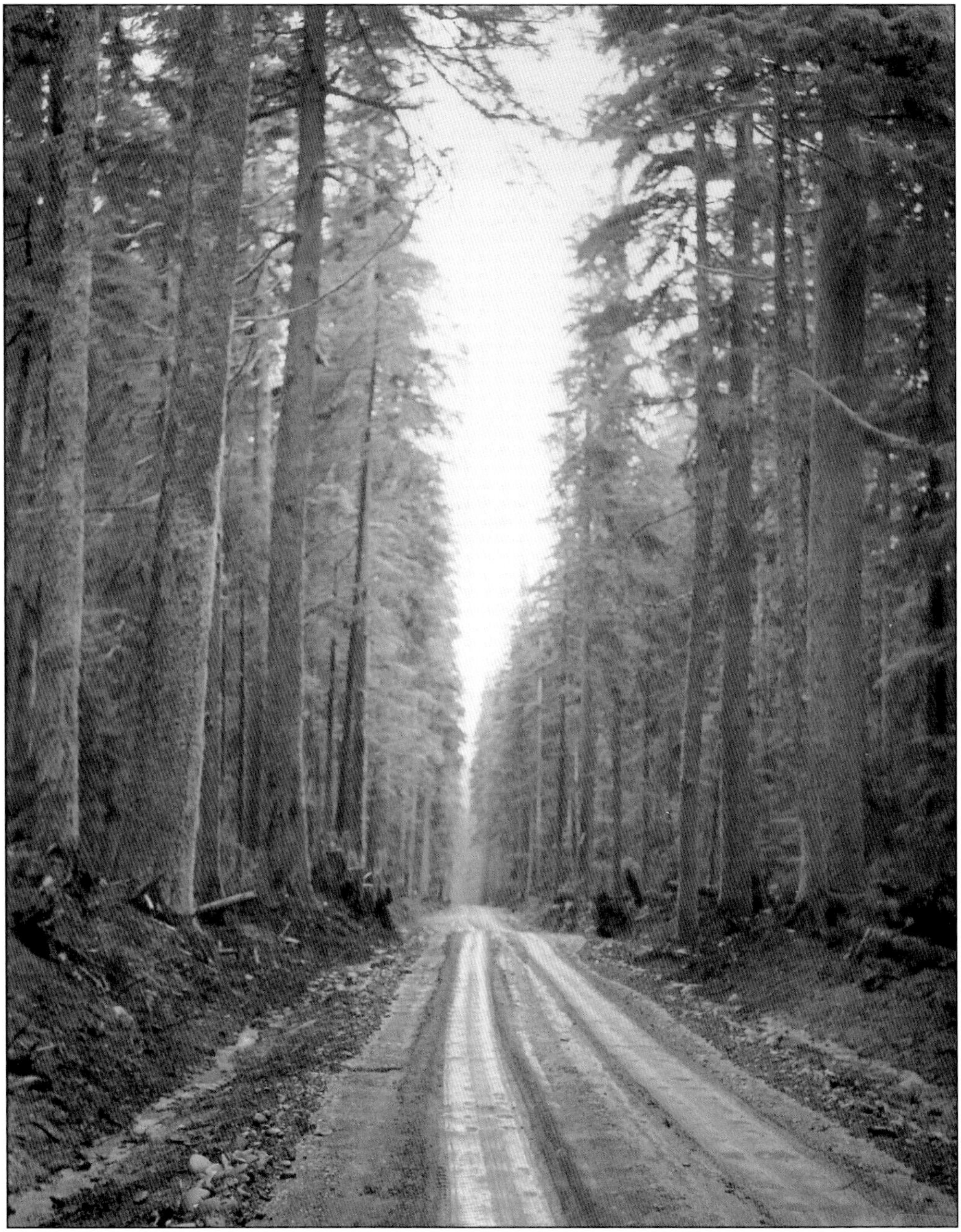

Narrow automobile tire tracks run down the dirt-road highway outside of Forks around 1915 to 1920.

Five

World War II and Postwar Years

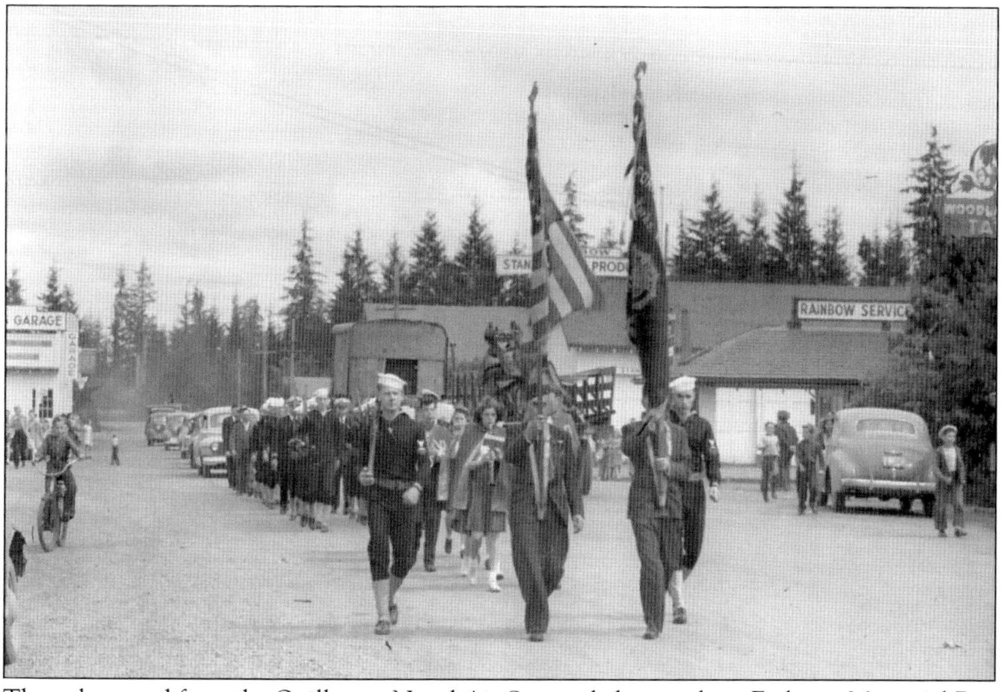

The color guard from the Quillayute Naval Air Station led a parade in Forks on Memorial Day 1944. The makeup of the parade displays the cooperation of the Navy personnel at the base with local folk, including the Quillayute Union High School marching band and, at the rear of the procession, older local veterans. The two men holding the flags may be local servicemen home on leave or Marines from the base.

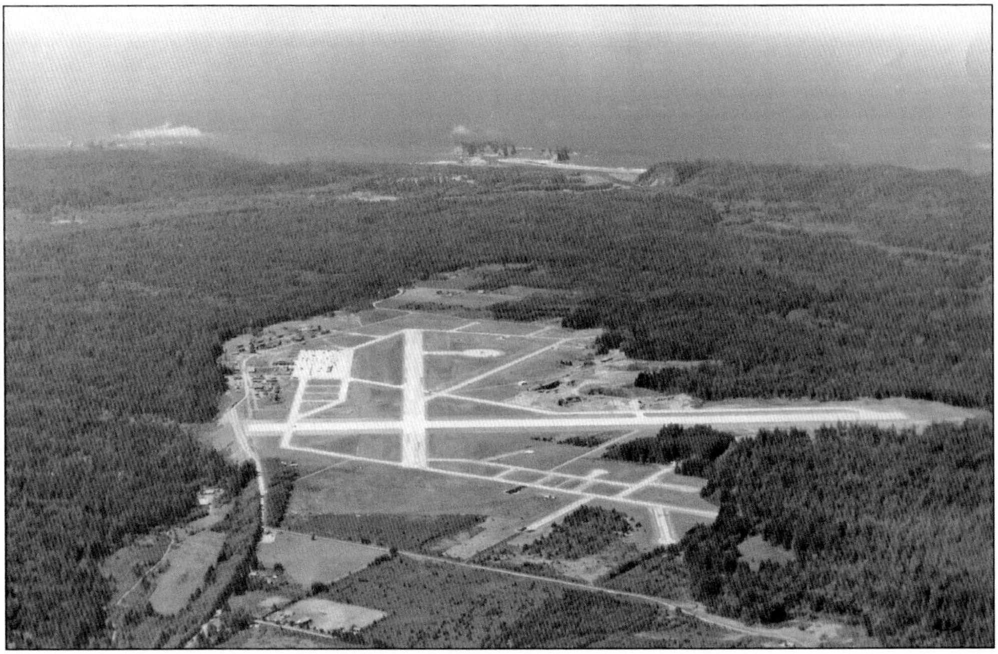

Here is the Quillayute Naval Air Station with its east-west and north-south runways during World War II. The self-sufficient base had electrical generators, fuel farms, a theater and chapel, barracks, and large hangers. Work on the field began in 1942; it would house up to 2,500 base personnel. The Navy field is likened to an aircraft carrier on land due to its coastal location.

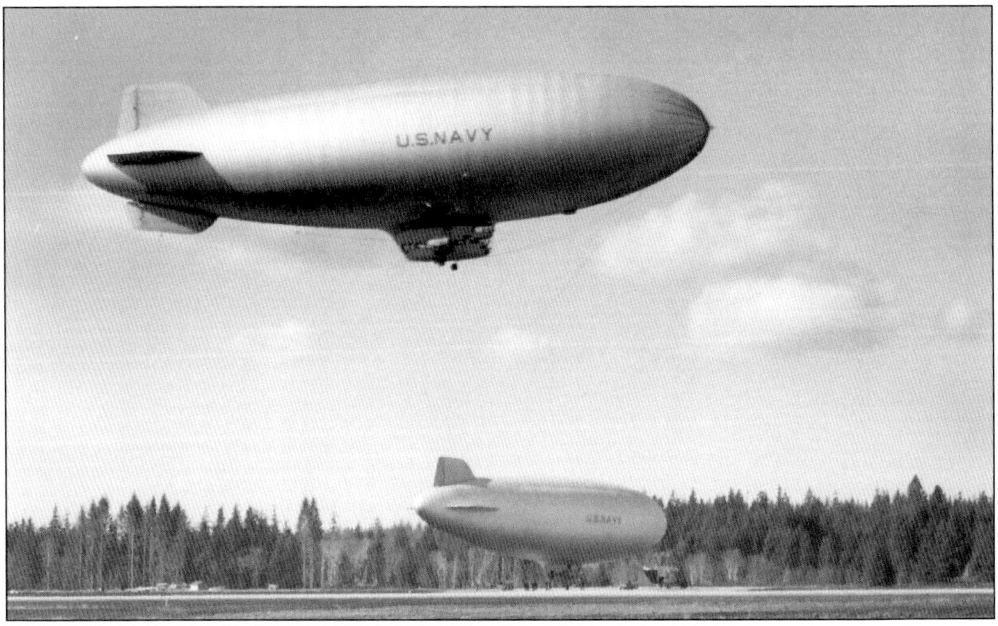

A Goodyear K-series blimp and its companion are on patrol from the blimp field at Tillamook, Oregon, and shown hovering over the Quillayute Naval Air Station runway during World War II. The blimps, about 250 feet long and filled with helium, made fueling and resupply stops here during offshore antisubmarine patrols. Portable masts were brought out for the landings. The two-engine blimps could reach 60 miles per hour in the air.

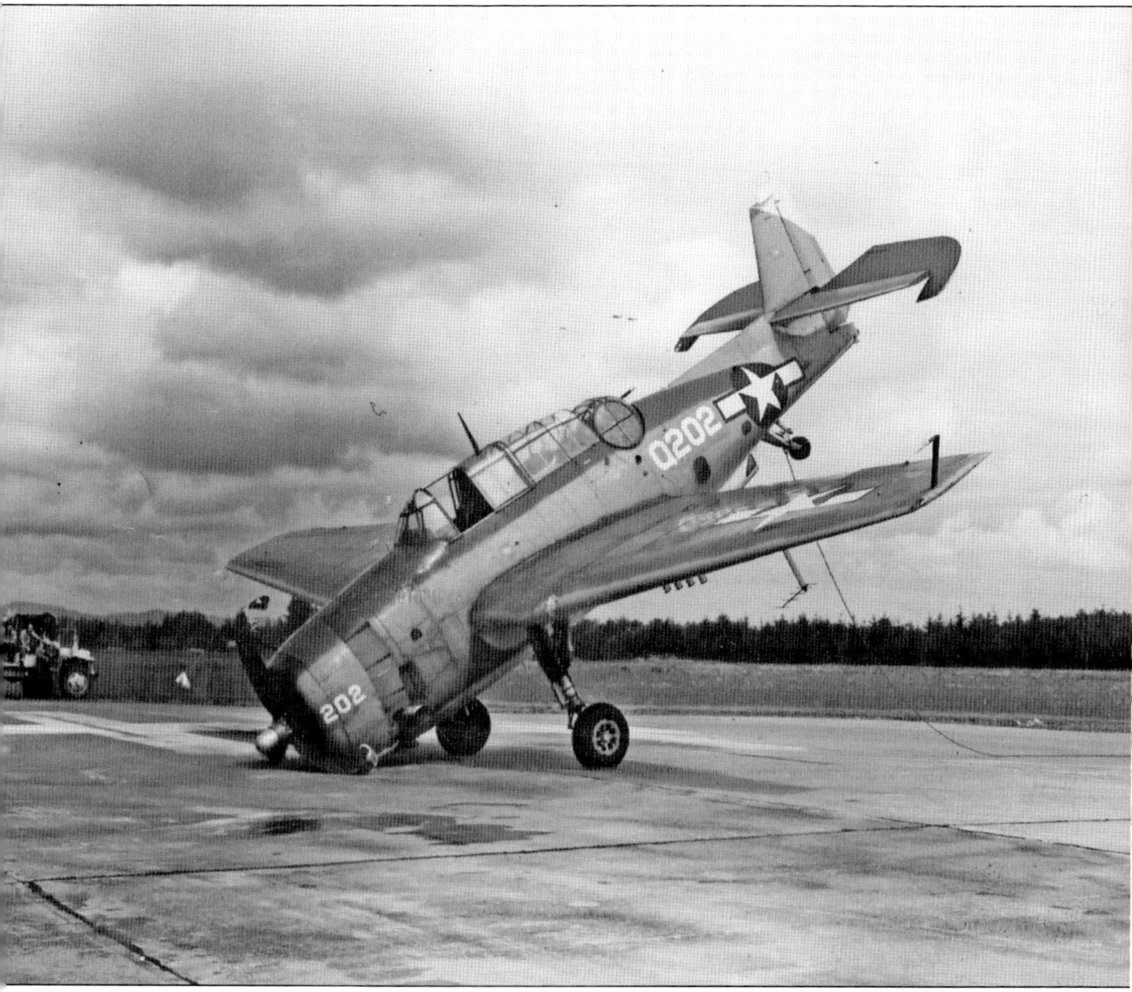

This TBM-3 Avenger torpedo bomber, made by General Motors under contract to Grumman, apparently fell forward due to a pilot's training error, either from wind or breaking too hard while taxiing. The plane carried a pilot, rear gunner, and a radioman who was also in charge of dropping bombs. It could carry four, 500-pound bombs or one torpedo.

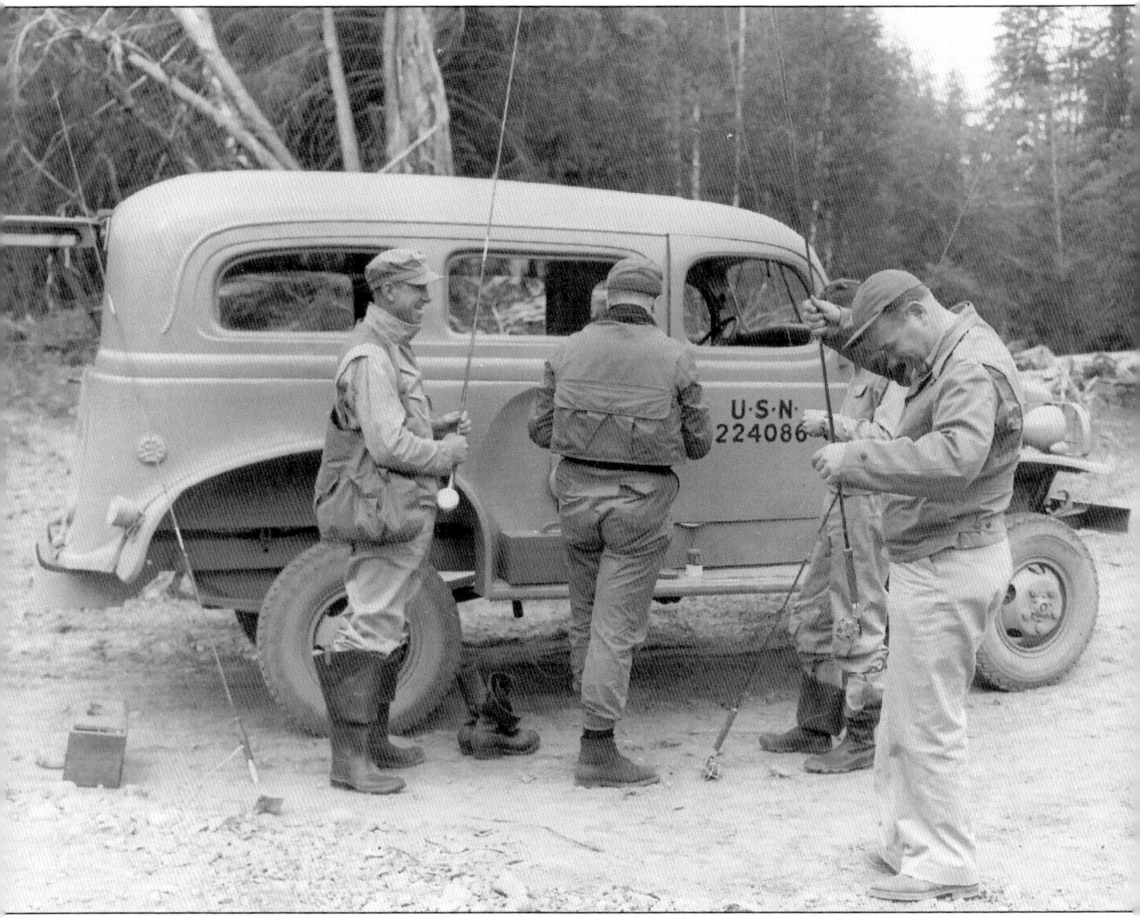

Four Navy fishermen head out in their Power Wagon to try their luck fishing in a river near Forks. The Quillayute Naval Air Station also served as a rest stop for servicemen and officers. This once classified photograph may portray an admiral or two who did not want the enemy to know they were on the Pacific Coast.

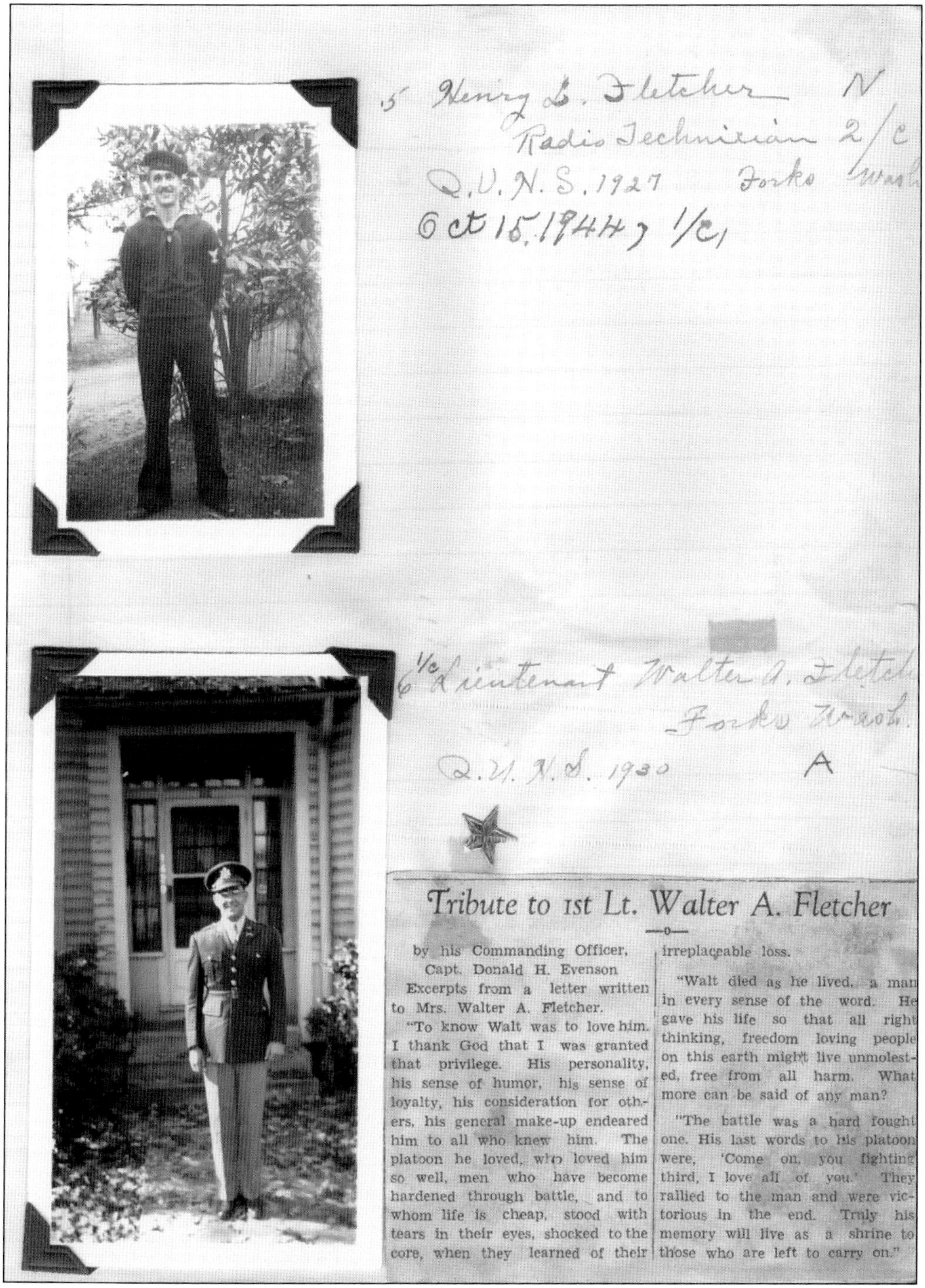

This scrapbook, kept during World War II, listed Forks's men in the armed forces and included snapshots of the men when they paid a visit home. Gold stars were placed next to photographs of men killed in the war, including Lt. Walter Fletcher, who was shot by a sniper on a German battlefield days before the end of the war.

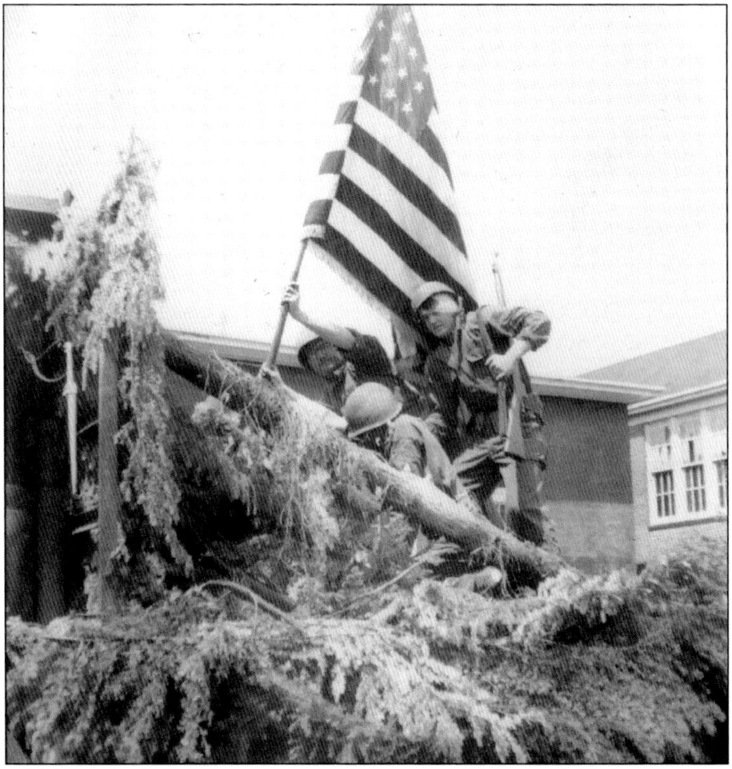

During a Forks parade, possibly celebrating V-J Day in August 1945, three young men, including John Leppell Jr. (with a bandage on his temple and a rifle slung over his shoulder), portray the iconic raising of the flag on Mount Suribachi in February 1945 at Iwo Jima. The parade float is decorated with logs and cedar boughs collected from local forests. A glimpse of the backside of Forks High School is in the background. (Courtesy Leppell family.)

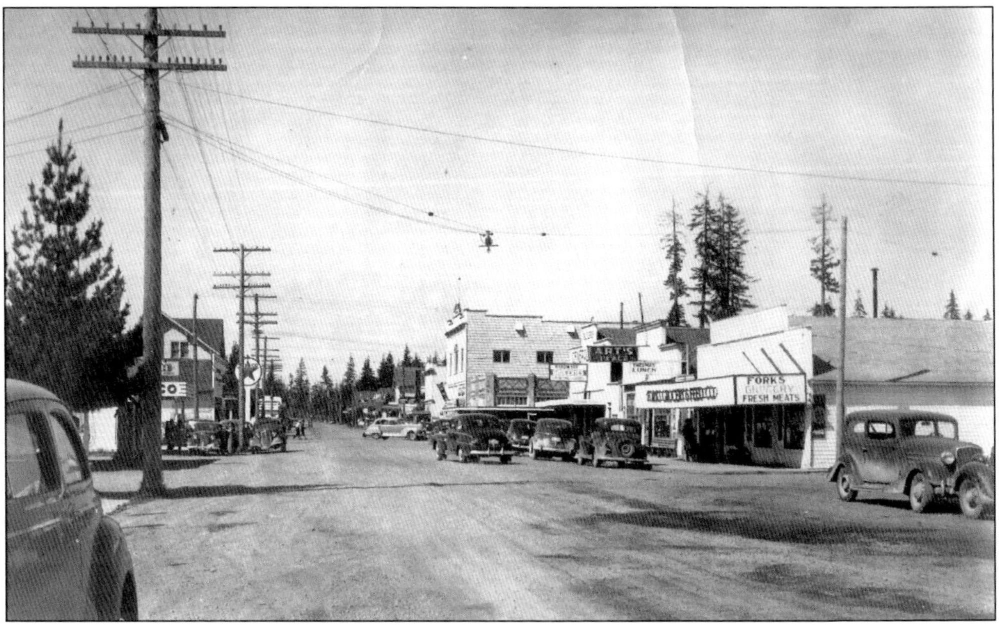

Downtown Forks prospered during World War II. The Odd Fellows Hall continued to be the tallest landmark in town. Dollars that were spent by Quillayute Naval Air Station personnel in stores and bars helped the economy, as did wartime logging work. Some timber industry workers were considered essential to the wartime defense industry and were exempt from the armed forces draft.

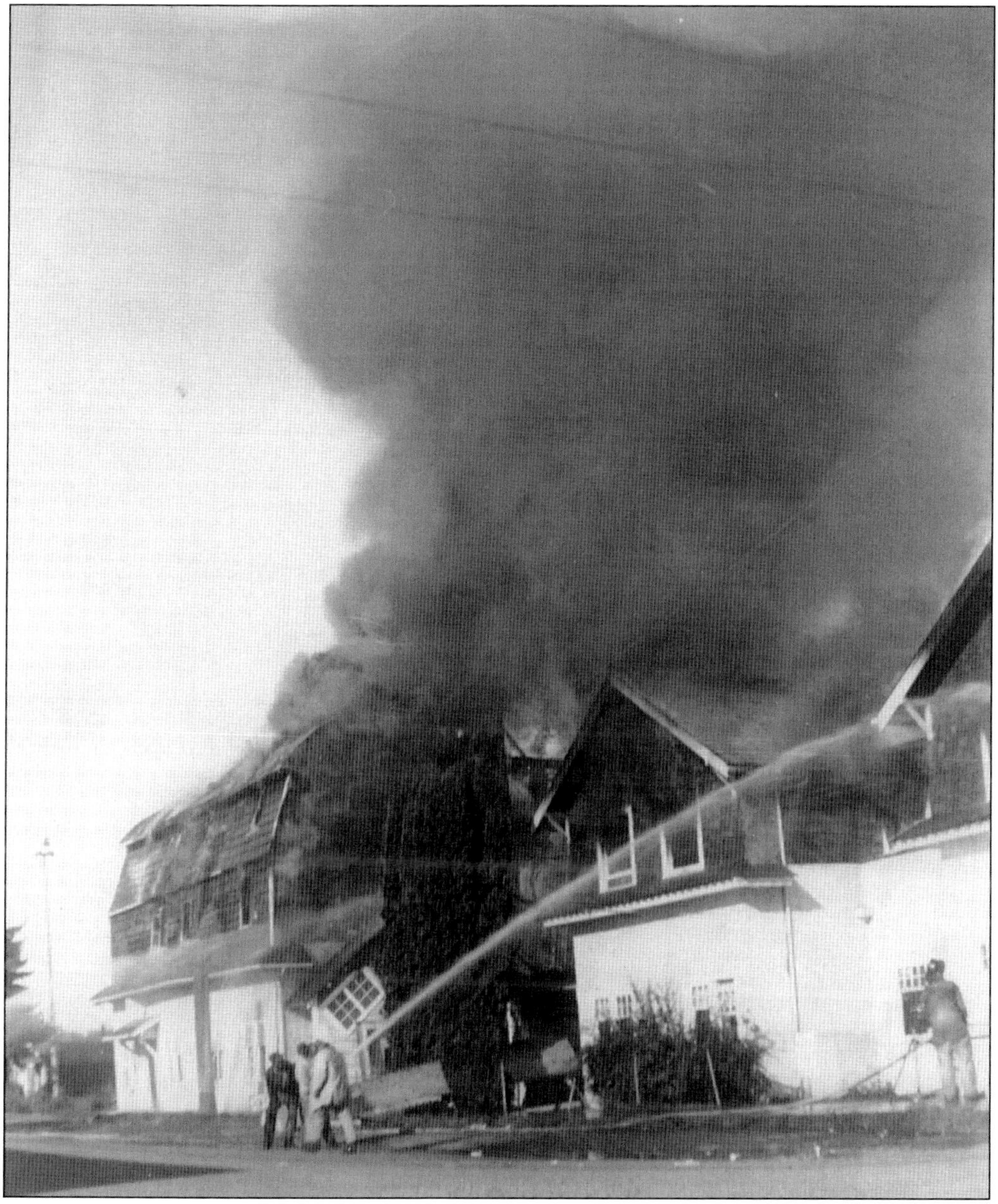

Firefighters in Forks typically battled blazes caused by wood-burning chimneys or electrical sparks in homes and businesses. However, occasionally, firefighters were called to extinguish fires in the forest. Fire spotters in towers located atop strategic peaks, such as Snider (east of Forks), were key in defeating these infernos. In the early days, bucket brigades fought blazes by passing pails of water. The downtown fire of 1925 spurred the creation of the first volunteer fire company, and by the 1930s, gas-fired pumpers had come into use. Clallam County Fire Districts organized in the late 1940s. Shown here, a Forks fire crew combats a building ablaze at the Olympic Apartments, formerly the Olympic Hospital, in 1954. A network of water lines and fire hydrants added to the modern capabilities of the firemen.

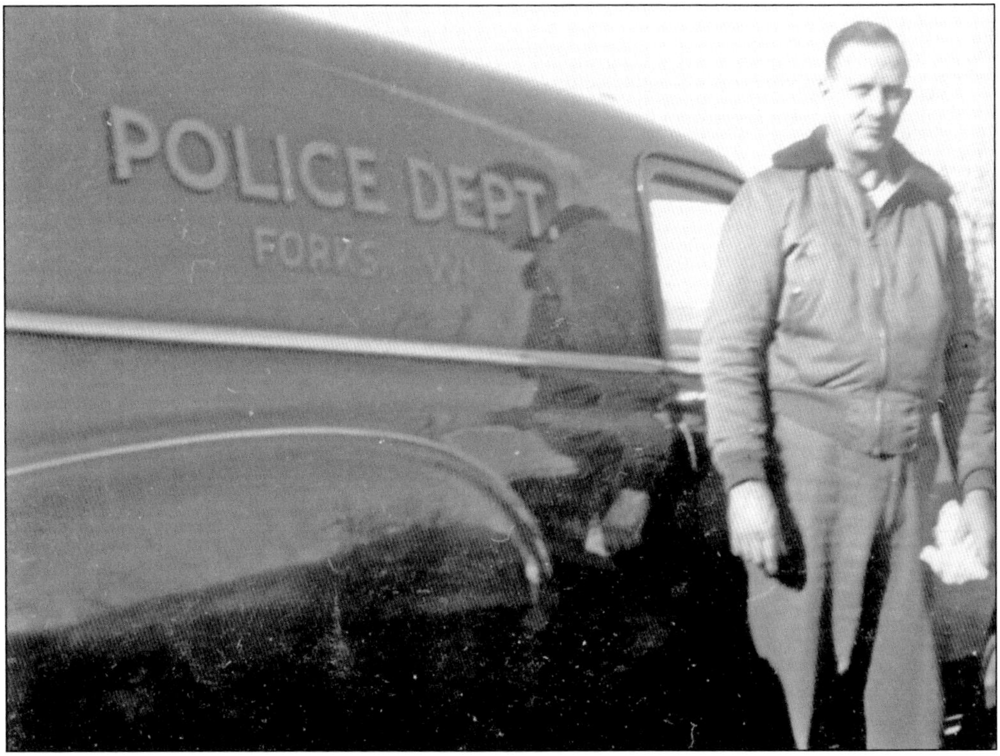

Forks policeman Elwood Leppell stands beside a Forks Police Department panel van wearing a park ranger–looking uniform. The city of Forks was incorporated in 1945. Elwood served as a town marshal. In earlier years, Washington State Patrol troopers, such as Boyd Rupp (who came to Forks at the outset of World War II), were stationed in Forks. Also at this time, Forks had a night watchman patrol the town. (Courtesy Leppell family.)

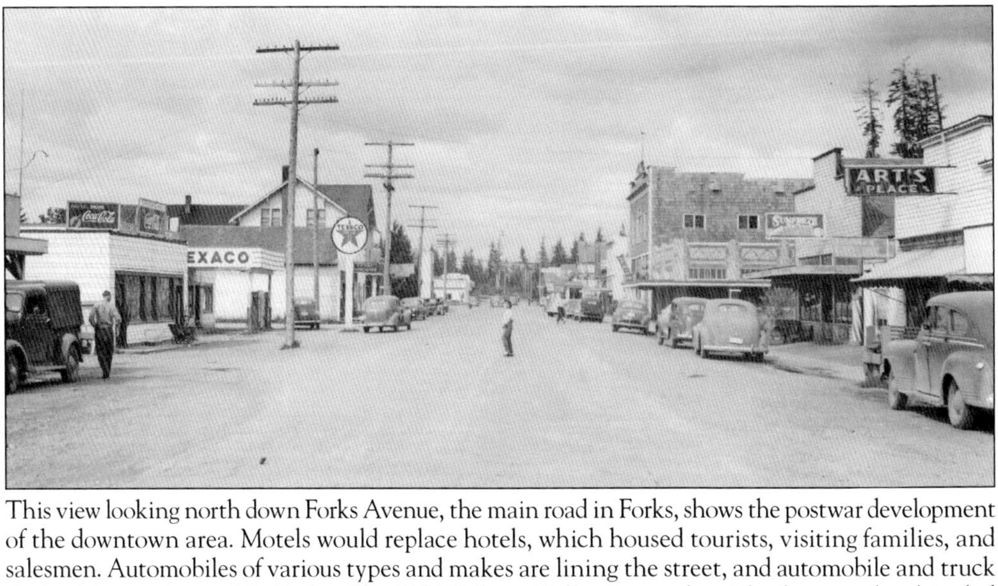

This view looking north down Forks Avenue, the main road in Forks, shows the postwar development of the downtown area. Motels would replace hotels, which housed tourists, visiting families, and salesmen. Automobiles of various types and makes are lining the street, and automobile and truck dealerships are located in Forks. The Odd Fellows Hall, seen to the right, has a cedar-shingled frontage and retail stores on the street level. Art's Place was a popular tavern.

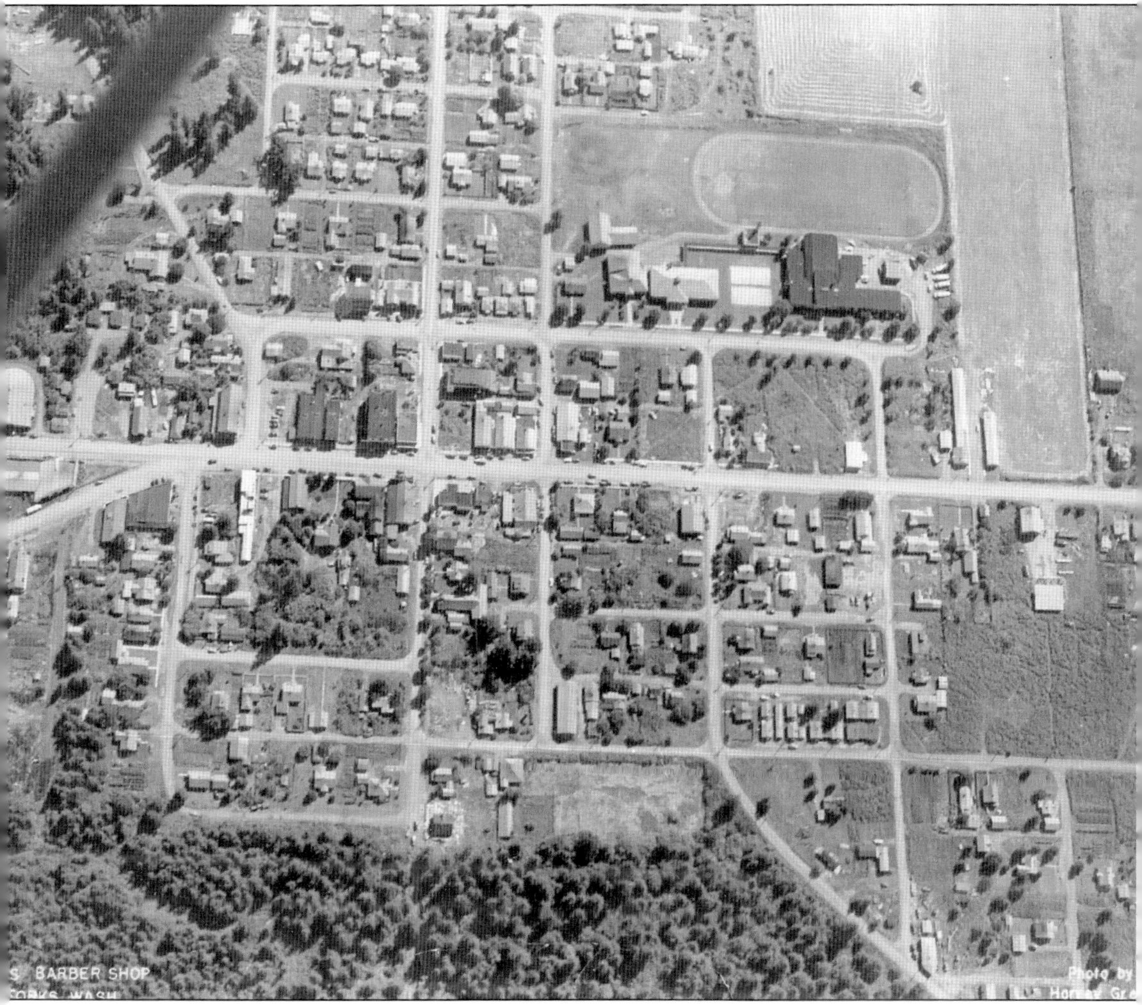

This aerial view of postwar Forks shows the growth of the town. The oval (top right) is the Forks High School football field adjacent to the high school. The American Legion Hall—a popular place for dances; boxing matches (also known as "smokers"), and roller-skating—is center left. The town lots and streets, laid out almost 50 years earlier, are still edged by the forest. Suburban-style homes would later be built in the surrounding subdivisions, which were mostly made up of pioneer family homestead tracts.

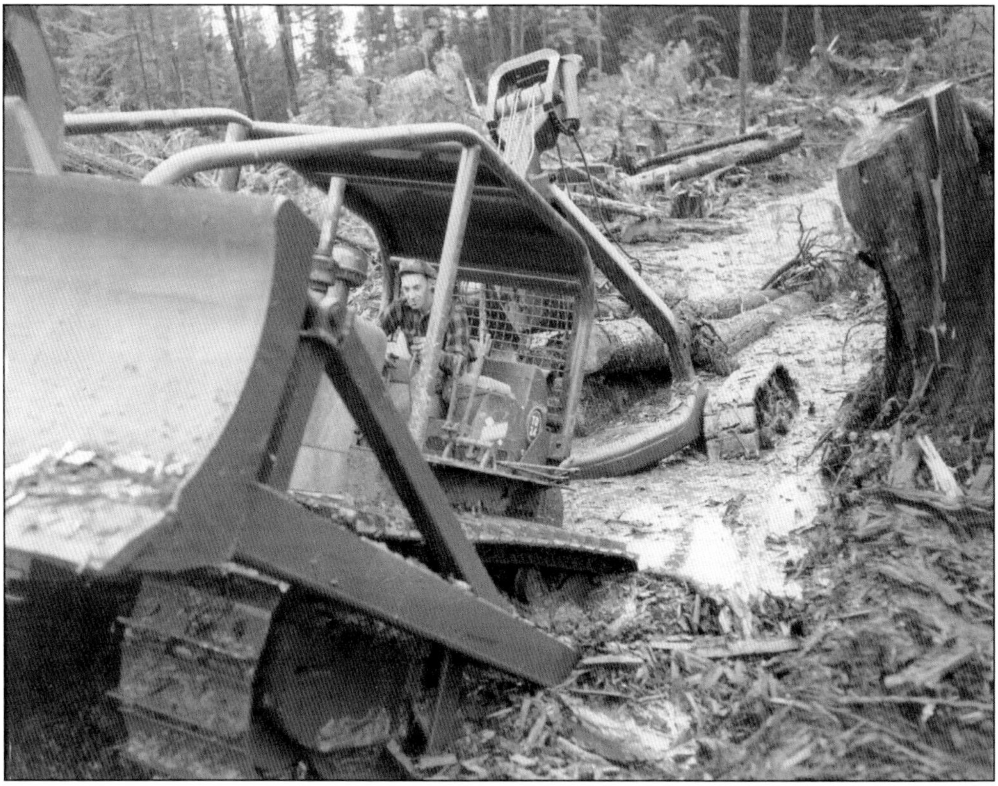

World War II helped step up the mechanization of the timber industry. Surplus war construction vehicles, like bulldozers, became readily available. Here, Gerald Miles uses a Caterpillar with a protective sheet-metal roof and a track-driven trailer to haul logs out of a West End forest. The logging-based economy continued to boom in Forks into the early 1990s. It was said that all one needed to do to get a job was show up on Forks Avenue early on a workday morning.

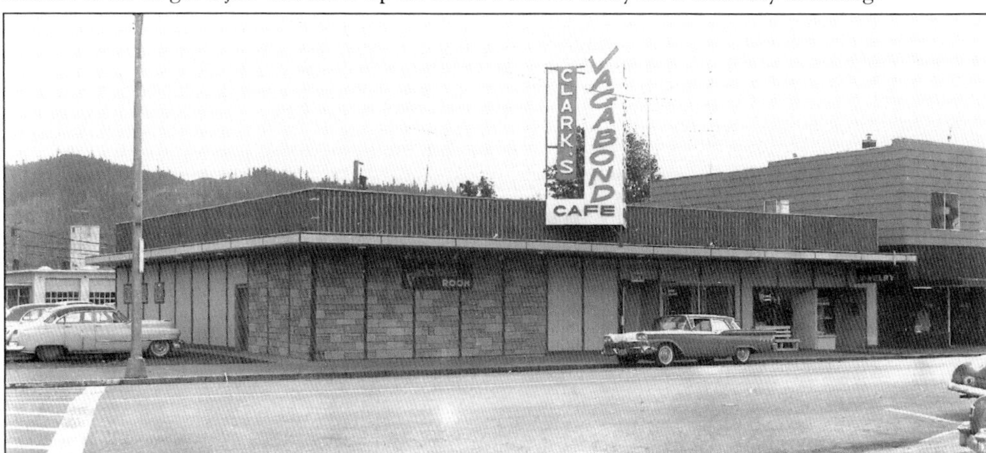

The 1950s brought new businesses and new sign graphics to downtown Forks. World War II and Korean War Navy veteran Claude Clark owned the popular dining spot Clark's Vagabond Café for 40 years, having taken over the Forks Café. An upstairs bar, the Top of the Rock, was later added. The popular logging show at the Forks Old Fashioned Fourth of July Celebration started as one of Clark's ideas.

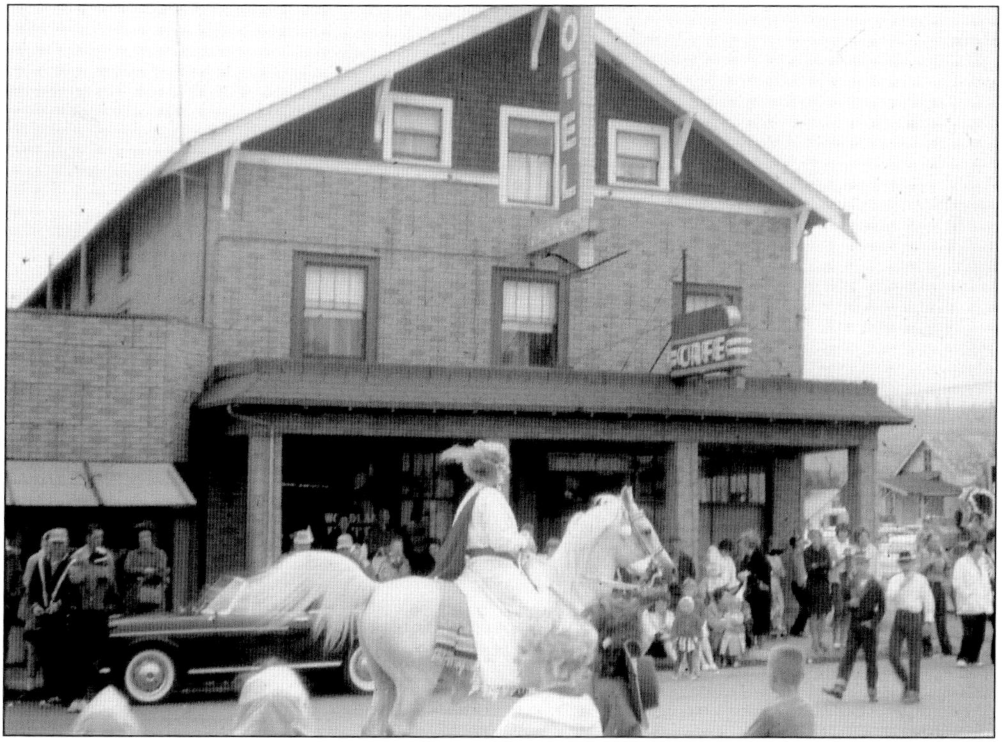

The Forks Fourth of July Parade is a long-standing tradition, drawing thousands of spectators each year. Here, a horse and rider gait down Forks Avenue in an early-1960s parade. In the 1890s, Forks began celebrations for the Fourth of July by singing patriotic songs and a reading of the Declaration of Independence, along with three-legged races, community picnics, and nightlong dances in barns, which included square dancing. The event grew into the top West End gathering of the year; people all across the West End gathered for the event, including Quileute and other tribes, who excelled in racing their ponies. Barrels were floated for miles down the Calawah River to Forks, and bets were placed on how long the barrels took. This pioneer float displays antique homesteading tools, including an elk rack (antlers) gun rack, a crosscut saw, and cast-iron pots.

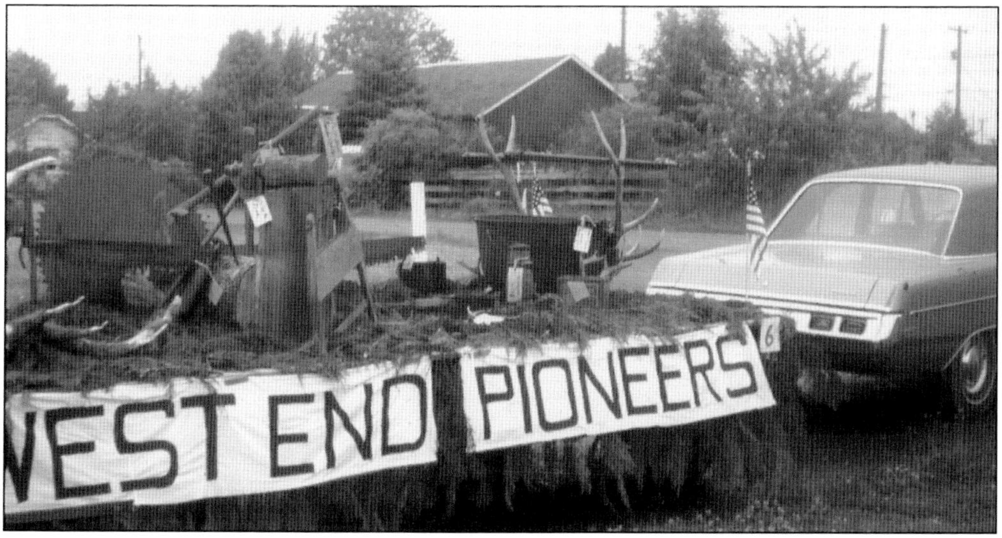

MODULE VII

Helitack Unit

"Airborne initial attack unit. Helicopter delivers crew and then may be used to airdrop water or retardant. Has capability of controlling class "A" fire. Hand tools and portable pump with crew. Capable of initial attacking any fire within 30 mile radius."

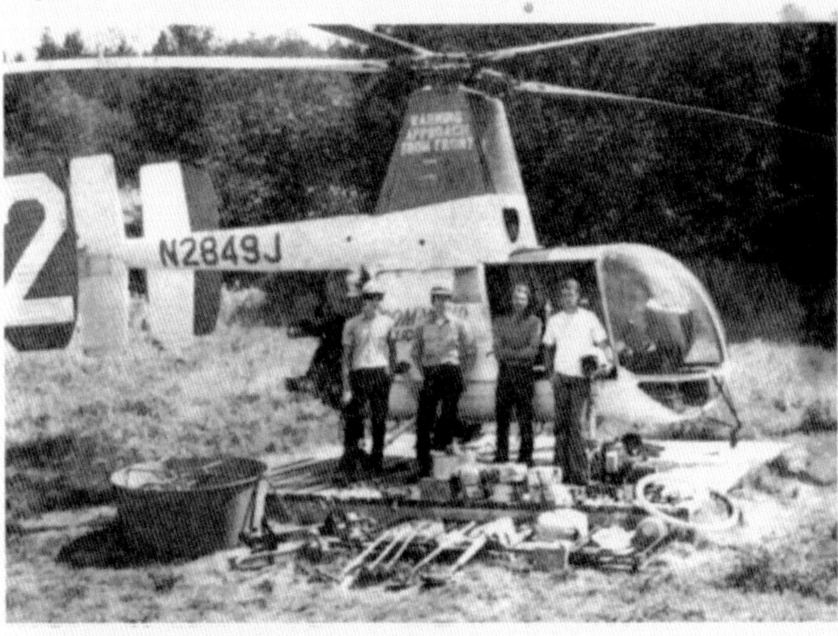

MODULE INCLUDES:

1 Foreman I

3 forest fire fighters

1 helicopter—4 men + pilot; 60 mph speed

1 mechanical trencher

In addition to cultivating and taking bids on revenue-generating state forestlands for schools and hospitals at its office in Forks, the state of Washington's Department of Natural Resources (DNR) focuses on firefighting. This page from the late-1960s fire suppression booklet pictures a firefighting crew. The helicopter would transport firefighters to help dowse fires.

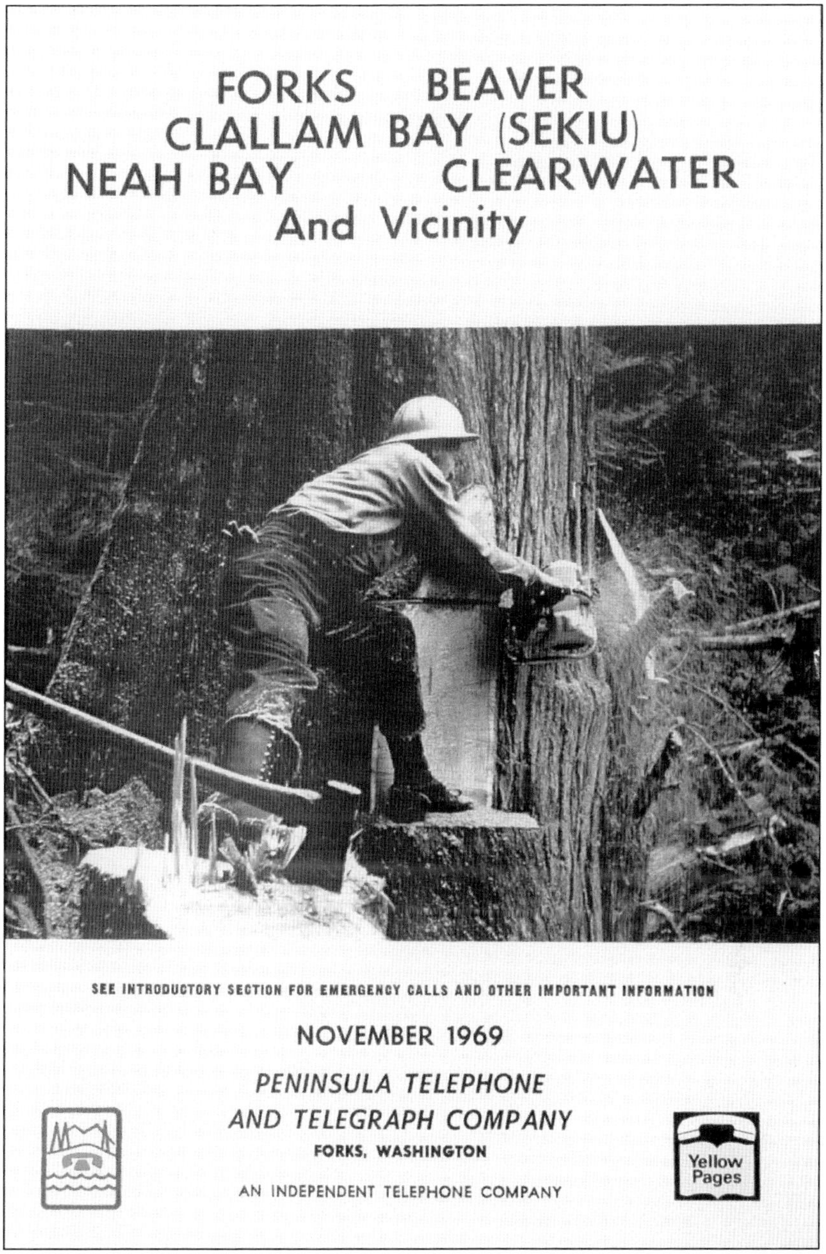

The business name of the locally owned Peninsula Telephone and Telegraph Company harkens back to the coming of telecommunications to Forks in 1909. Telegraph and phone lines strung from Clallam Bay allowed for instant outside communication. A small switchboard was located in Jim Henry's grocery shop. Residential lines and a commercial network linked several dozen subscribers, all of whom used crank phones with a combination of rings identifying who a call was for. Today, Gates Foundation–funded high-speed digital Internet connection links Forks to the world. The installation served as a prototype for rural communities across the nation. This photograph, which was featured on the cover of a phone book, shows timber feller Creighton "Slim" Fouts using a chain saw as his ax stands ready. Well-known Forks photographer Lonnie Archibald, who worked for Peninsula Telephone, provided cover images for some of the phone books.

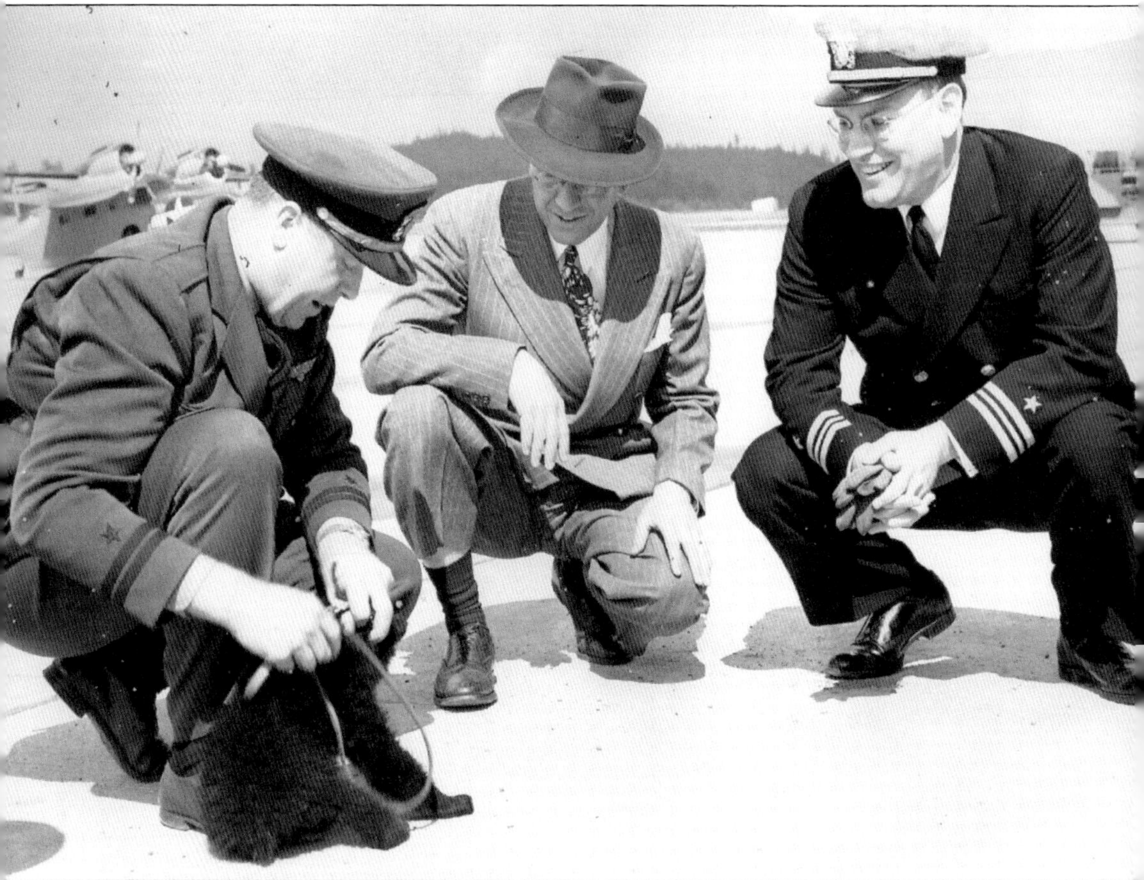

Lieutenant Commander Dobbins (left), commander of the Quillayute Naval Air Station, plays with either "Tuffy" or "Taffy," one of the bear cubs that were given as a gift to the base brass. Looking on is a visiting Department of Defense official. A declassified Navy document reported that the mother of the cub showed up at the base gate searching for her cubs.

Six

The Forks Fire

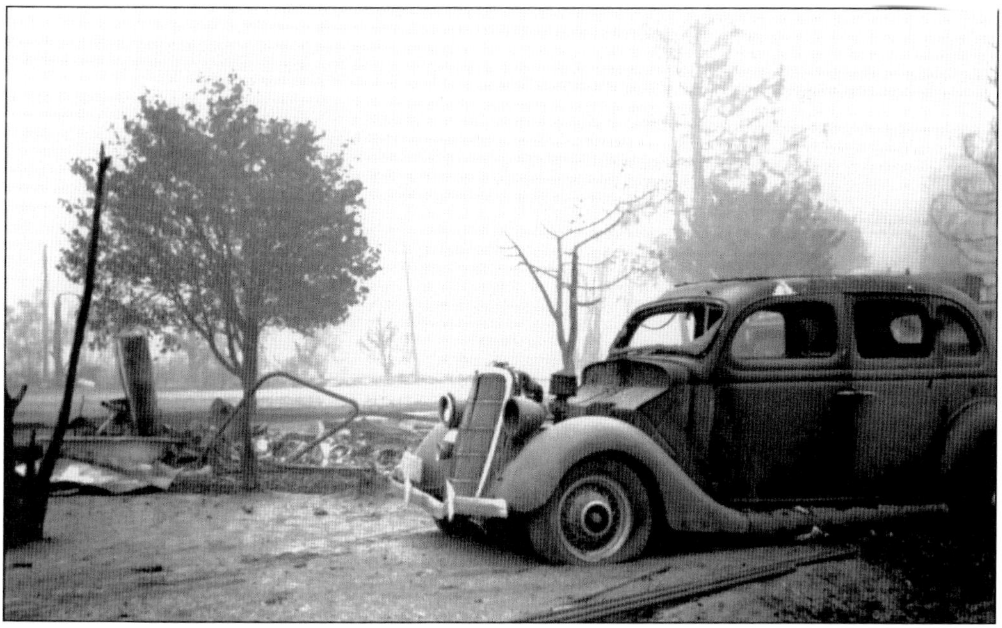

The Forks fire destroyed homes and businesses on the north side of town, roaring up the Calawah River valley toward downtown Forks, burning west across 18 miles in eight hours and consuming 30,275 acres. A total of 32 buildings burned, including the Spoelstra brothers' logging business warehouse. Here, the gutted body and frame of a sedan stands next to the charred remains of a home with only a porcelain bathtub still intact.

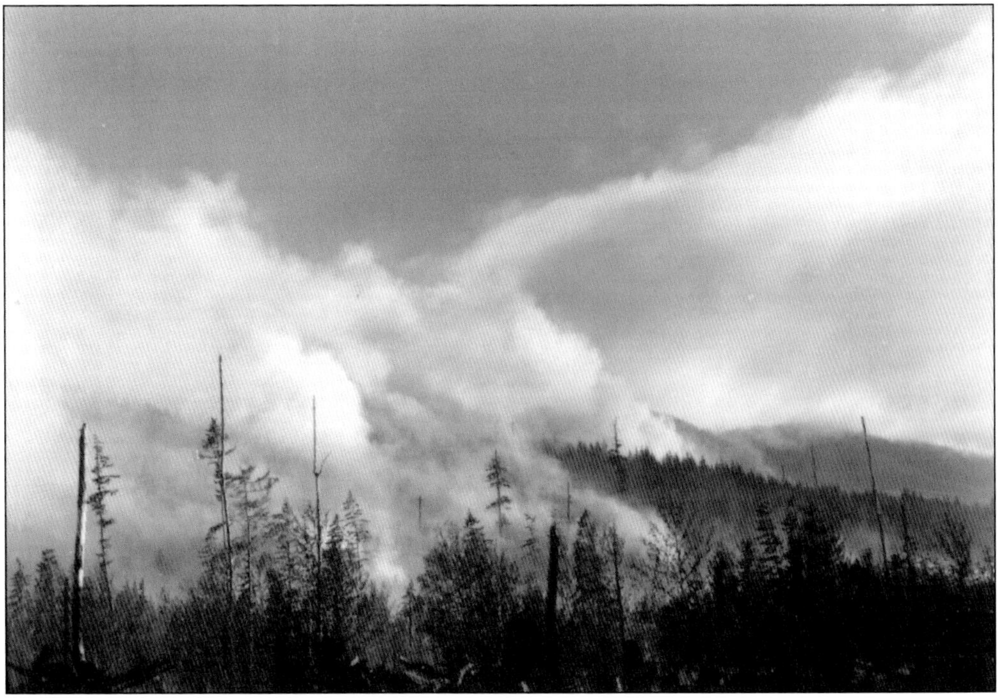

The summer months of 1951 were very dry ones with just over one inch of rainfall, compared to a summertime average of about eight inches. In early August, a forest fire (above) burned just east of the Snider National Forest camp, likely set by sparks from a Port Angeles and Western Railroad logging train. The fire burned hundreds of acres of forest over several days. Hot spots from the fire were likely fanned into flames the fateful morning of September 20, 1951, when an east wind picked up and the air became dry. The blaze spread rapidly, beginning at about 3:00 a.m. and heading west toward Forks through the Calawah Valley. An estimated $100 million in timber was burned. (Above, courtesy US Forest Service; below, courtesy Washington State Department of Natural Resources.)

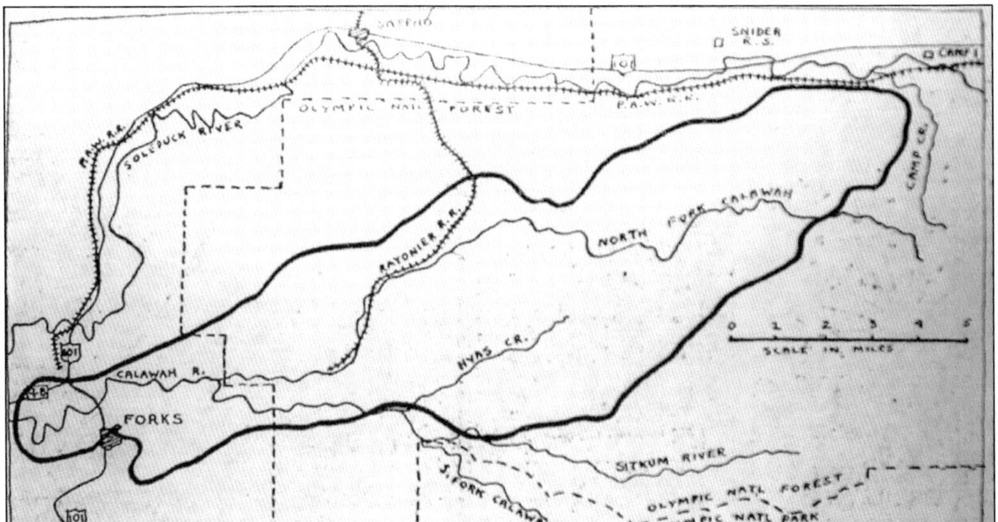

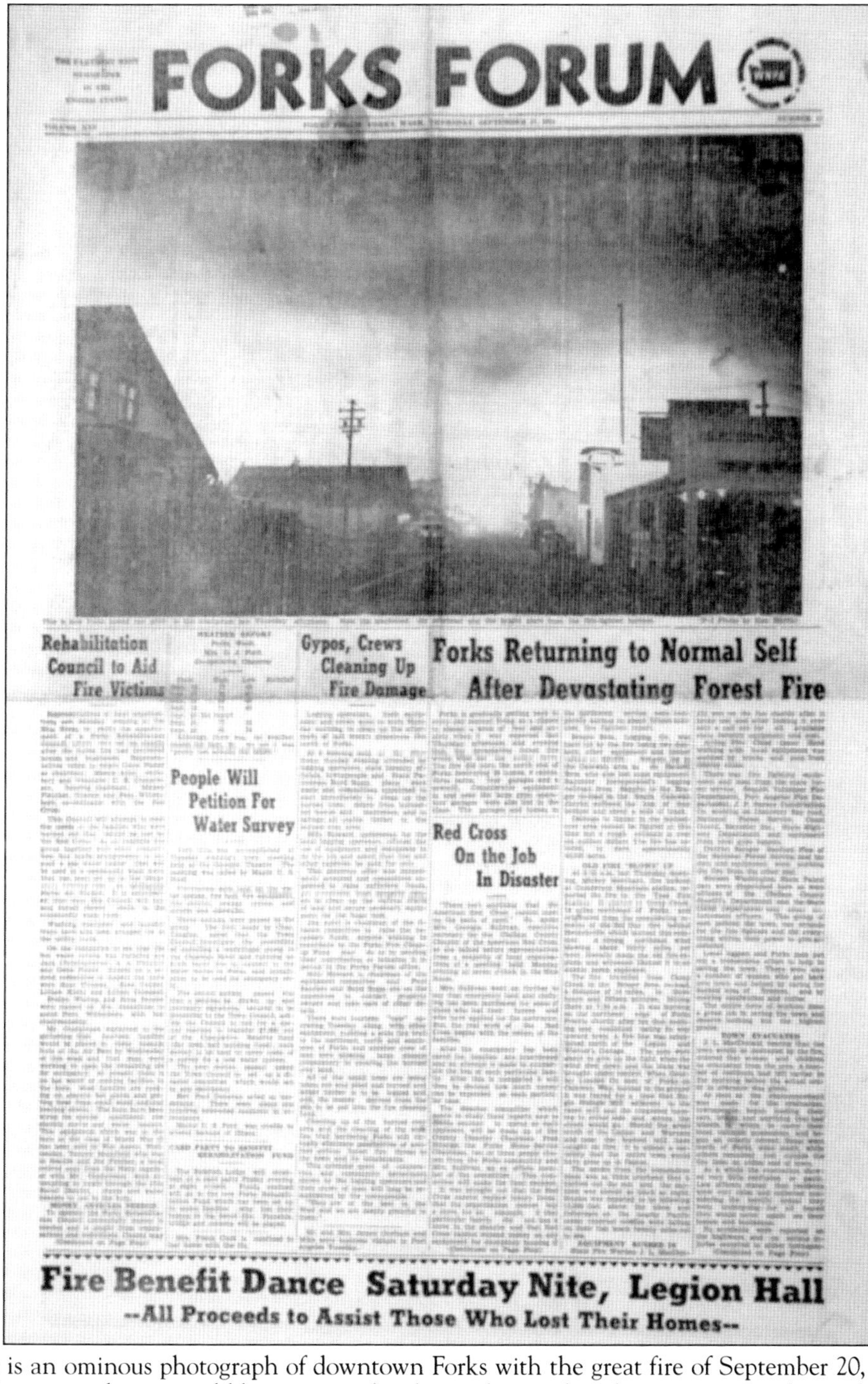

FORKS FORUM

Rehabilitation Council to Aid Fire Victims

Gypos, Crews Cleaning Up Fire Damage

Forks Returning to Normal Self After Devastating Forest Fire

People Will Petition For Water Survey

Red Cross On the Job In Disaster

Fire Benefit Dance Saturday Nite, Legion Hall

--All Proceeds to Assist Those Who Lost Their Homes--

Here is an ominous photograph of downtown Forks with the great fire of September 20, 1951, heading toward town and blotting out the sky to the north—the street seems doomed. This September 27, 1951, issue of the *Forks Forum* weekly newspaper described the fire and its aftermath and sought help for local folks who lost homes and businesses to the raging fire. The newspaper began publishing weekly news of Forks and other towns on the West End of the Olympic Peninsula in 1930. (Courtesy *Forks Forum* newspaper.)

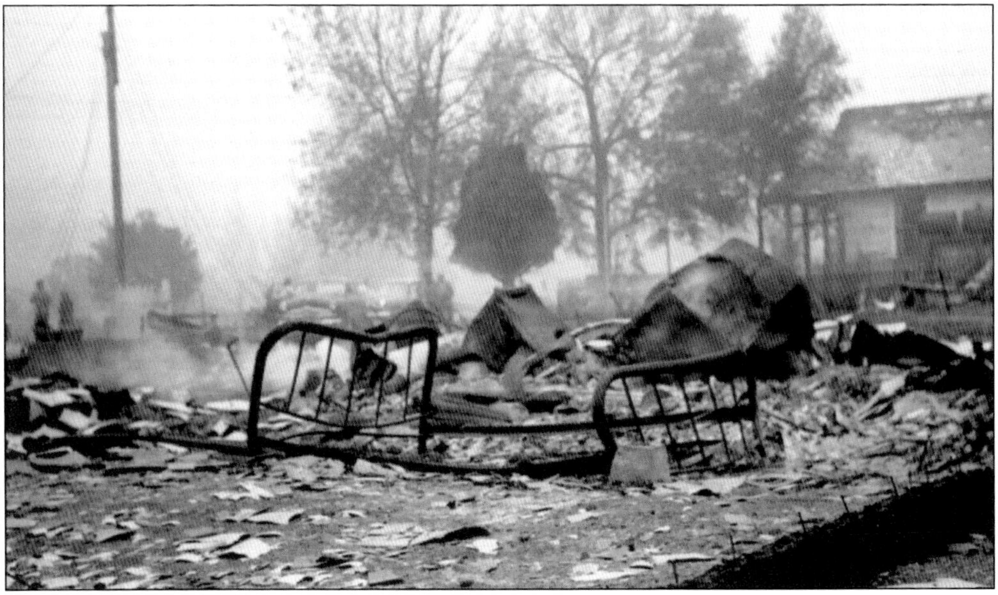

Beyond this pile of smoldering debris, local residents stand in shock and awe in the smoky background, pondering why their world in the middle of the west Olympic Forest almost burned to the ground in less than a day. The charred cedar-shake roof of a building to the right stands as evidence as to where the fire halted its advance and how closely the town came to total devastation. Thanks to a damp ocean wind, the fire was able to be controlled.

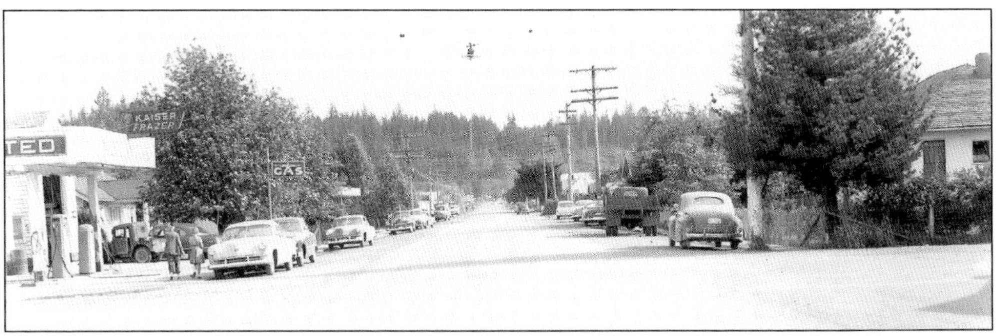

Arthur "Art" Anderson owned the Kaiser Frazer automobile dealership in Forks. Knowing the fire was on its way, he loaded his wife, Pat, who was pregnant with their son Dan, in the family car and sent her to the Coast Guard station at LaPush. She was helicoptered out. He later loaned all the new cars from his agency to people desperately fleeing the fire. "I got back every one of the cars," Anderson later recalled.

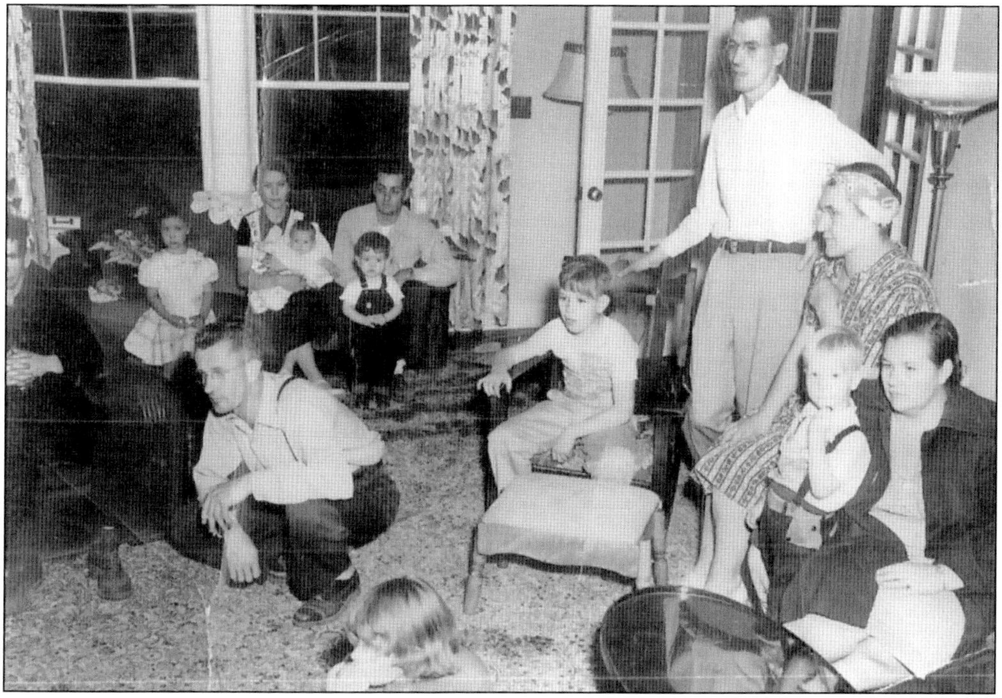

As the Forks fire threatened the town, laundry owner Leo White of Port Angeles (the man kneeling in the foreground) invited the Brown and Guyll families of Forks into his home. The Brown family members joked that their baby son Jerry got his teddy bear at a fire sale.

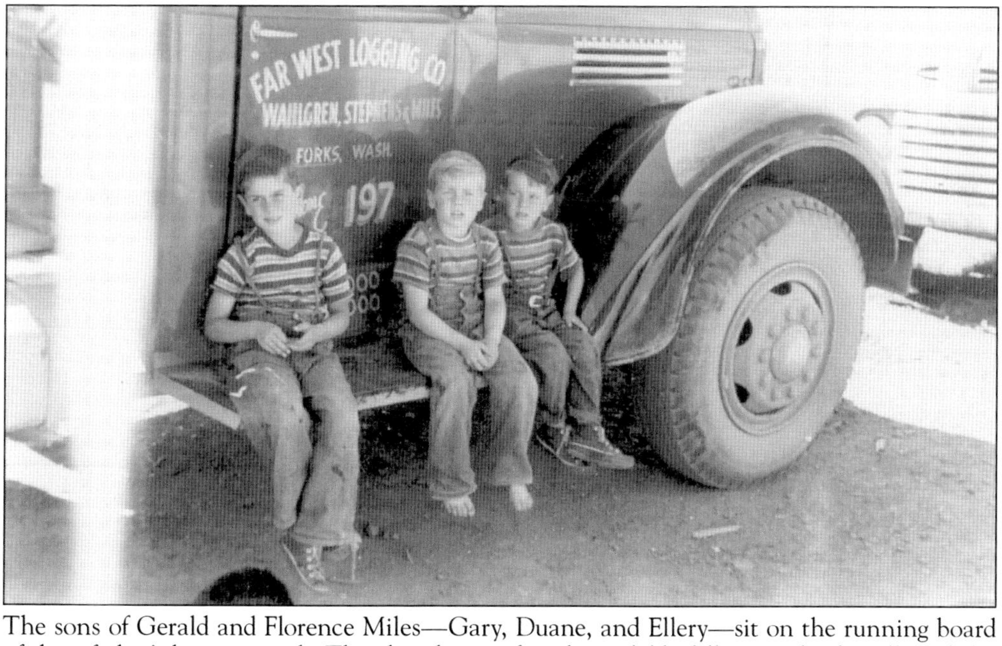

The sons of Gerald and Florence Miles—Gary, Duane, and Ellery—sit on the running board of their father's logging truck. The abundance of work available following the fire allowed the family to return to Forks from living in Brinnon due to a housing shortage prior to the fire. Gerald was a partner in Far West Logging Company with Carl Wahlgren and Van Stephens. (Courtesy Miles family.)

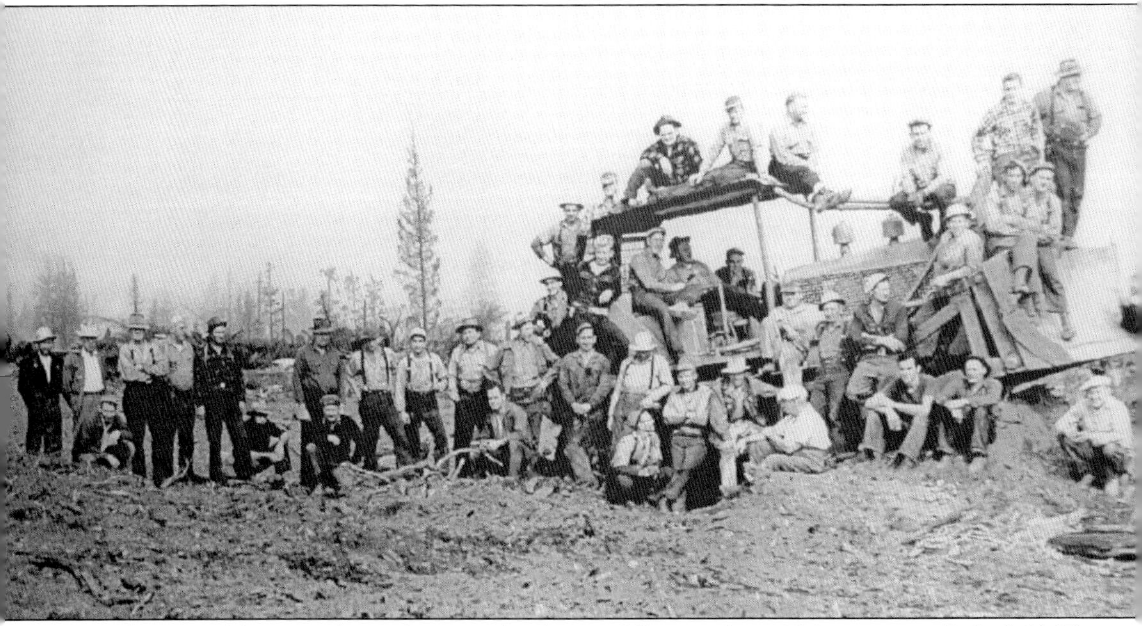

About 45 of the men who took part in the cleanup following the 1925 fire pose in a Forks field. The community response to the disaster included using logging company bulldozers to work fire lines, feeding men fighting the fire, and evacuating people from the area. When needed, the self-sufficient, hardworking Forks residents come together in a big way to tackle community emergencies. The bulldozer in the photograph belongs to Forks resident and former logging company owner Ted Spoelstra. Some of Spoelstra's properties in Forks were destroyed in the fire.

VOLUNTEER CLEAN-UP CREW AFTER THE FAMOUS FORKS FIRE OF SEPTEMBER 20, 1951

1. Carl Wahlgren
2. Johnny Wike
3. Danny Stephens
4. Jim Silcox
5. Sam Rasmussen
6. Nansen Anderson
7. Warren Rideout
8. Bill Smith
9. Albert Wasankari
10. Gene Fraker (?)
11. Bill James
12. Frank Fletcher
13. Pete Hallman
14. Noble Hobbs
15. Carl Klahn
16. Gordon Allen
17. Louis Klahn
18. Kenny Chambers
19. Jack Edwards
20. Leroy Johnson
21. Howard Wilson
22. (unknown)
23. Emil Haugen
24. Ted Spoelstra
25. Jim Klahn
26. Carl Wallace
27. Roland Lewis
28. Jerry Miles
29. Wayne Miller
30. Scotty Gossage
31. Jimmy Mansfield
32. Myron Simmons
33. Bill Beebe
34. Roland Undi
35. Paul Sanders
36. John Spoelstra
37. Paul Atkinson
38. Dick Mottner
39. Jimmy Mason
40. Harris Twiss
41. Jack James
42. Charlie Marshall
43. Billy Howard
44. Wayne Kline
45. Frank Willett

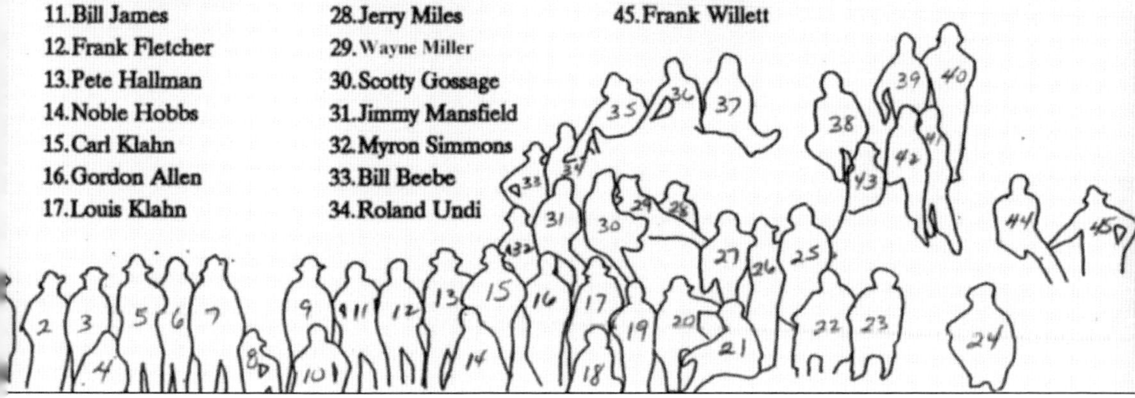

This chart provides the names of the Forks fire volunteers pictured on the previous page.

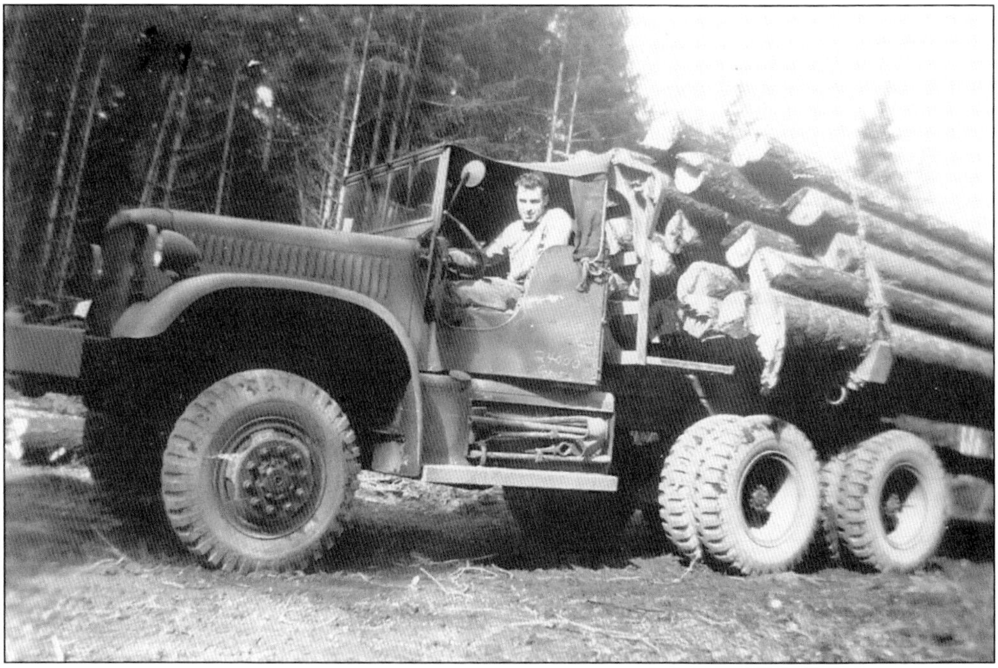

Fred Shaw, a veteran of World War II Navy Aviation duty, is shown in the canvas-top cab of his six-wheel surplus Army truck, which he bought at auction at Fort Lewis following the war. Like other veterans, Fred started out in the log-hauling business with a surplus truck, a second truck for parts, and a desire to get ahead after completing military service. (Courtesy Shaw family.)

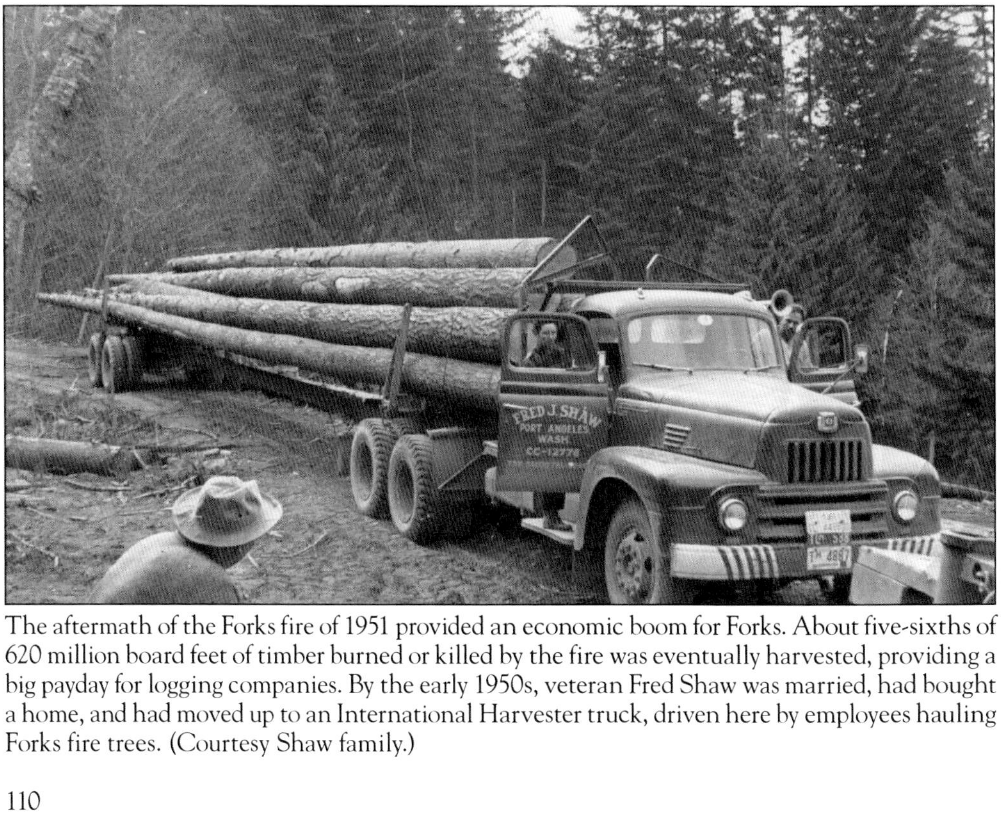

The aftermath of the Forks fire of 1951 provided an economic boom for Forks. About five-sixths of 620 million board feet of timber burned or killed by the fire was eventually harvested, providing a big payday for logging companies. By the early 1950s, veteran Fred Shaw was married, had bought a home, and had moved up to an International Harvester truck, driven here by employees hauling Forks fire trees. (Courtesy Shaw family.)

Seven

FORKS AND *TWILIGHT*

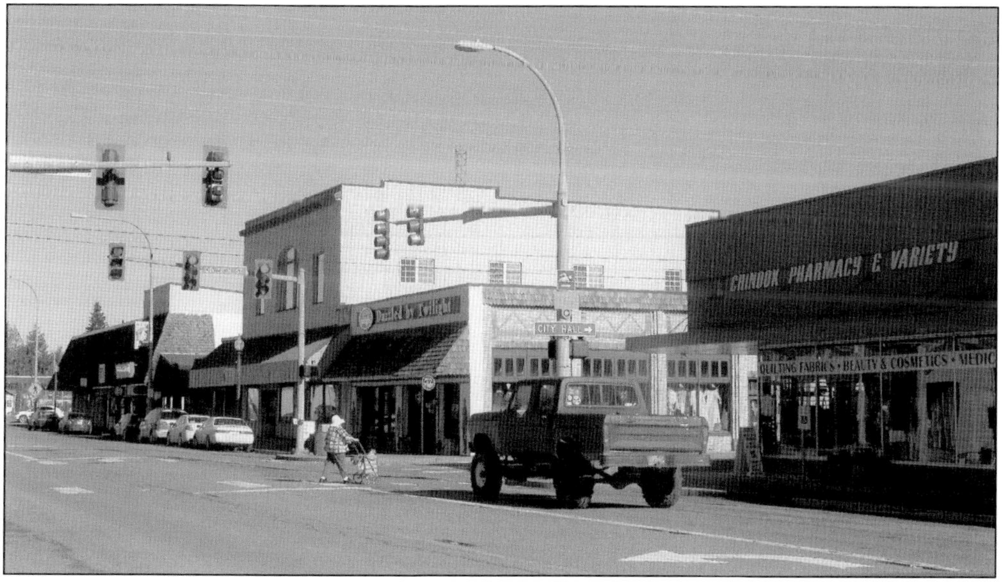

Fans of the global best-selling *Twilight* series by author Stephenie Meyer created demand for an overlay to the retail stores of downtown Forks in 2006. The distinctive lines of the historic Odd Fellows Hall in the center of the photograph continue to anchor the crossroads of Forks Avenue and Division Street. Dazzled by Twilight, the largest *Twilight*-only store in the world, is now located in the former Olympic Pharmacy building. Forks's drugstore (previously Chinook Pharmacy and Variety), a vendor of *Twilight* souvenirs, is located across Division Street. The cars of the book's fans line this section of downtown Forks on summer days and during special events, such as the Forks Chamber of Commerce's Bella's Birthday-Stephenie Meyer Day, held over a mid-September weekend.

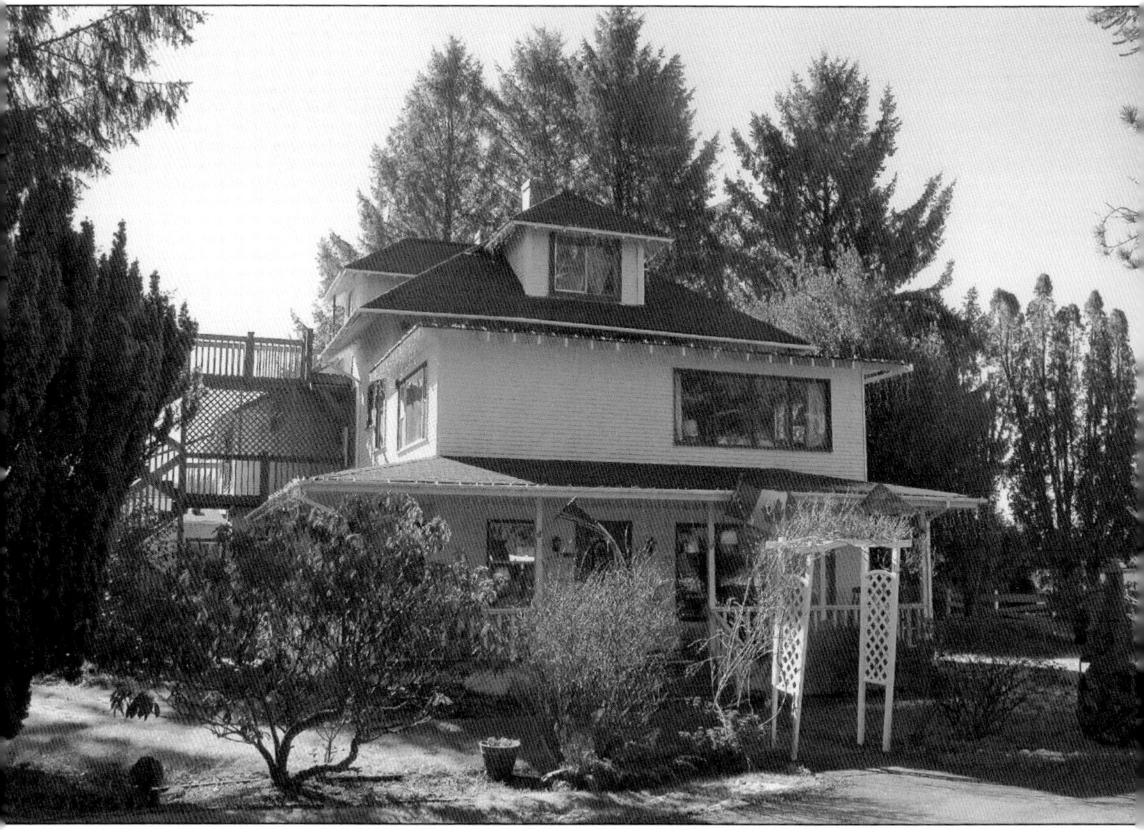

The historic Miller Tree Inn plays the role of the Cullen house for visiting *Twilight* fans. Owners Bill and Susan Brager post notes at the front door that tell of the whereabouts of the fictitious Cullen family of *Twilight* fame, and the rural route mailbox out front is marked "CULLEN" in black letters. The historic home is traditionally known as the Winifred Ford Peterson home. Land was cleared on the pioneering Peterson-Ford family dairy and cattle homestead in 1916, and the building's foundation was laid in 1917. Unfortunately, Eli Peterson, Winifred's husband, passed away in an automobile accident near Lake Crescent in 1916. Winifred and her daughter Myrtle continued to run the family farm and hired workers to run the dairy. During World War II, the family helped alleviate the local housing shortage by taking in boarders. In 1943, Dr. and Mrs. Edwin Leibold purchased the home from Winifred, who moved to Port Angeles. Dr. Leibold uncannily had many similarities to Dr. Cullen of *Twilight* fame, including being on staff at a Forks hospital. The name Miller Tree Inn comes from the 1984–1999 era when Ted and Prue Miller owned the home and created what is believed to be the first bed-and-breakfast in Forks.

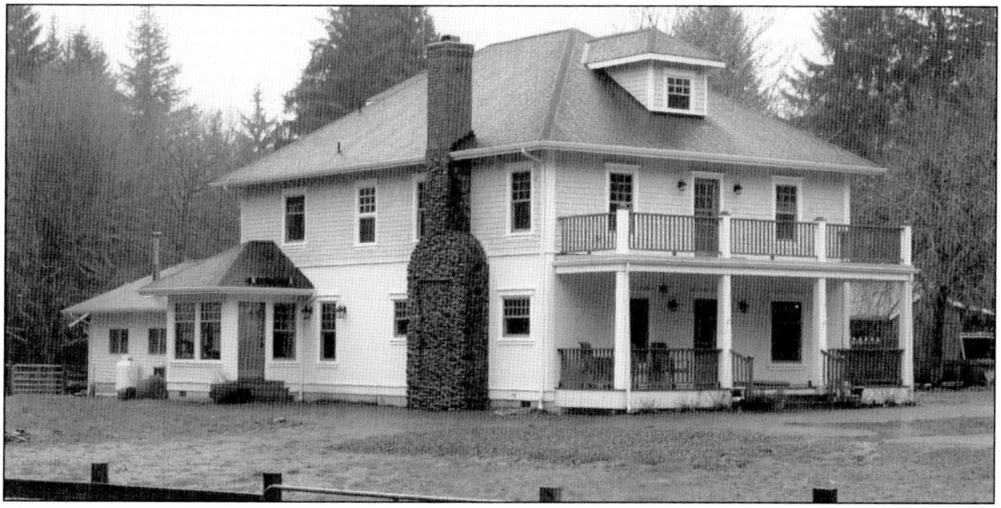

This foursquare c. 1914 home is known as Westlands. John and Michelle Simpson restored the home, finishing in 2010, after a devastating fire destroyed most the building in March 2009. Westlands is located in Sappho, a once bustling logging camp located about 12 miles west of Forks. A portion of the home was first built as the headquarters of the Clallam Logging Company. Later, ownership was passed on to the family of Theodore Rixon, an Englishman who surveyed much of the Olympic Peninsula for resources potential in the early 1900s. The home was for sale when author Stephenie Meyer wrote her groundbreaking first *Twilight* book. Local *Twilight* followers believe Meyer used photographs of Westlands that appeared on the website of realtor Carrol Lunsford (far right) of Lunsford & Associates in Forks for the setting of the Cullen family of vampires' home around the time she was writing her first book. In this image, Lunsford joins the West End historical society on a visit to the restored home. The club is a continuation of the Pioneers Club of Forks.

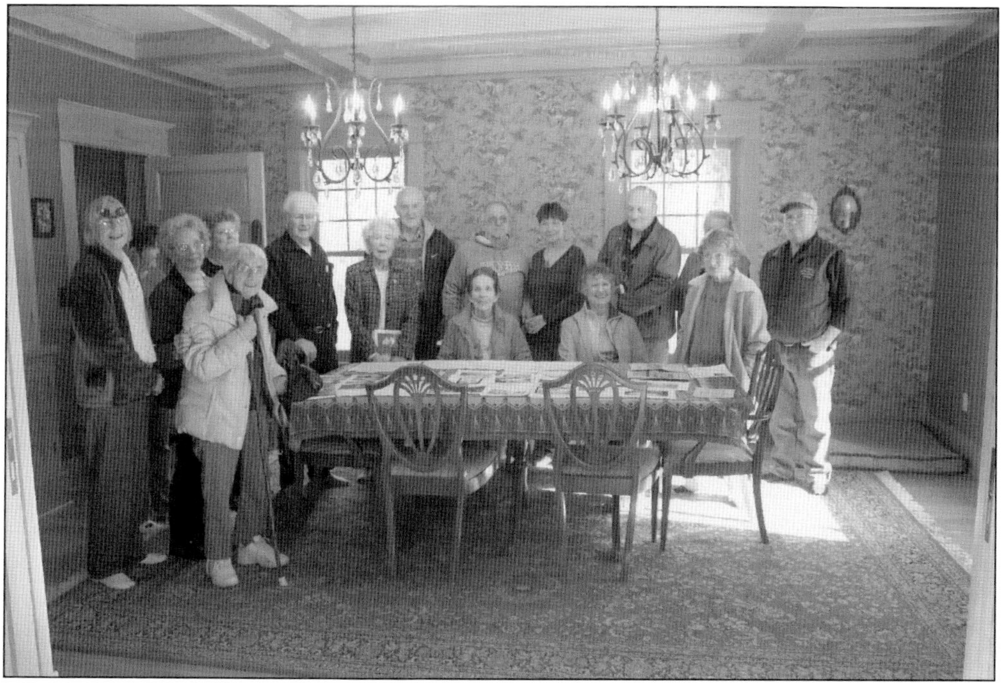

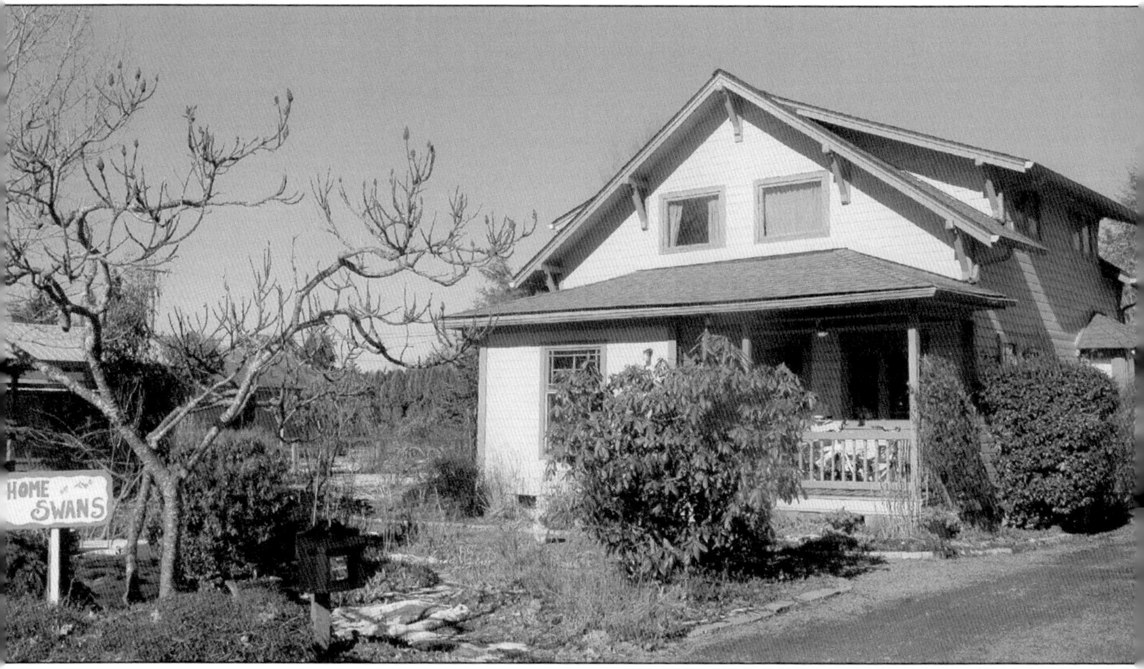

Bella Swan's home is portrayed in Forks by the home of Dave and Kim McIrvin and family. The home reflects the style of Forks's residences built in the 1920s and 1930s and retains touches of Craftsman-style bungalow architecture, as well as that of a comfortable and practical pre-World War II middle-class home. The home originally stood closer to Highway 101, but it was later moved to its present location in a suburban-like Forks neighborhood near Russell Road. Moving buildings and converting buildings for different uses are both common practices in Forks's history.

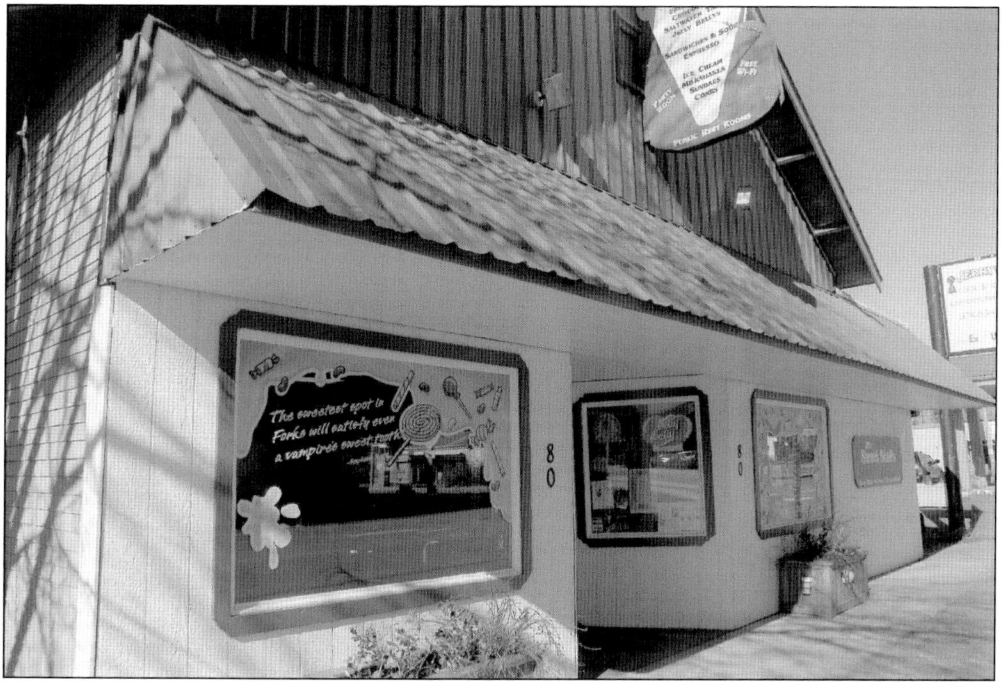

J.T.'s Sweet Stuffs is a candy, ice cream, and luncheon shop. Tom and Janet Hughes's store has benefited from its *Twilight* connection. The 1916 building served as a hardware store, barbershop, soda fountain, and the Hangup Tavern, which had the rear end of a stuffed elk on its street-side wall and the front of the elk across the street in the Vagabond bar. The Ruel & Hammer Hardware sign once hung outside the building, but now it resides in the Forks Timber Museum.

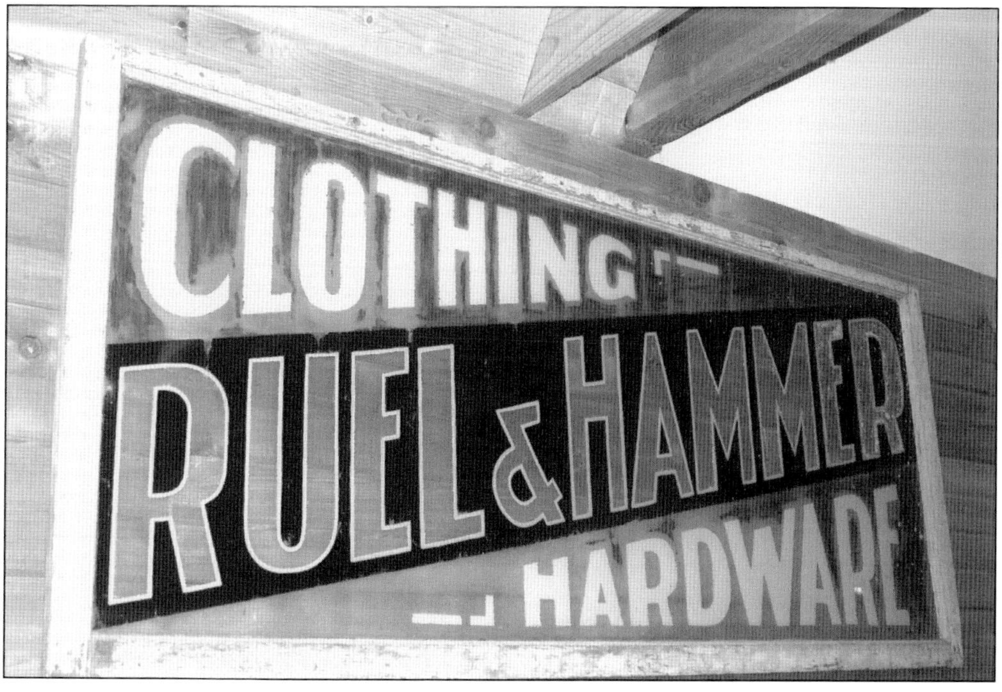

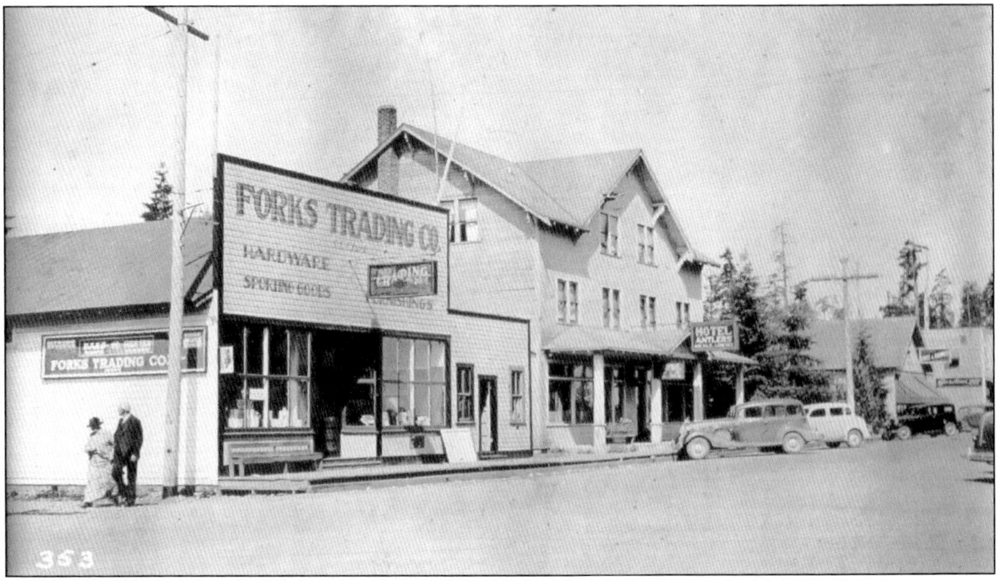

Native to Twilight is a gift shop featuring *Twilight*-themed crafts and tribal design items in a building once used as a trading post in downtown Forks. Native to Twilight exemplifies the rebirth of a long-vacant main street retail building, thanks to the *Twilight* boost to the local economy. A Peterson family member, Anna Matsche, opened the store. The building was previously known as Coast to Coast and sold hardware. This 1920s photograph of the building shows its earlier use as a trading post.

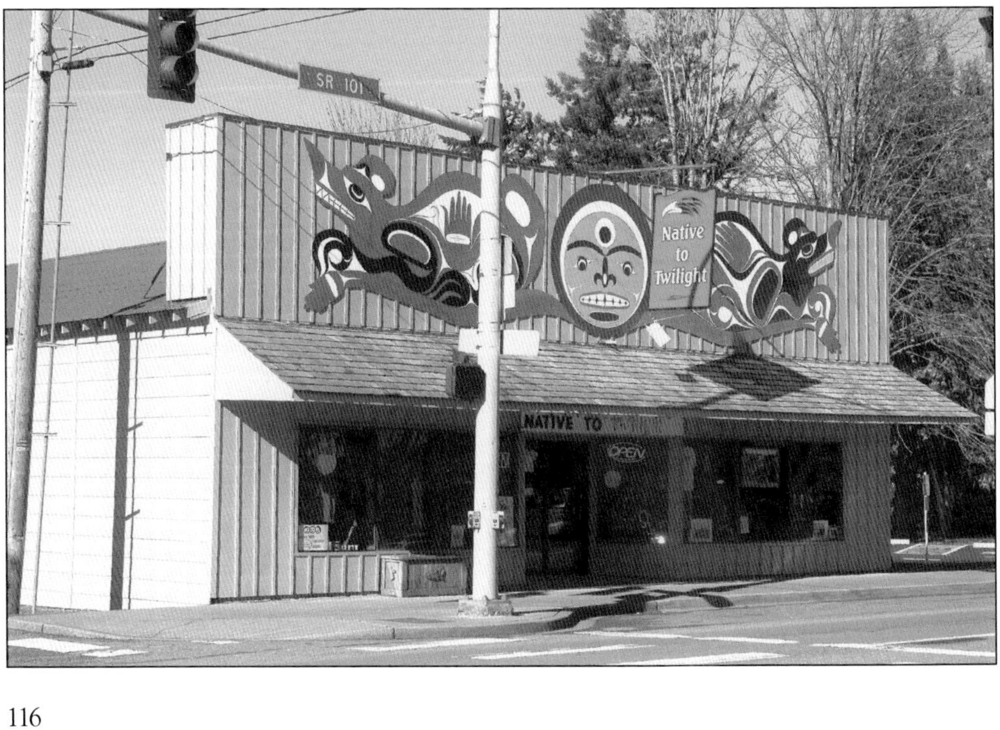

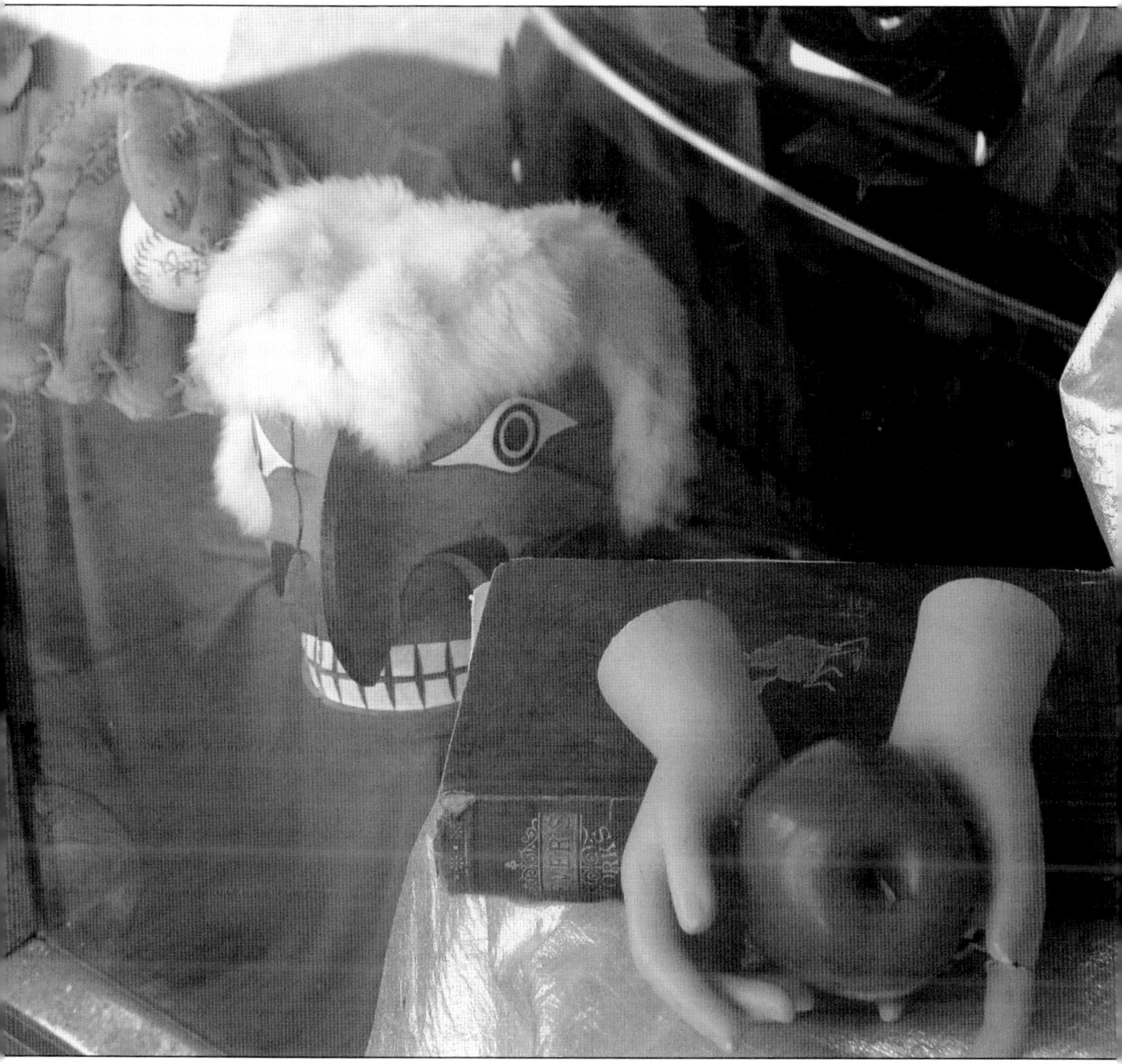

Symbolic objects, including a coastal tribal mask, are artfully arranged in the window of Leppell's Flowers and Gifts on South Spartan Avenue in Forks. The florist business continues the Leppell family's small-business operating tradition in Forks and features a selection of *Twilight* souvenirs and gifts presented with a touch of the Northwest crafts style found among Forks quilters and artisans.

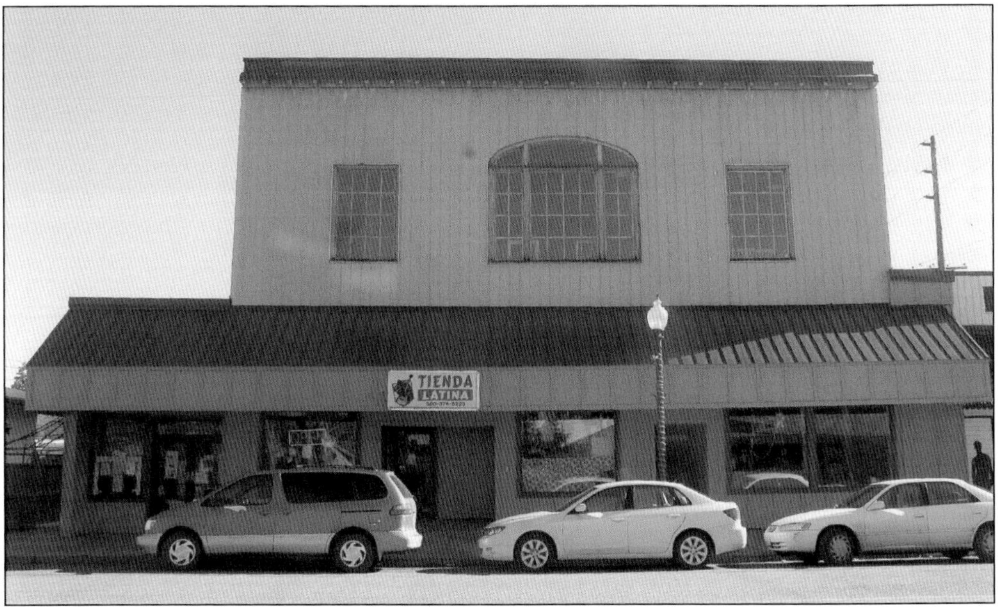

Forks's Odd Fellows Hall continues to play its century-old role as a landmark and is still an actively used building in downtown Forks. Today, the old West–looking building is home to the nonprofit Rainforest Arts Center. Here, plays are regularly staged upstairs by the Rainforest Players, an acting troupe. In addition, the Hispanic community gathers at this building for dances featuring bands usually from the Seattle area. The Tienda Latina store, the first Hispanic community-focused store in Forks, fills a retail shop on its first floor—as other shops have done throughout the century-long existence of the hall, helping to underwrite its costs of operation. Leppell family members ran the City Cash Market butcher shop on Forks Avenue and a milk delivery business in the past, and today, family members operate a logging supply and equipment rental business.

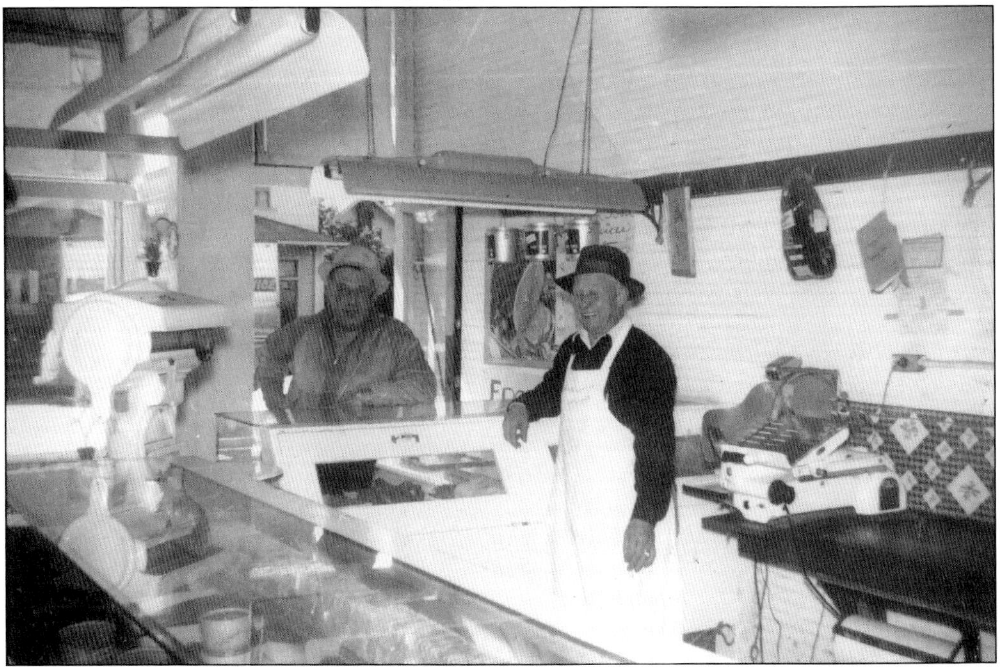

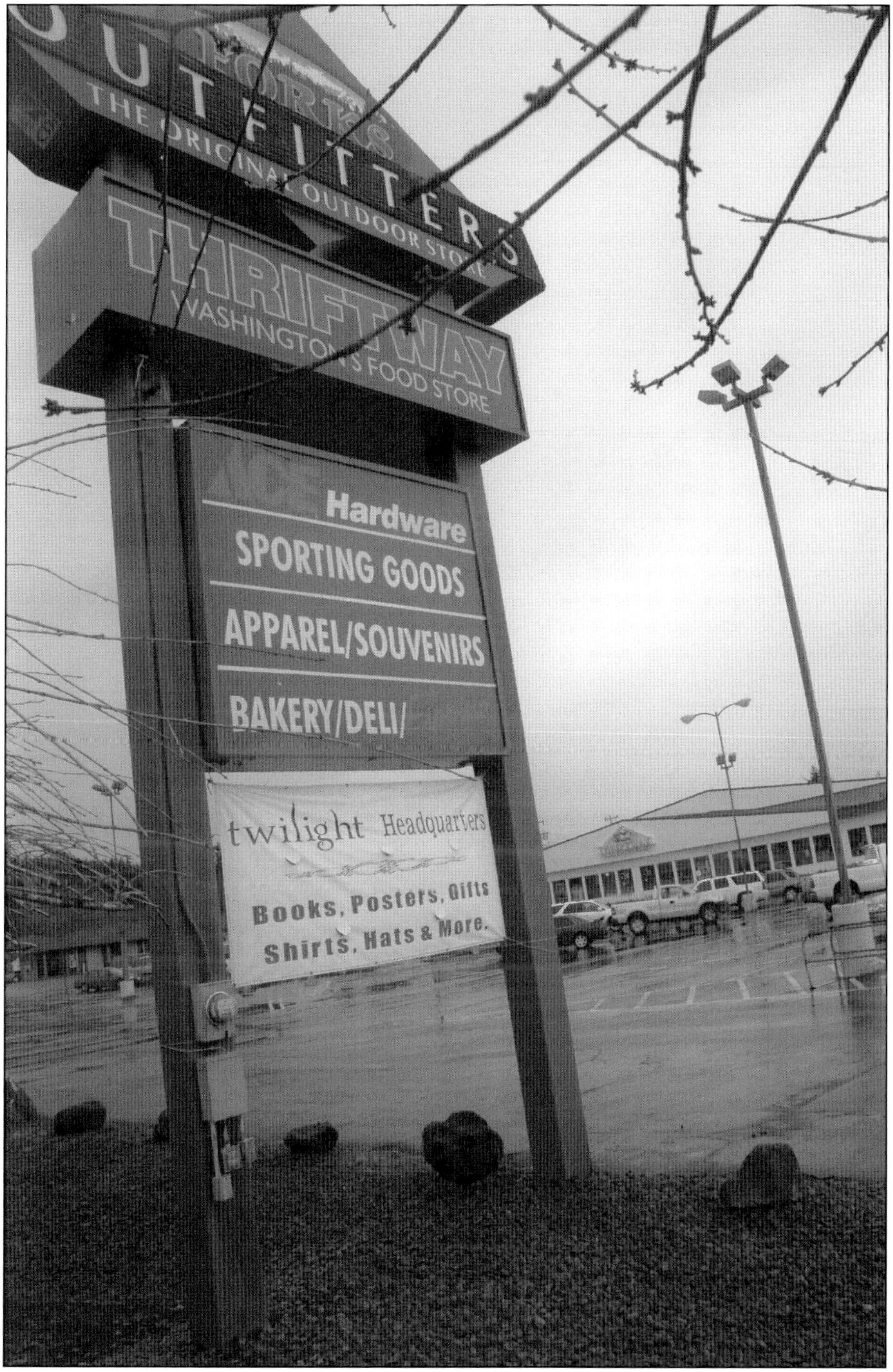

Forks Outfitters is Forks's general store evolved into the 21st century. A wide selection of *Twilight* clothing and souvenirs is sold at Forks Outfitters, alongside groceries and logging clothing. Bert Paul and Bruce Paul and their families own and operate Forks Outfitters. The family opened Forks Grocery and Feed in 1951 at the location of the Forks extension of today's Peninsula College. In 1973, Warren Paul and partners moved the store to its present location on the south end of Forks.

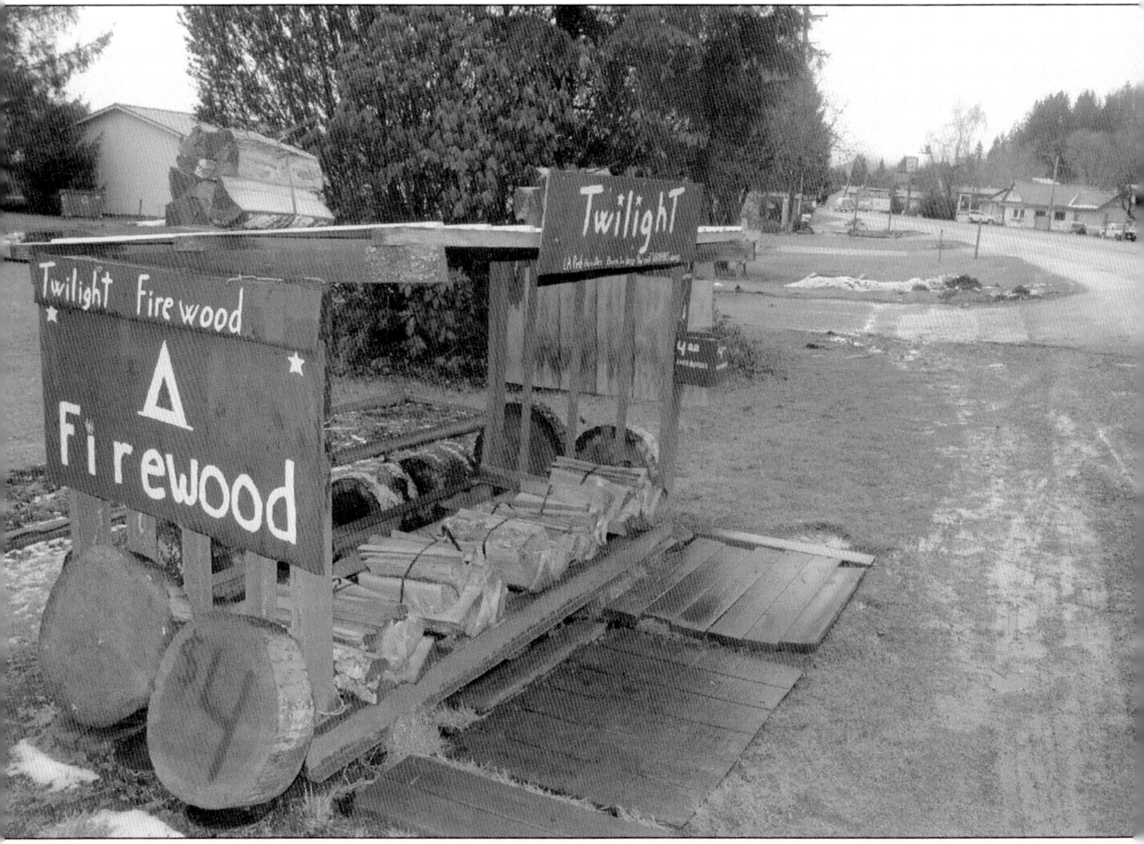

The *Twilight* firewood, located along South Forks Avenue, with its hand-lettered for-sale signs, continues the Forks's traditions of making a dollar from the timber that surrounds the town and catering to visitors traveling to town from near and far. In 2010, well over 70,000 visitors stopped in at the Forks Chamber of Commerce's visitor center, many of them lured by the *Twilight* tie-in to Forks.

Eight

FORKS TIMBER MUSEUM

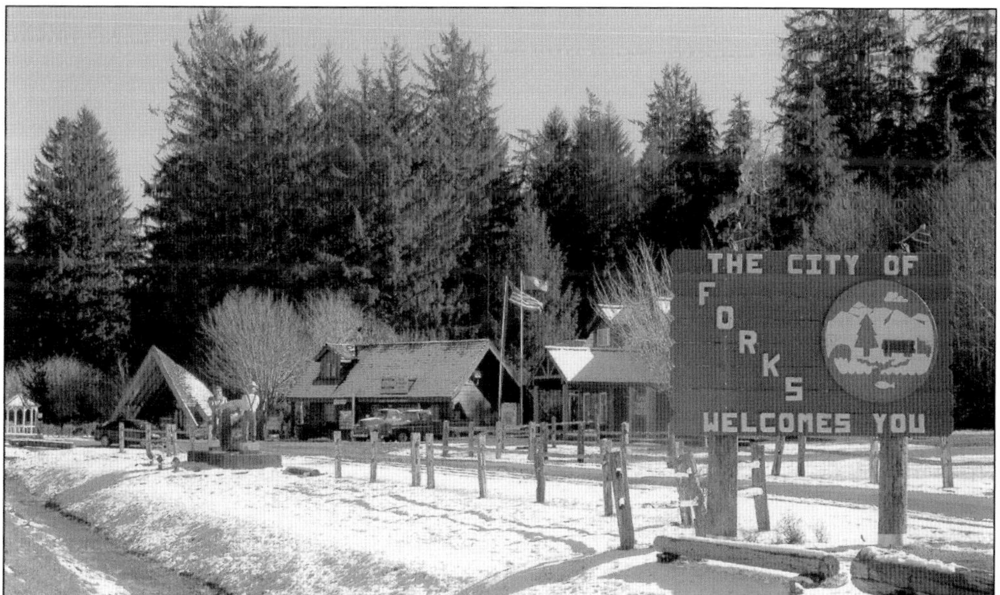

The Forks Timber Museum (the building to the right) is set along Highway 101 on the south end of Forks in a complex of buildings that serves as a heritage center for local residents, as well as Forks's main visitor greeting area. The Forks welcome sign, along with its almost identical companion located near the Calawah Bridge on the north end of Forks, is noted as one of the most-photographed signs in the world due to its connection to the *Twilight* books and movies. The Forks Logger's Memorial is the A-frame building on the left, and the Forks Chamber of Commerce's visitor information center and chamber headquarters is in the middle.

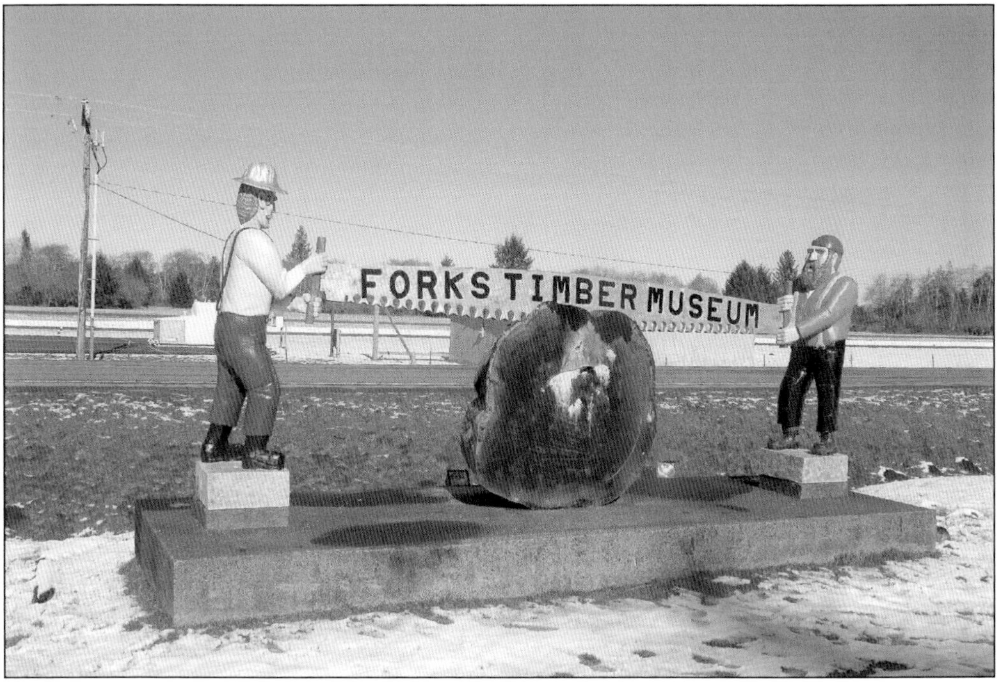

Made from hand-carved West End timber, two loggers with their crosscut saw decorate the Forks Timber Museum sign, which is located along Highway 101 south of Forks and across from the Forks Municipal Airport.

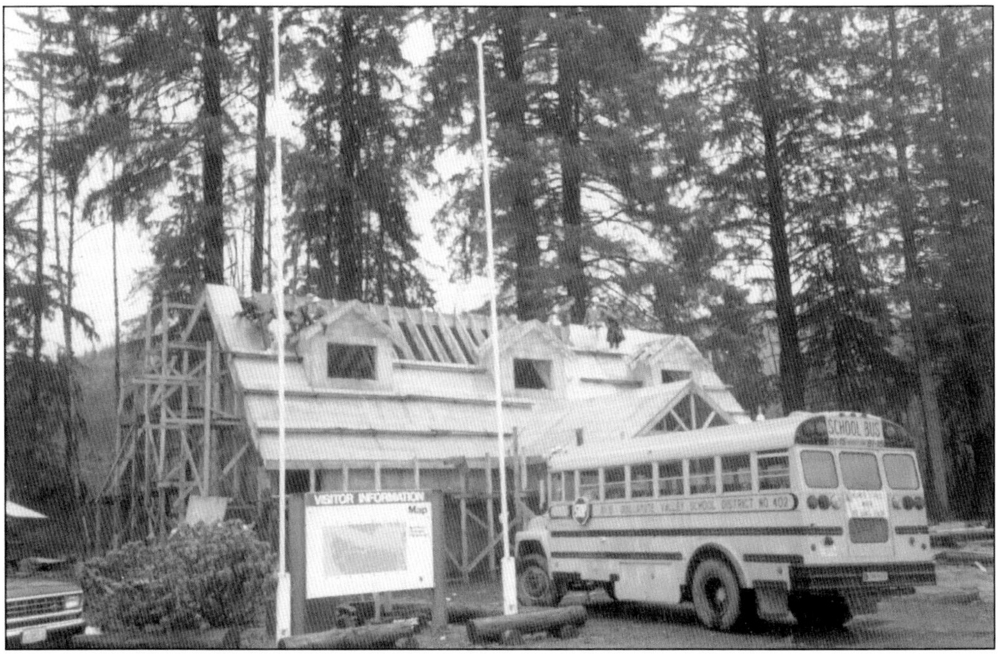

The Forks Timber Museum is shown under construction in 1989. Along with volunteer carpenters and subcontractors, the Forks High School carpentry class erected the building. Lumber milled from local wood and logs of area trees were used in its construction.

The late, renowned West End artist Elizabeth "Missy" Fletcher Barlow painted this nostalgic Forks Old Fashioned Fourth of July award marker on a slab of local red cedar. The scene shows loggers with an ax and a crosscut saw felling a huge first-growth tree, along with pioneer mother, daughter, and father. This depiction recalls, perhaps, the artist's family who lived along the Lower Hoh River on the Fletcher homestead.

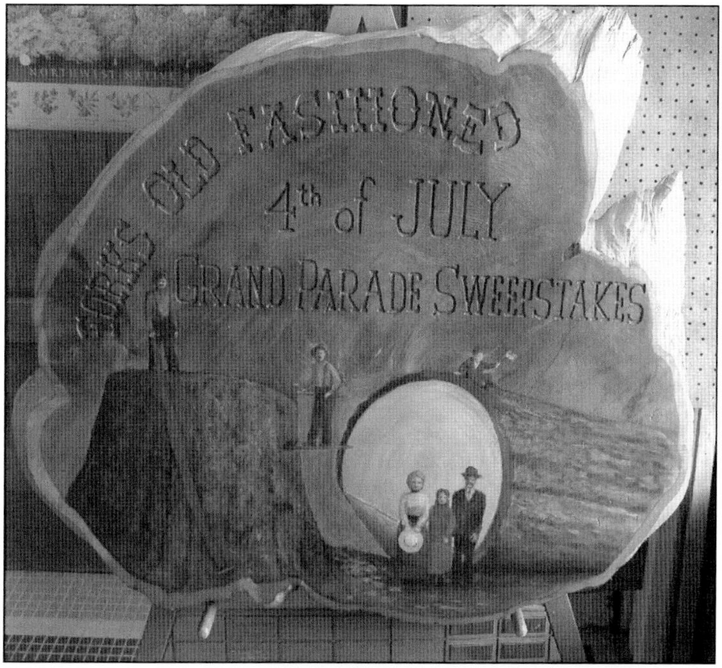

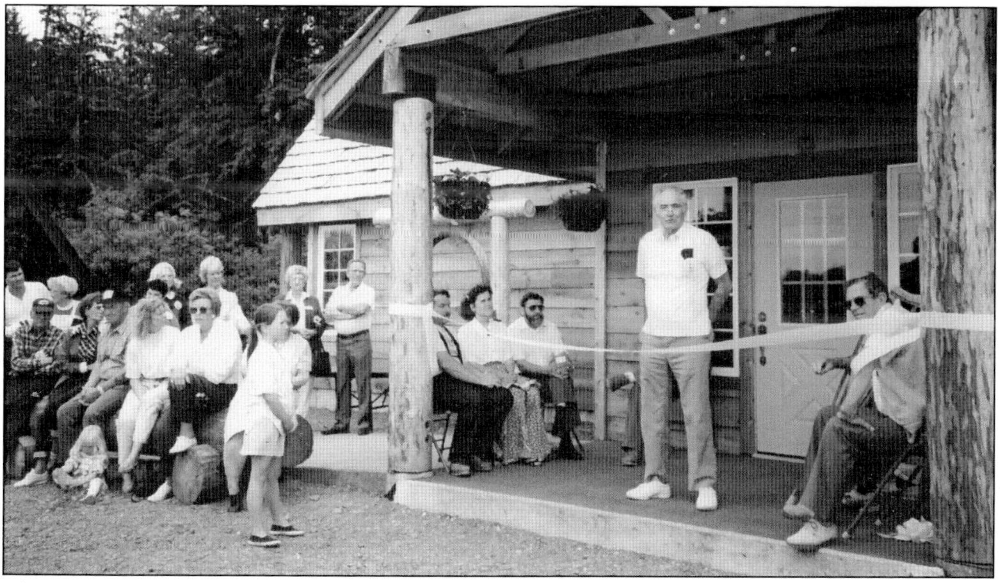

The Forks Logger's Memorial was dedicated on Memorial Day, May 25, 1992, after an almost five-year effort by community members in creating it. The memorial was established to honor Olympic Peninsula timber workers who perished while working in the industry and other deceased timber workers who devoted their lives to providing wood products for the nation. Pictured is Warren Paul, speaking to timber workers and their friends and families gathered for the dedication of the memorial. Today, a committee made up of his daughter-in-law Martha Paul, June Cassell, and Jo Marie Miller continues to collect names and maintain the memorial. The late Evelyn Bryson served on the committee prior to Jo Marie. Family, friends, and coworkers have submitted nomination forms for over 650 forest product industry workers. The origins and vocations of the workers were many and varied, spanning the time period from the late 1800s to the present day.

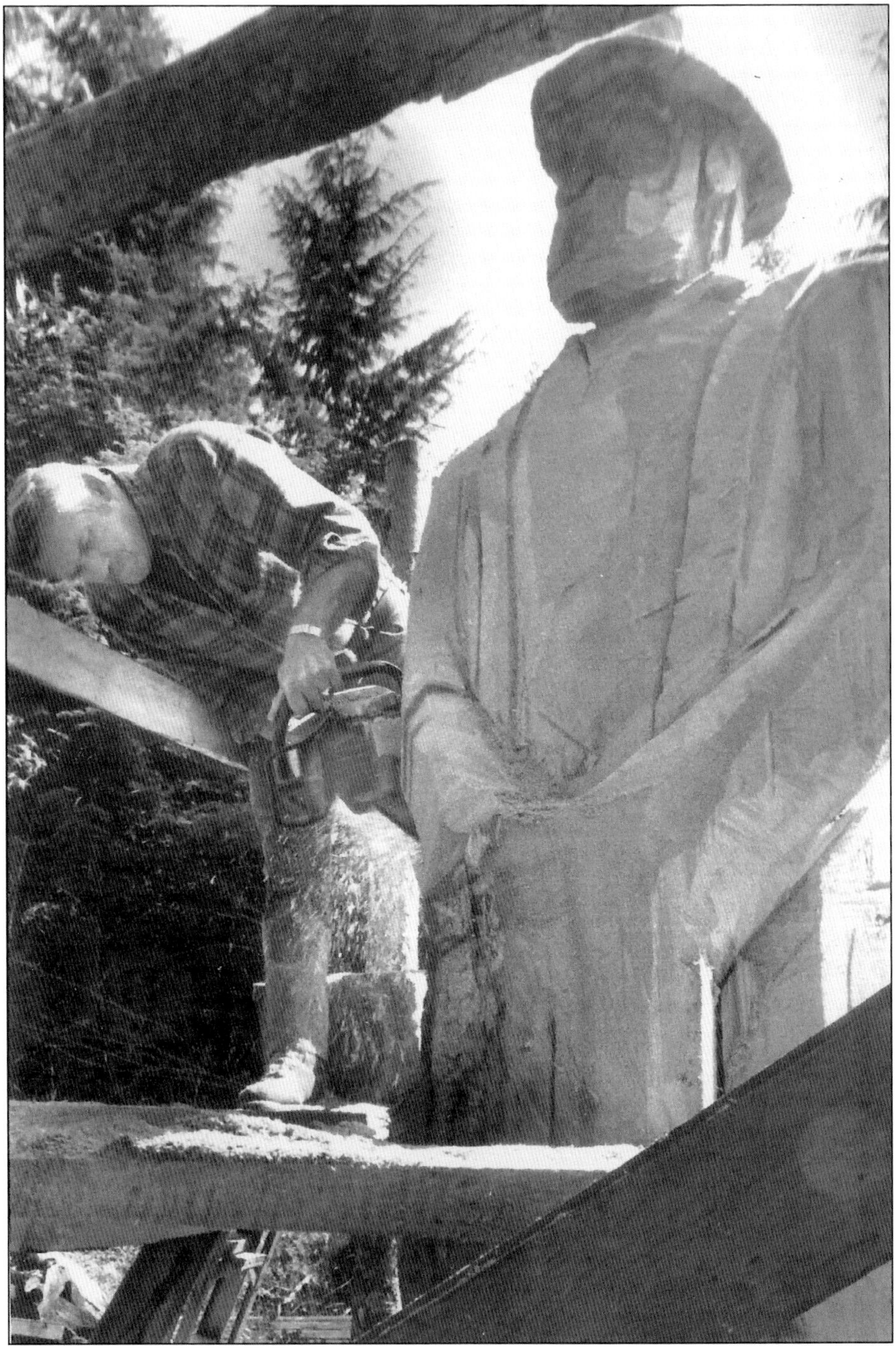

Chain saw carver Dennis Chastain roughs out the Forks Logger's Memorial logger on-site. Chastain is based out of his Den's-Wood-Den located at his homesite south of Forks along Highway 101, near the turnoff for the Olympic National Park's Hoh Rain Forest interpretive center. Chastain's carvings of loggers, eagles, bears, and other figures found on the West End are on display throughout Forks and around the world. Dennis and his wife, Margaret, carved the 12-foot-tall statue out of western red cedar.

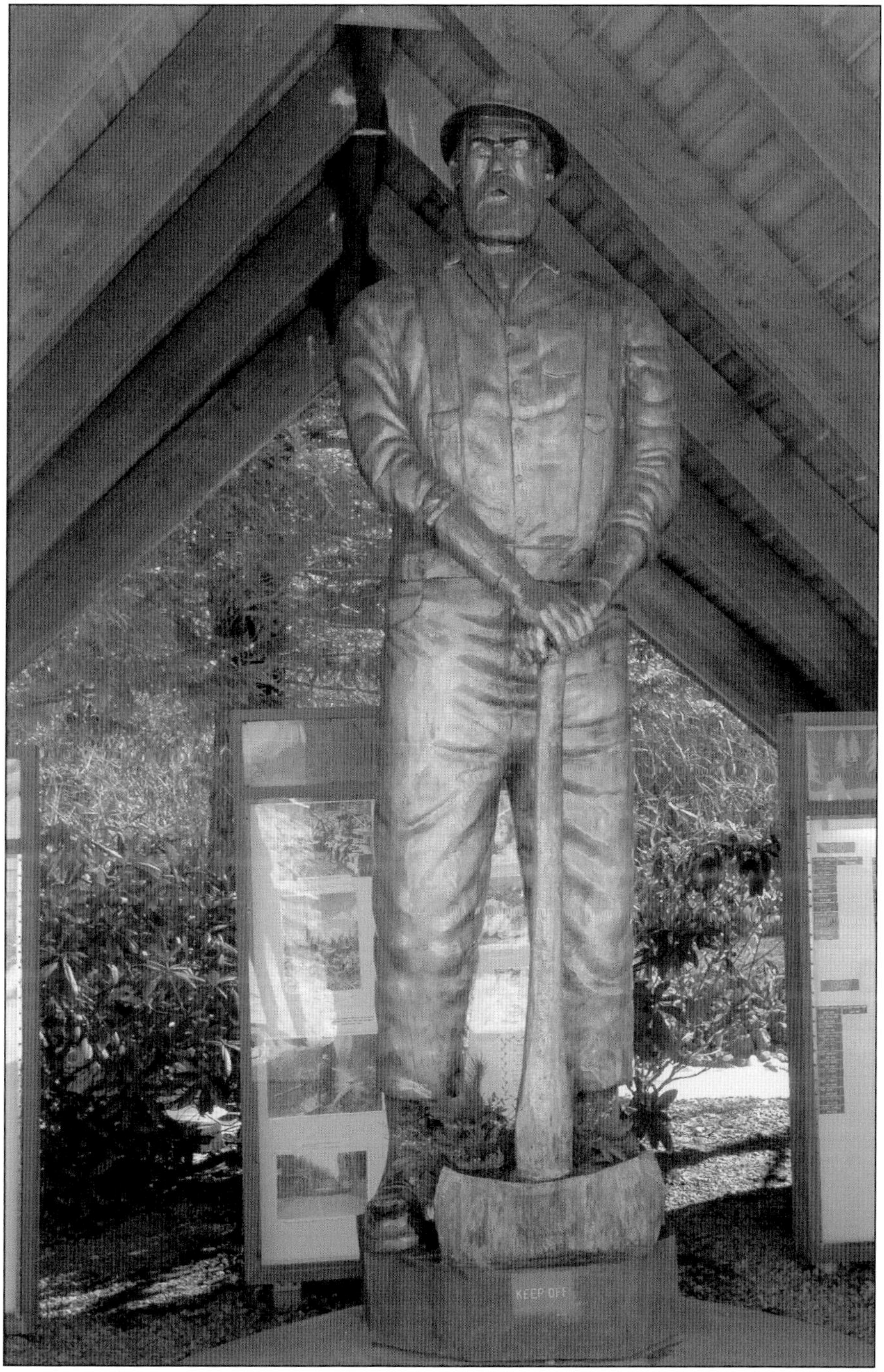

This oversized logger stands proudly under the A-frame roof of the Forks Logger's Memorial. Display cases alongside the statue are regularly updated with donated photographs of West End logging scenes. Names of timber industry workers who have passed on or who died working in the forest are proudly displayed in adjoining cases. The following is the motto of the memorial: "In tribute to those in the timber industry who perished providing the materials for the backbone of America's greatness. In gratitude to those working there now."

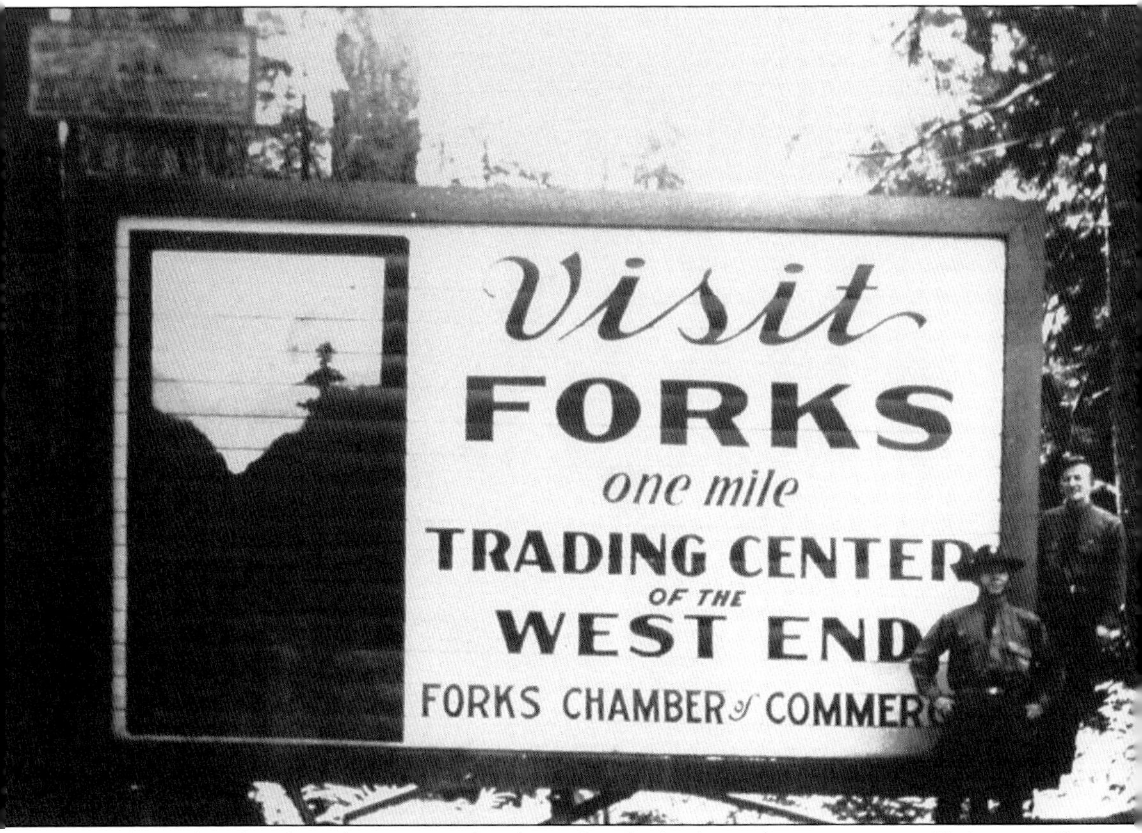

The Forks Chamber of Commerce has long played a leading role in promoting Forks, as well as the West End of the Olympic Peninsula. Here, law enforcement officers stand by a "Visit Forks" sign located near the Port Angeles side and north entrance to town. Use of the term "trading," as opposed to "shopping," reflects the pioneer heritage of the town.

Bibliography

Amundson, Mavis. *The Great Forks Fire*. Port Angeles, WA: Western Gull Publishing, 2003.

Archibald, Lonnie, and Susan Goff. *There Was a Day: Stories of the Pioneers*. Forks, WA: Olympic Graphic Arts, 1999.

Bryson, Evelyn, June Cassell, Susan Goff, and Martha Paul. *Forks Loggers Memorial: A Tribute*. Forks, WA: Forks Loggers Memorial, 1994.

Clallam County Historical Society. *Clallam County, Washington*. Chicago, IL: Arcadia Publishing, 2003.

Clallam County Historical Society. *Jimmy Come Lately History of Clallam County, a Symposium*. Port Orchard, WA: Publishers Printing, 1971.

Cook, Chris. *Twilight Territory: A Fan's Guide to Forks and LaPush*. Sequim, WA: Olympic View Publishing, 2009.

Dietrich, William. *The Final Forest: Big Trees, Forks, and the Pacific Northwest*. Seattle, WA: University of Washington Press, 2010.

Fish, Harriet U. *Tracks, Trails, and Tales in Clallam County, State of Washington*. Carlsborg, WA: H.U. Fish, 1983.

Forks Forum (newspaper archives), Forks, WA, 1933–2010.

History Link. "The Free Online Encyclopedia of Washington State History." *HistoryLink.org*. www.Historylink.org

Peterson, Gary L, and Glynda P. Schaad. *Women to Reckon with: Untamed Women of the Olympic Wilderness*. Forks, WA: Poseidon Peak Publishing, 2007.

Smith, LeRoy. *Pioneers of the Olympic Peninsula*. Forks, WA: Olympic Graphic Arts, 1977.

University of Washington Libraries. *Olympic Peninsula Community Museum: A Web-Based Museum Showcasing Aspects of the Rich History and Culture of Washington State's Olympic Peninsula Communities*. University of Washington Libraries. www.communitymuseum.org.

University of Washington. *University Libraries*. www.lib.washington.edu

Wahlgren, Iva H. *Memories of a Quillayute and Sol Duc Country Pioneer*. Forks, WA: West End Pioneers Club, 1998.

Discover Thousands of Local History Books Featuring Millions of Vintage Images

Arcadia Publishing, the leading local history publisher in the United States, is committed to making history accessible and meaningful through publishing books that celebrate and preserve the heritage of America's people and places.

Find more books like this at
www.arcadiapublishing.com

Search for your hometown history, your old stomping grounds, and even your favorite sports team.

Consistent with our mission to preserve history on a local level, this book was printed in South Carolina on American-made paper and manufactured entirely in the United States. Products carrying the accredited Forest Stewardship Council (FSC) label are printed on 100 percent FSC-certified paper.

MADE IN THE USA